DARTMOOR
MOODS

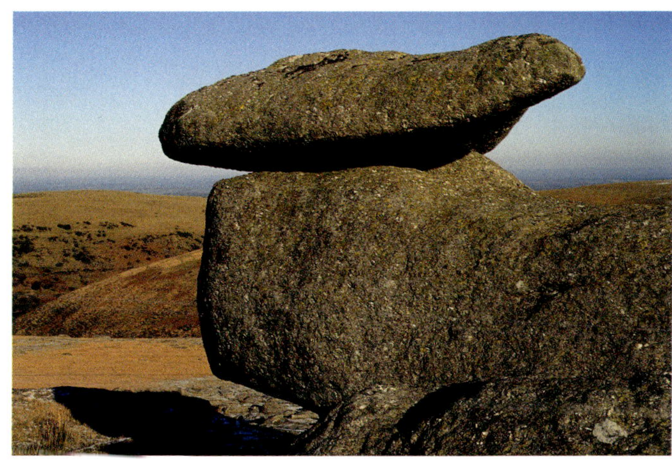

PETER WHITE

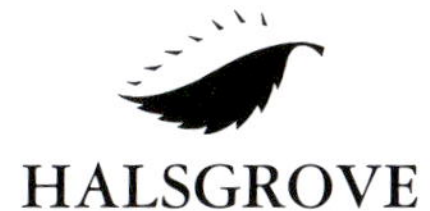

HALSGROVE

First published in Great Britain in 2003

British Library Cataloguing-in-Publication Data
A CIP record for this title is available from the British Library

ISBN 1 84114 266 2

HALSGROVE

Halsgrove House
Lower Moor Way
Tiverton, Devon EX16 6SS
Tel: 01884 243242
Fax: 01884 243325
email: sales@halsgrove.com
website: www.halsgrove.com

Printed by D'Auria Industrie Grafiche Spa, Italy

CONTENTS

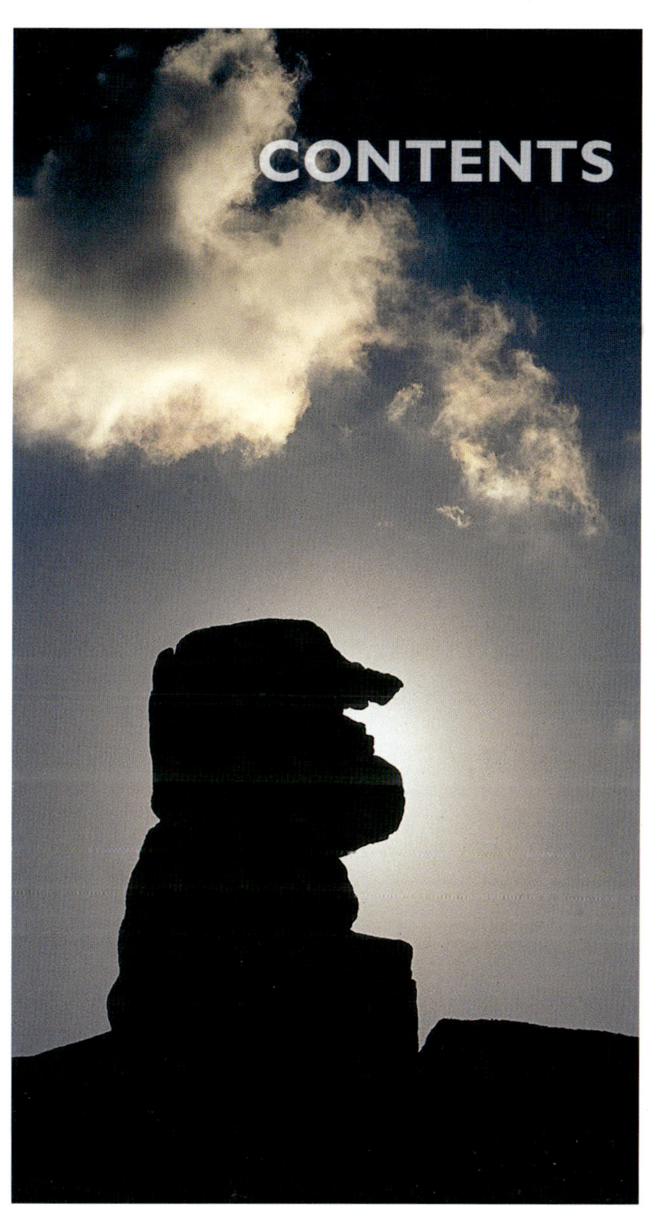

Bowerman's Nose on Hayne Down

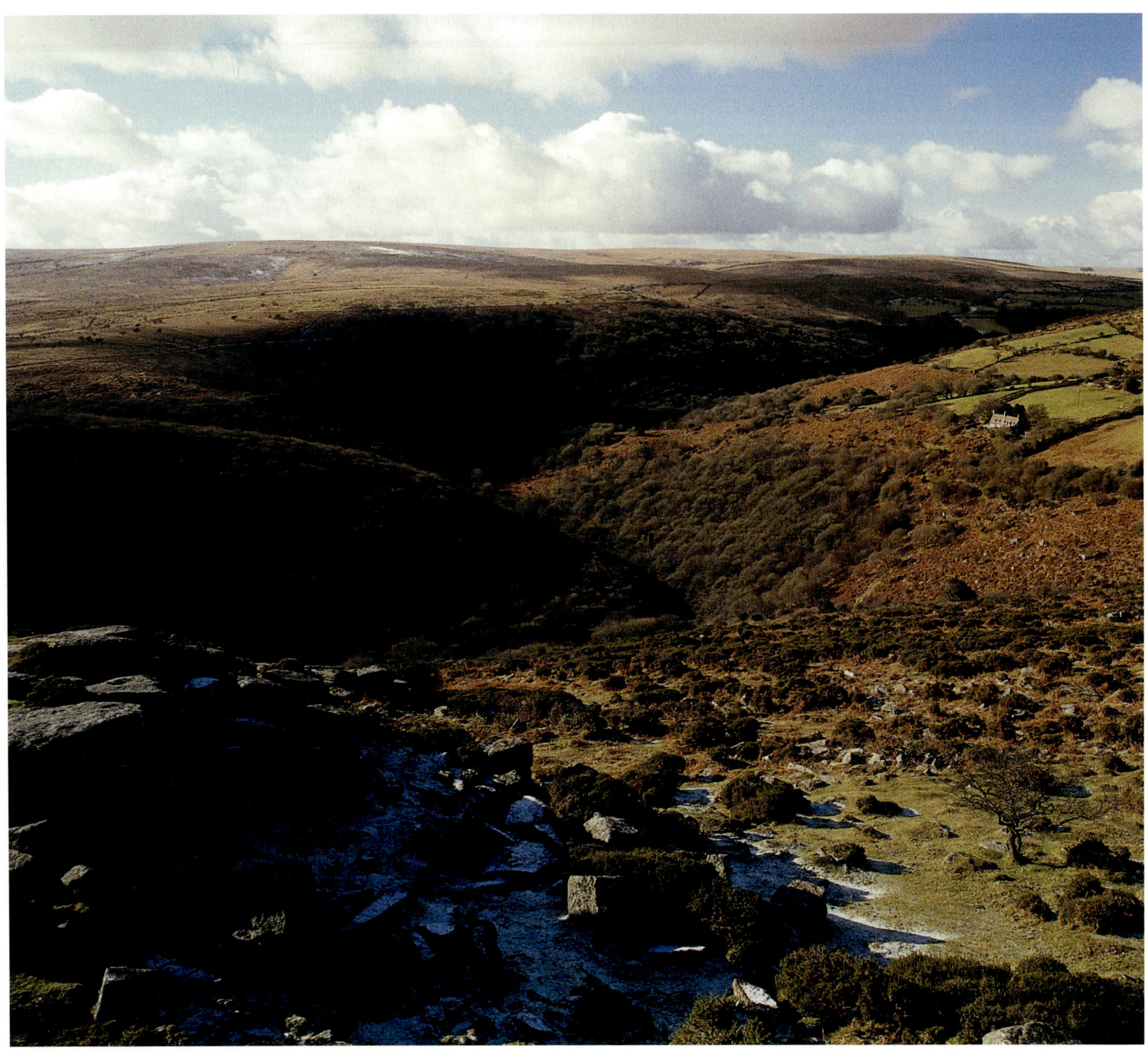

The Dart valley from Mel Tor

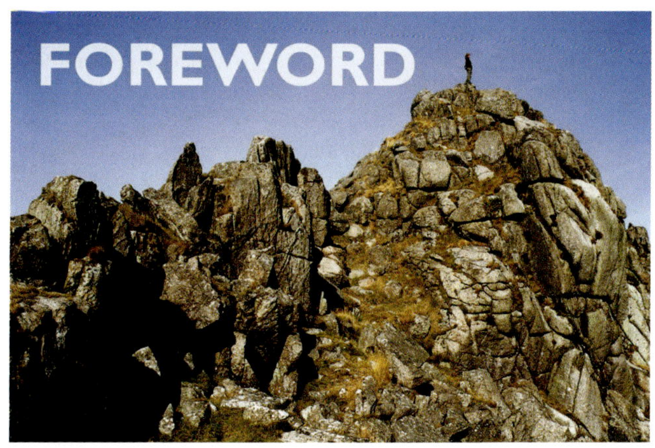

Me and my photography

I first came to Dartmoor in 1957 at the age of eleven, on a cycling tour of Devon, and I was not impressed. It rained, the cloud hung low, I was terrified by the warden of Bellever Youth Hostel and my pocket money only ran to a packet of mint imperials rather than the cream tea I really wanted! I did not return until 1967 when I left London to start my first job in Devon. By then I had acquired a real yearning to explore upland Britain and the prospect of having Devon's hills and coasts on the doorstep was exciting. On my first weekend, on a glorious frosty day, I walked up the Dart from New Bridge to Dartmeet and back over Spitchwick Common, and I was hooked! That walk is still one of my favourites; it has beauty, drama, remoteness, variety and a huge amount of detailed interest – all of the elements that make Dartmoor's landscape so appealing.

In 1974 I was fortunate enough to start work with the National Park Authority and from then until early retirement in 1999, I was able to make my own small contribution to keeping that landscape special – a rare privilege. Retirement gave me more time for photography, an interest since the age of twelve when my father gave me my first camera. Since then I have always enjoyed walking with a camera because if I am searching for that special image, I am looking at the landscape and all that is in it, rather than simply seeing it pass by. In 2000 I put on my first Dartmoor exhibition, which lead to others, and then to magazine articles and the wonderful opportunity to do this book.

I use an ancient Olympus OM1 with various zoom, close-up and wide-angle lenses. I never use a tripod or flash and nothing is 'tweaked' on the computer. The natural world is beautiful enough without me trying to improve it. I travel light and cover a lot of ground. I know the country and I watch the weather forecast. The satisfaction is in being in the right place at the right time and taking a shot that does justice to what I see. My thanks to Linda, who has patiently waited for the sun to come out many times and has offered constructive criticism throughout. With her help I have enjoyed putting this book together. I hope that you will enjoy the result, either as a portrayal of a place you know and love, or as inspiration to get out there and experience the real thing.

DARTMOOR NATIONAL PARK

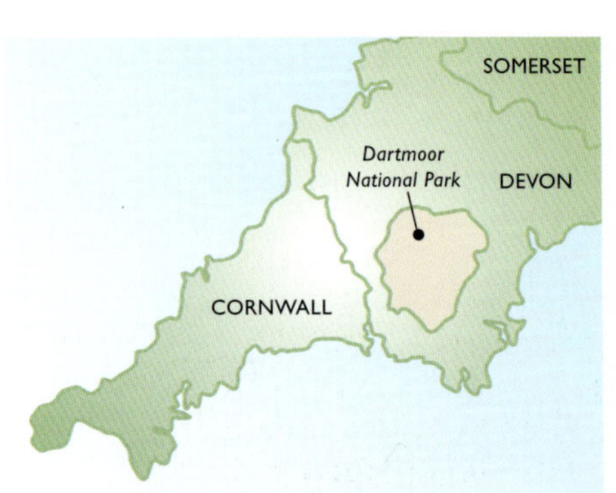

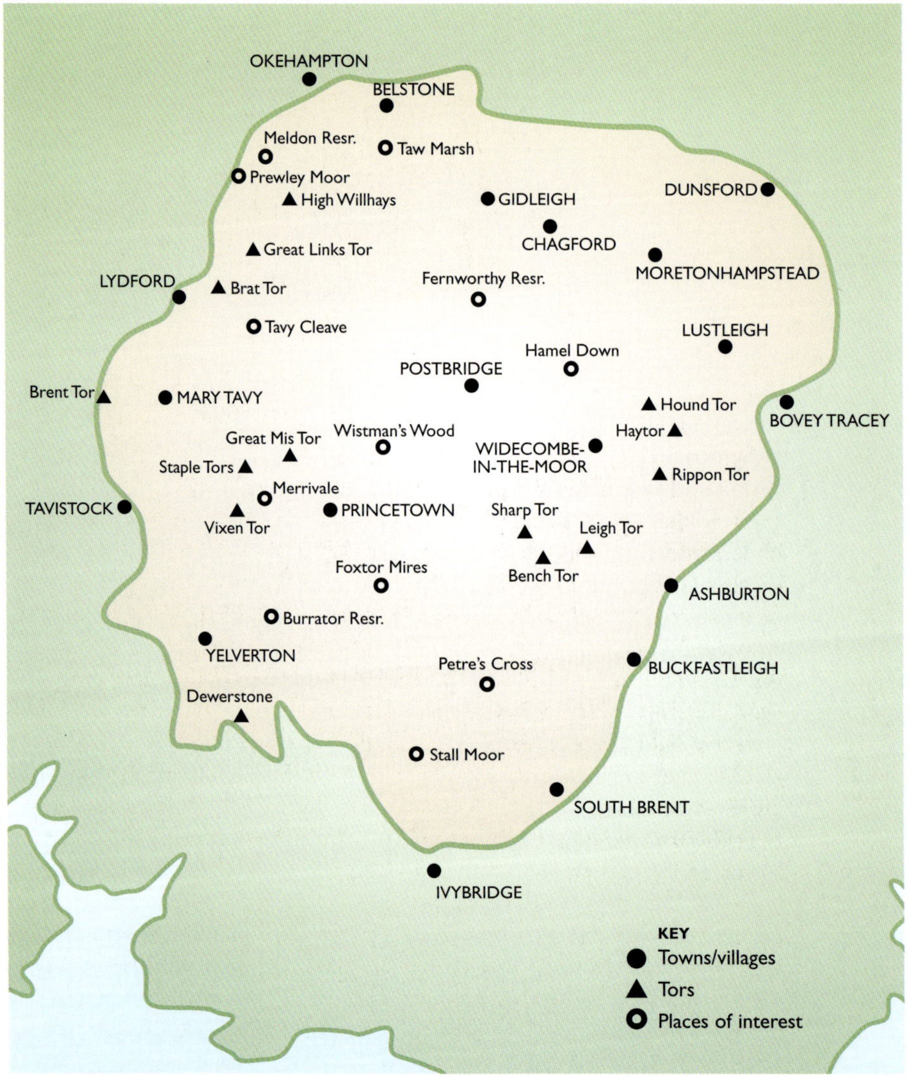

6

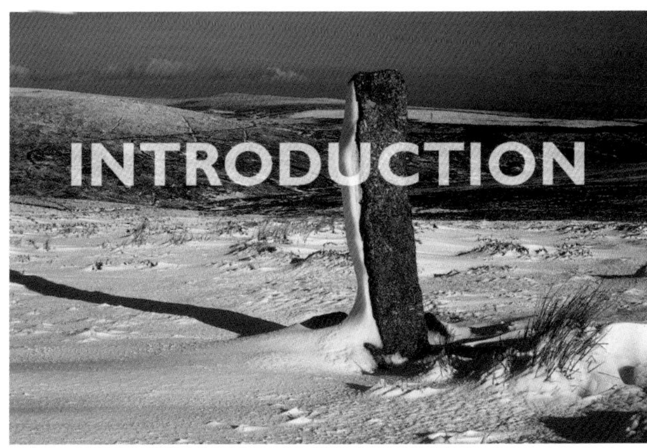

My Dartmoor

Dartmoor is a magical landscape. It stands proud over the rest of Devon, an outpost of upland Britain – an island of granite in a sea of softer rocks. It is in many ways a harsh landscape, often described as 'the last great wilderness in southern Britain'. Walk into the centre of the northern or southern plateau and you will understand why. You will find vast expanses of open moorland, bogs made more fearsome by images of Conan Doyle's Grimpen Mire, huge skies, unpredictable weather and, above all, remoteness from human habitation. All of these combine to offer escape, challenge, or spiritual refreshment to those who seek them.

But Dartmoor is much more than that. The streams that rise on the high ground and ooze across the peat bogs suddenly steepen and tumble off the edges of the plateaux in dramatic rocky gorges. As rivers they become more powerful, with falls and rapids linking pools of golden peat-coloured water. Downstream, the lower slopes become clothed in beautiful soft woodland and side valleys cut the surrounding moorland into smaller, steeper blocks, often crowned with dramatic tors. Farmland, won from the moor, begins to appear; and as the valleys broaden the pattern of fields, farms and villages becomes more dominant. Eventually the rivers flow out of Dartmoor, through the market towns on its fringes and into the farmland of Devon which laps up against the granite all around its boundaries.

So here is a landscape which has an identifiable character, woven from granite, altitude, upland vegetation and weather. But within that overall character it offers a huge variety of experiences. If you want the challenge of a 20-mile hike over continuous moorland, it is there. If you want a family picnic you can find some of the most beautiful riverside spots in England. You can lose yourself in the woods or take granny to Widecombe for a cream tea. The choice is yours.

Almost wherever you go you will be aware of history and prehistory. The hardness of granite as a building material, and the huge areas which have never been cleared or ploughed, have left Dartmoor with an amazing legacy of remains dating from many thousands of years ago to the present day. Bronze Age field systems with hut circles and stone rows stretch for miles over what is now moorland. Iron Age hill-forts, medieval villages and the farming, mining and industrial remains of more recent centuries are all superimposed on each other, creating a vast archaeological landscape.

Very little of Dartmoor is a natural landscape. With the exception of blanket bog on the highest parts, and the tors themselves, its present appearance has been shaped by man. Forest was cleared from what is now moorland, and it only remains as moorland because of our stock grazing. Many woodlands only look as they do now because of past management by coppicing for charcoal and timber; and of course all of the pattern of walls, hedges, lanes, farms and villages has evolved over centuries as a response to man's needs.

In recent times those needs have sometimes led to very controversial landscape changes – usually when the requirement has arisen from outside the Dartmoor community. Reservoirs, roads, firing ranges, quarries and communication masts have all provoked anger and a protective reaction. Some have happened, others have not. Where they have, I leave you to judge the effect for yourself.

So Dartmoor is a landscape of many parts, very distinctive, even unique. Its value to the nation as a whole was recognised in its designation as a National Park in 1951. Post-war idealism led the movement to protect our most treasured landscapes and make sure that ordinary people could enjoy them. The principle still holds good, and has matured and been developed over time. Landscape quality and the enjoyment of it remain as the fundamentals, but the concept of landscape has been expanded to embrace all of the elements which combine to produce it – geology, plants and wildlife, the cultural heritage of many centuries of human use, and the Dartmoor community of today which not only maintains the landscape through farming, forestry and other activities, but which is itself as much a part of Dartmoor as the tors.

The National Park covers 368 square miles. It is more or less circular in shape and only some 25 miles across. When you are in it, it feels much bigger, because there is so much that is over the horizon and never seen from the road, and because when you set out to explore there is such a wealth of interest on the way. In this book I have tried to look beyond superficial impressions and picture-postcard views to explore not only the well-known beauty spots, but also the lesser-known parts of the Park, and the elements which make up its landscape – the weirdness of a rock formation, or the wind-blasted tree that speaks volumes about its harsh environment; the tranquillity of still water or the power of a river; the majesty of a moorland sky or the magic of ice and snow.

I have tried to capture the feel of the place too. It has moods. It can be frightening, it can be uplifting, it can make your spine tingle with its power and beauty. It is one of those places, rare in England, where the landscape is bigger than you. It fulfils that basic human need for wild places – places that have not been tamed by man; places which you need to know are still there even if you are unable to penetrate their remotest parts.

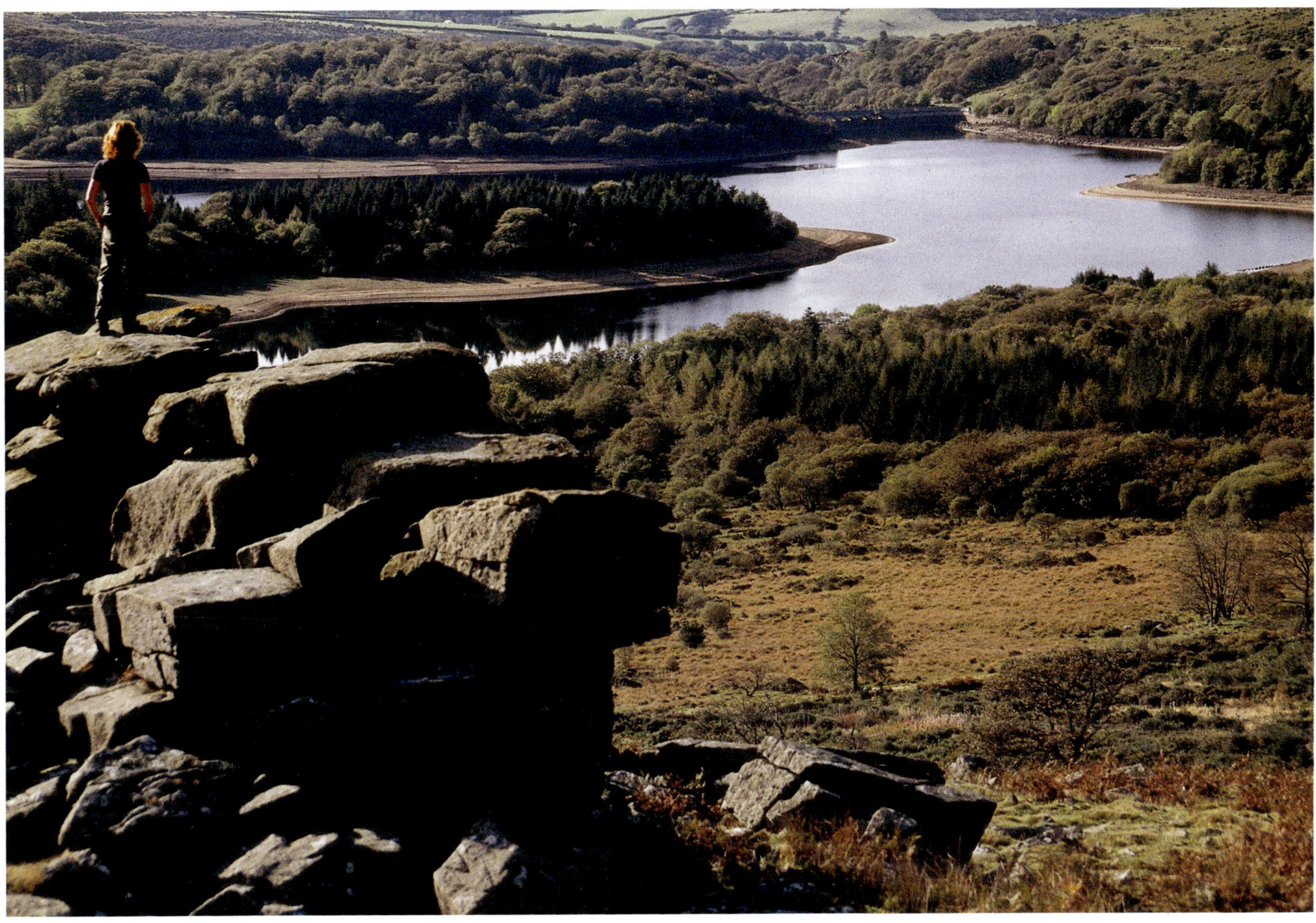

Burrator Reservoir from Leather Tor

Overleaf: *A lonely tree and a winter sky*

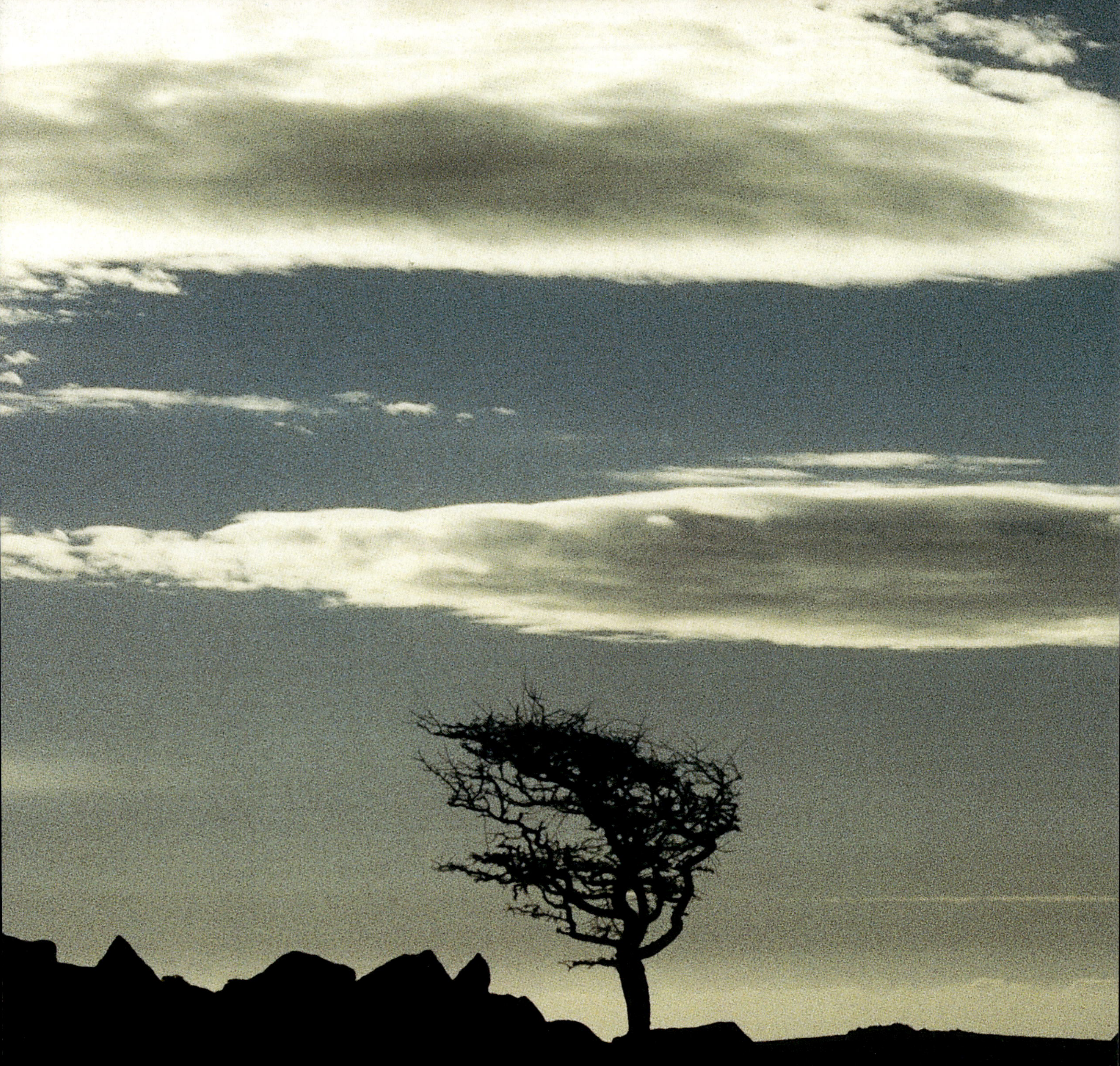

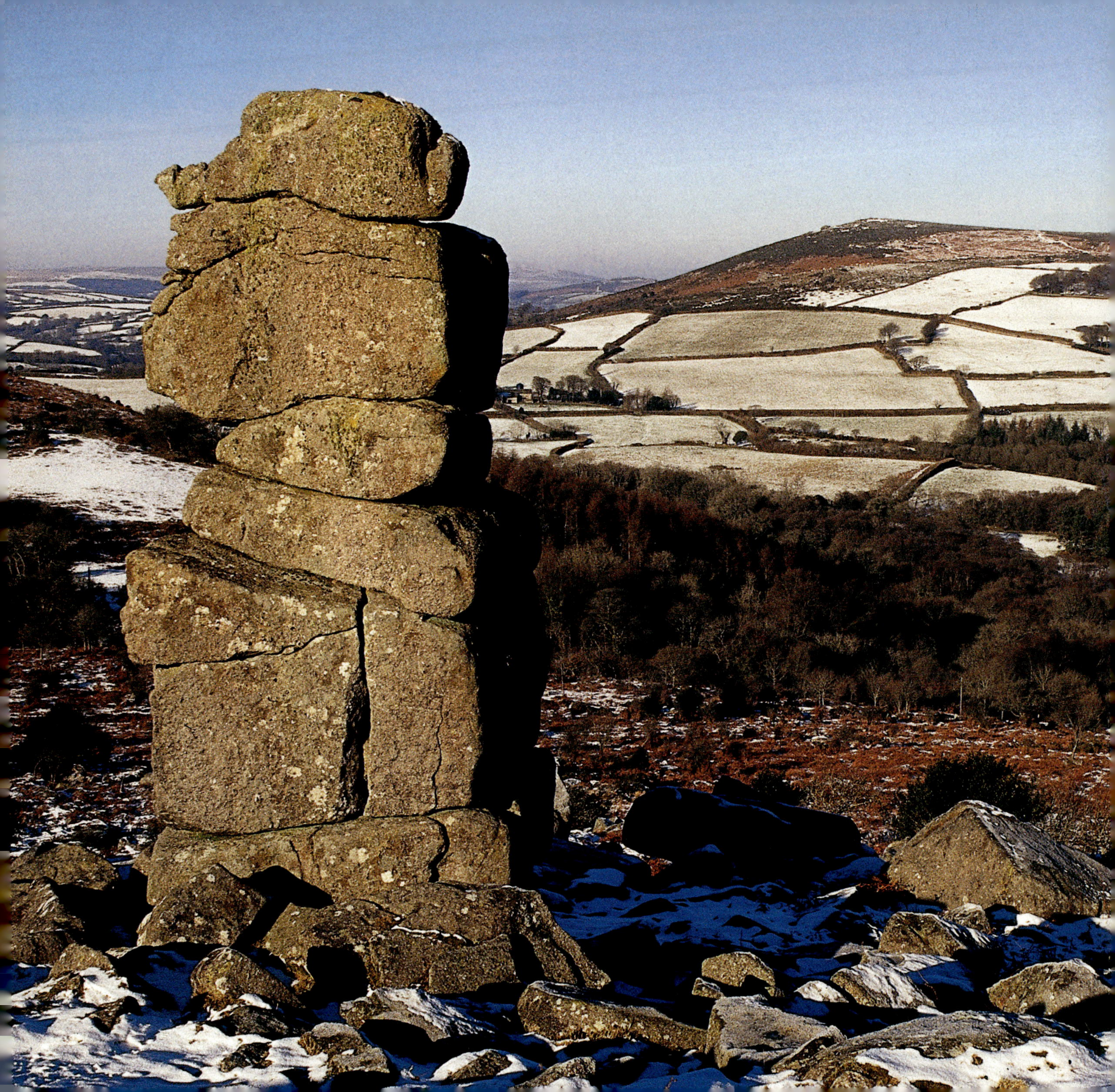

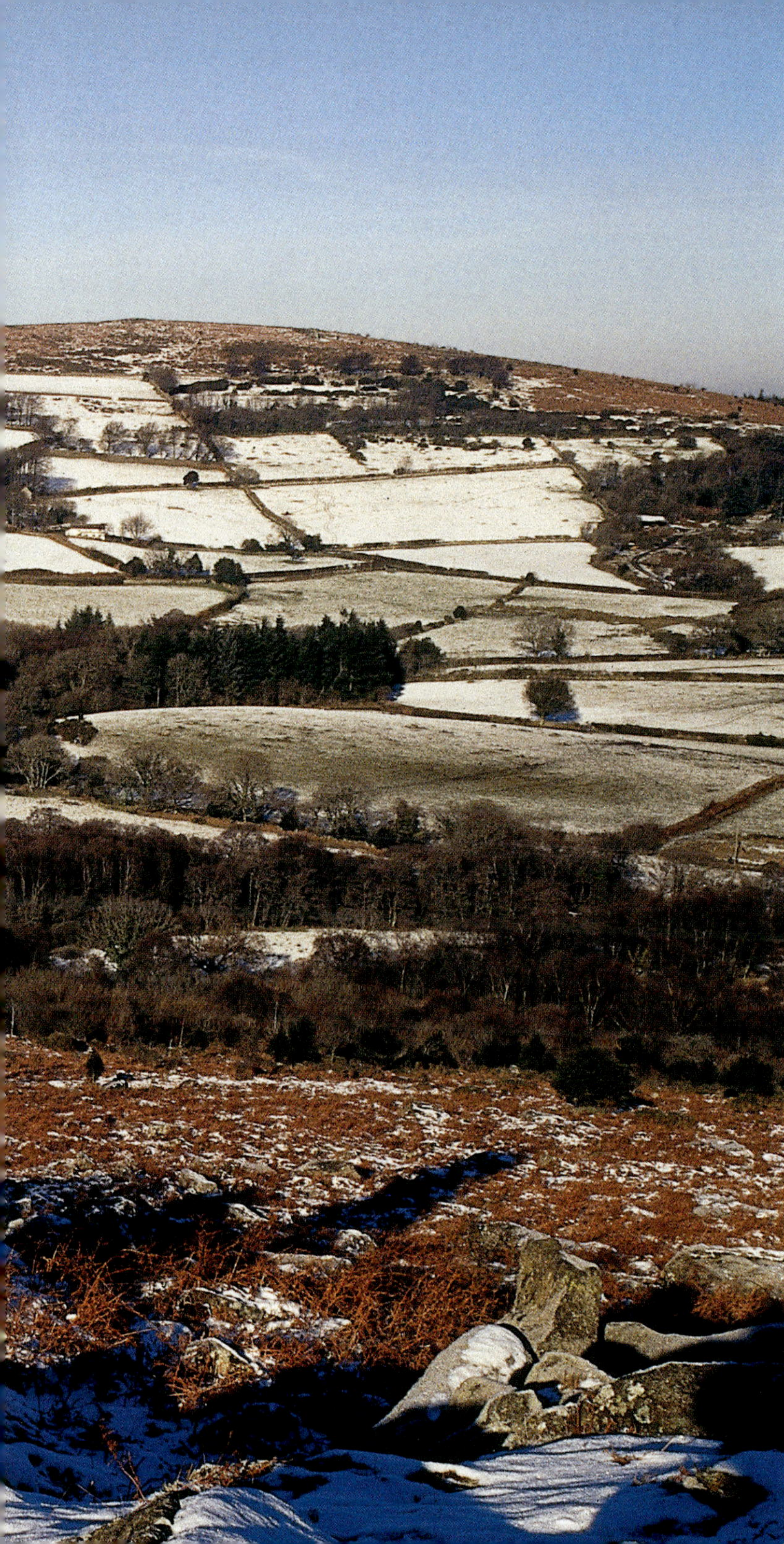

Bowerman's Nose and Easdon Down

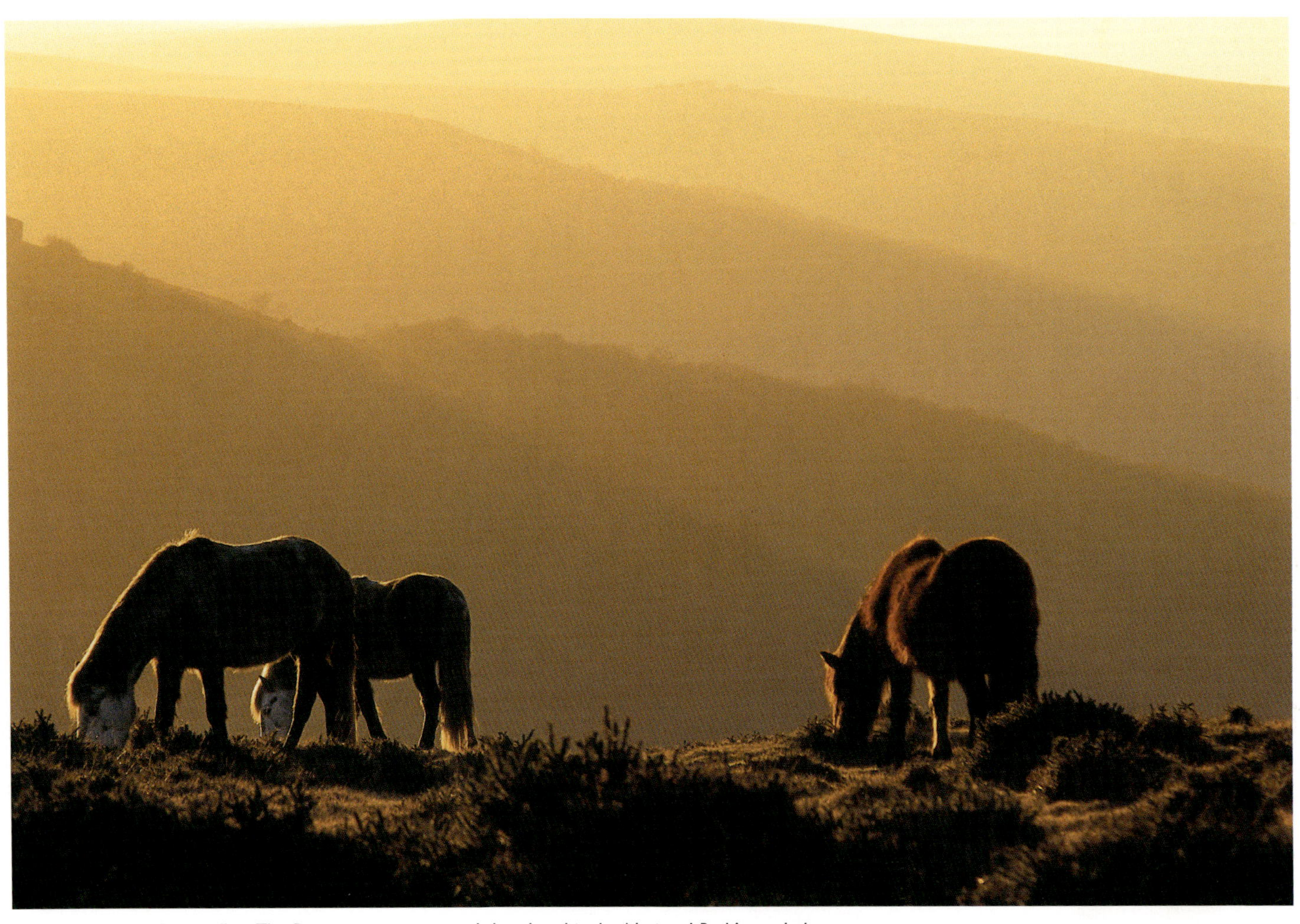

Ponies above the Dart valley. The Dartmoor pony is much loved and is the National Park's symbol

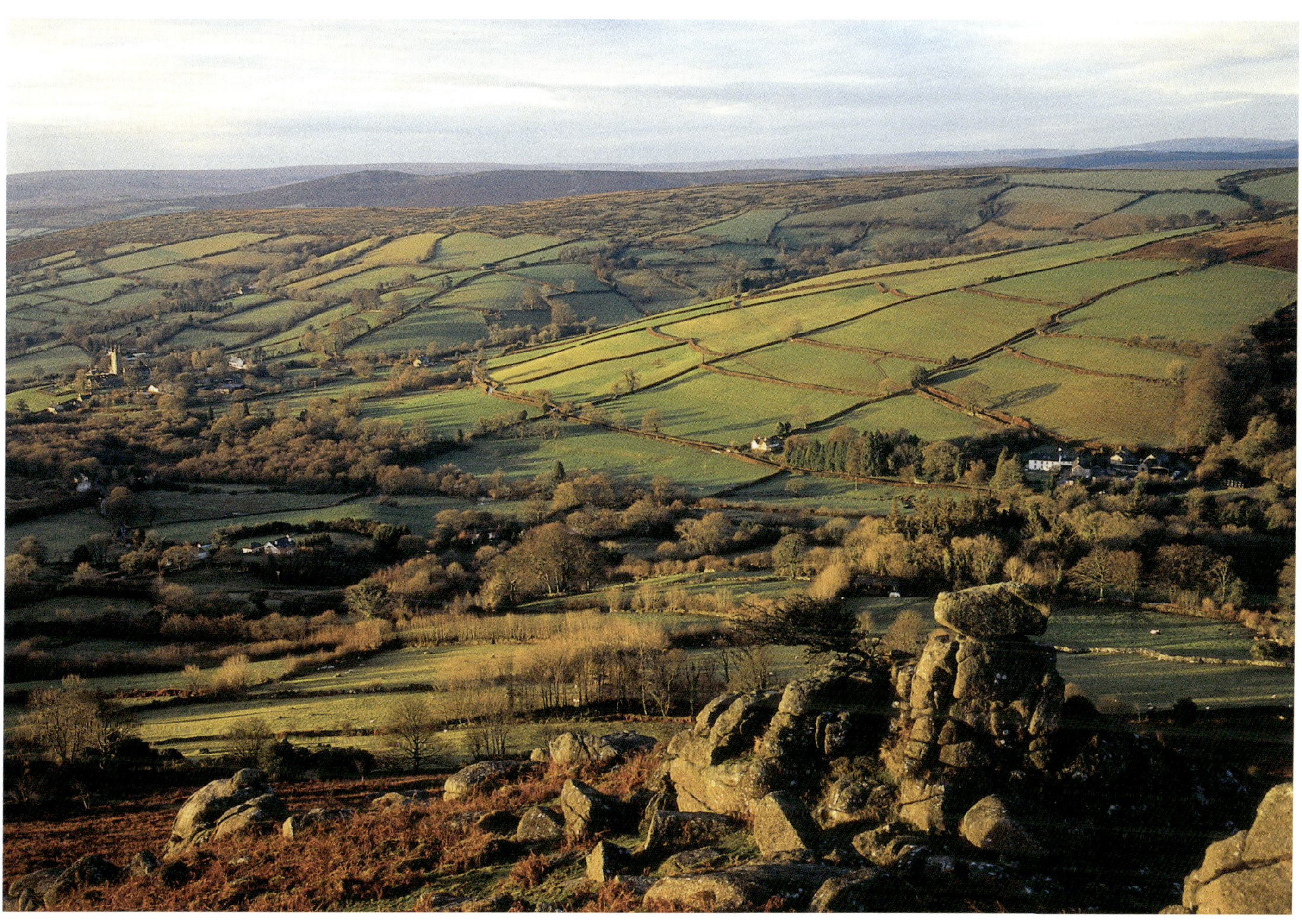

The Widecombe valley from Bell Tor, with the village sitting prettily in the field patterns

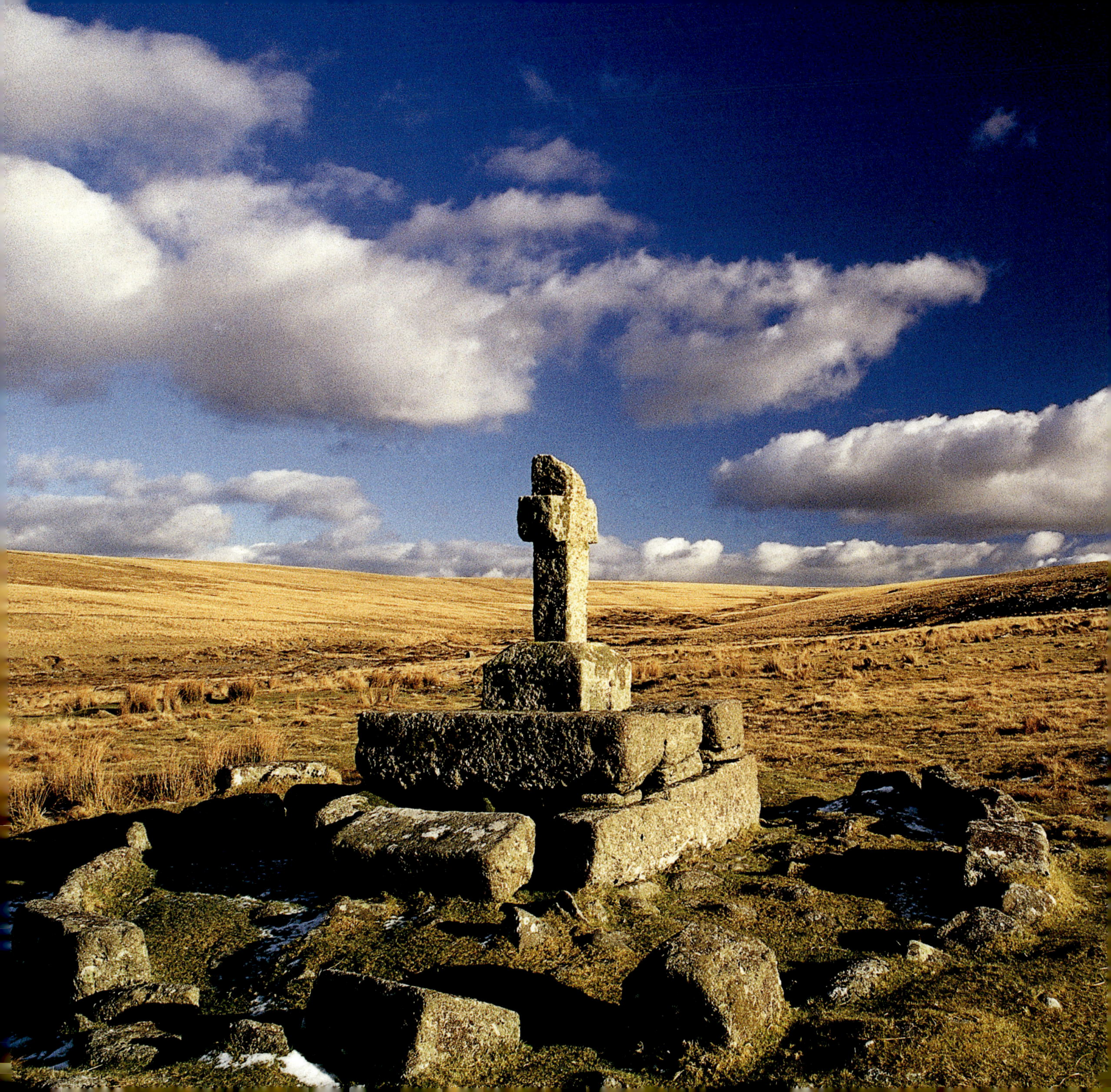

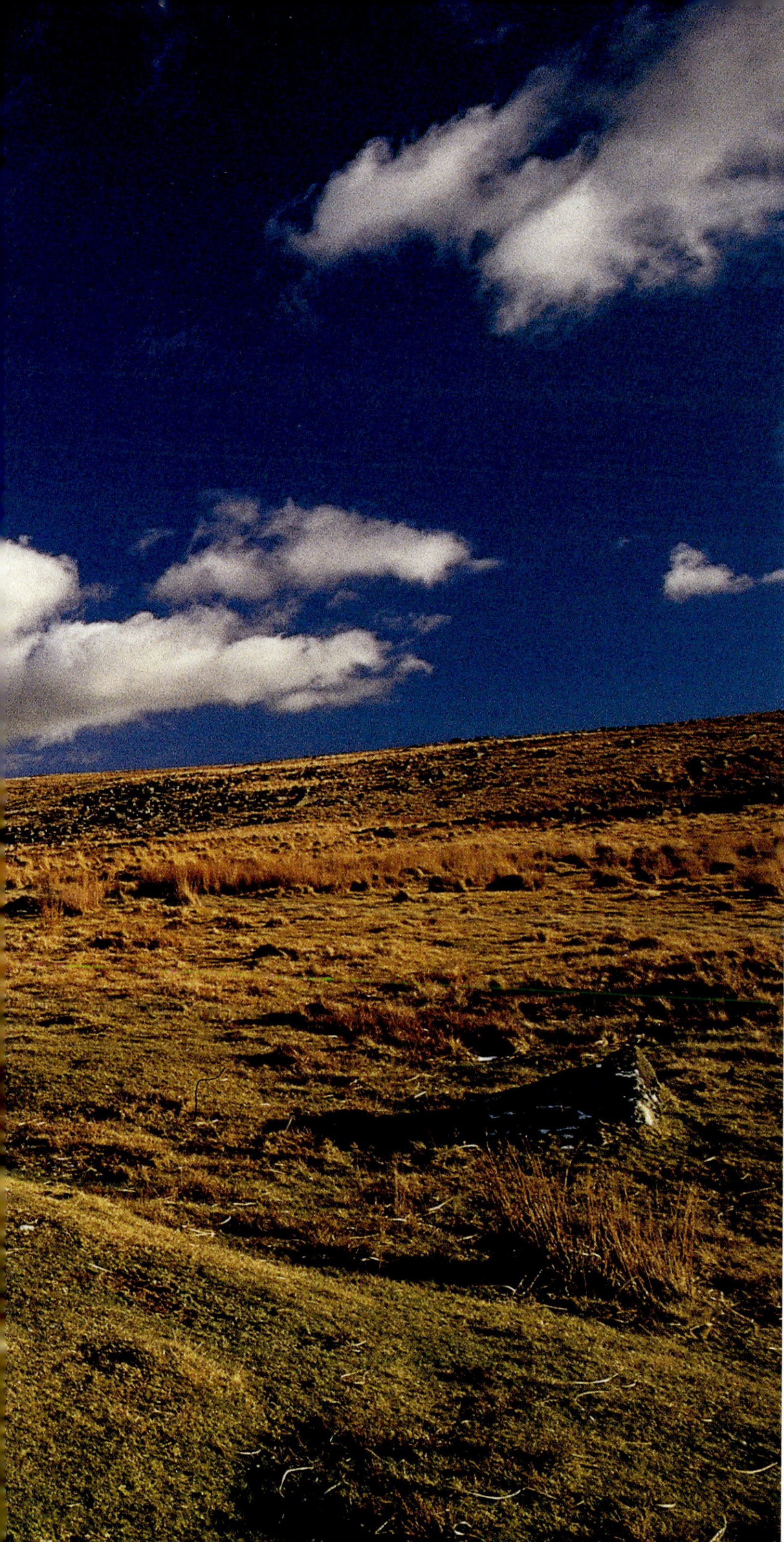

Childe's Tomb, overlooking Foxtor Mires. Legend has it that Childe the Hunter, lost in a snow storm, disembowelled his horse and sheltered in the carcass, but nevertheless died

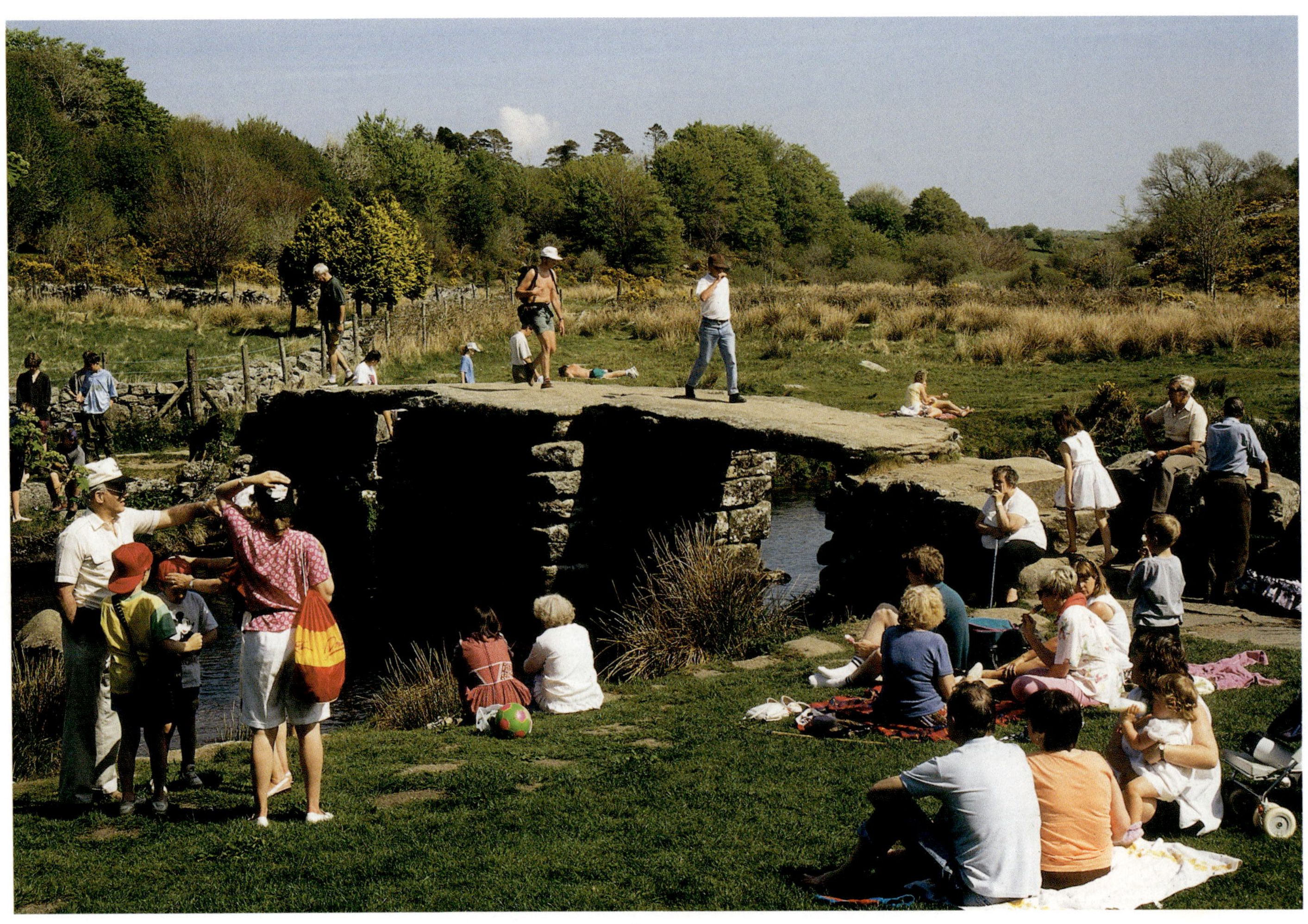

The clapper bridge at Postbridge. These ancient granite bridges span many Dartmoor rivers

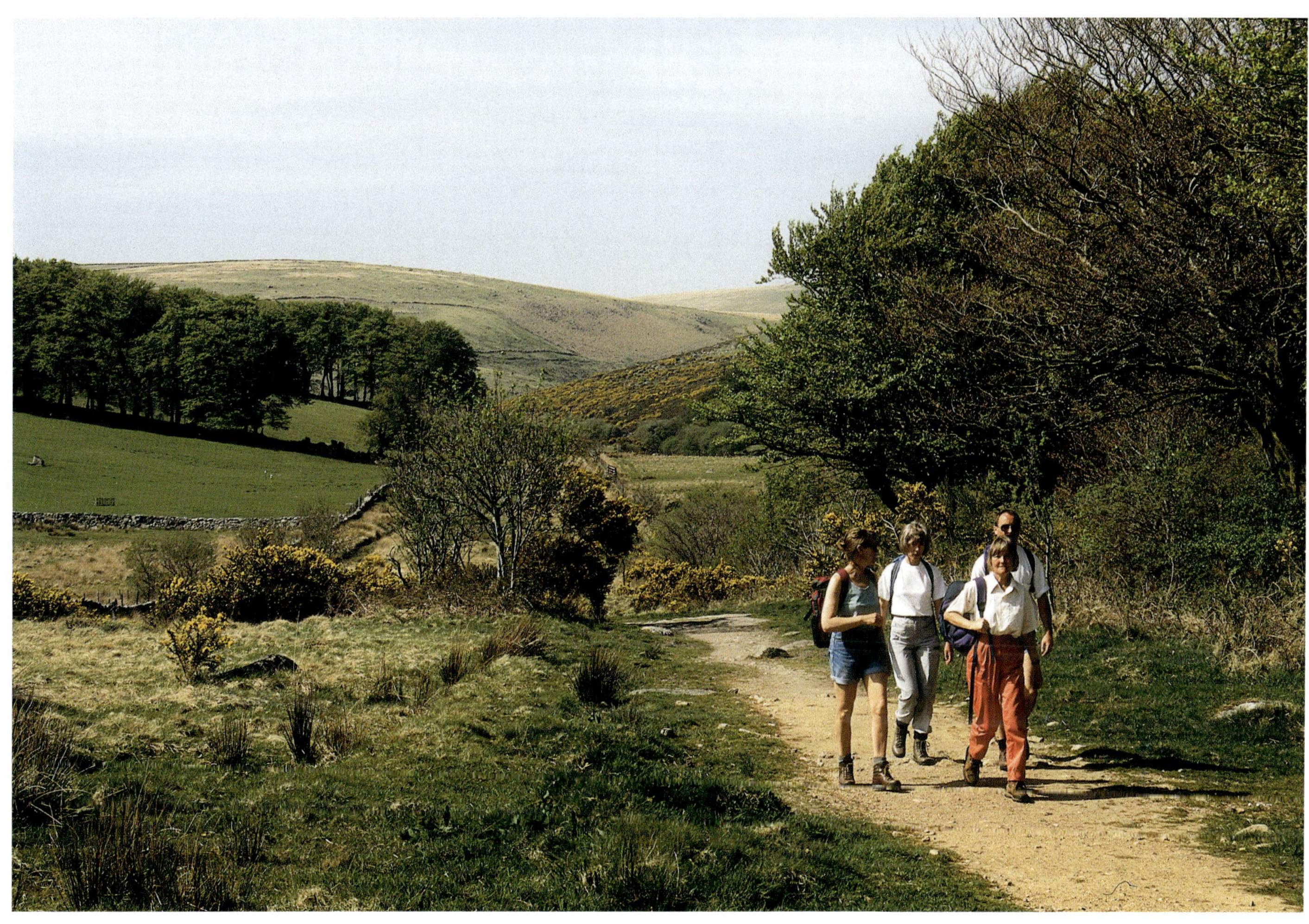

Postbridge is a popular place, but is the starting point for many quiet walks

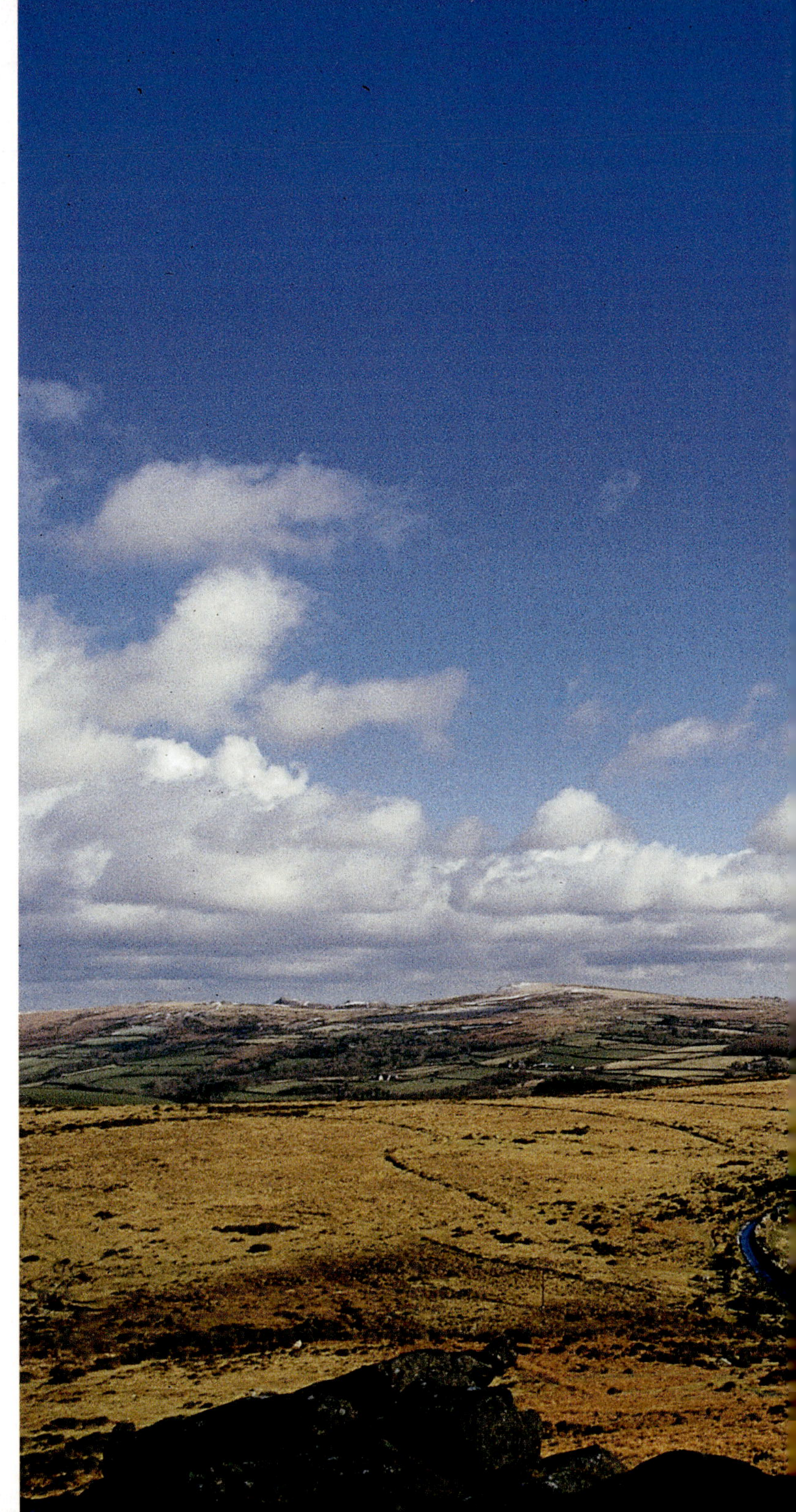

Looking east from Sharp Tor on Spitchwick Common

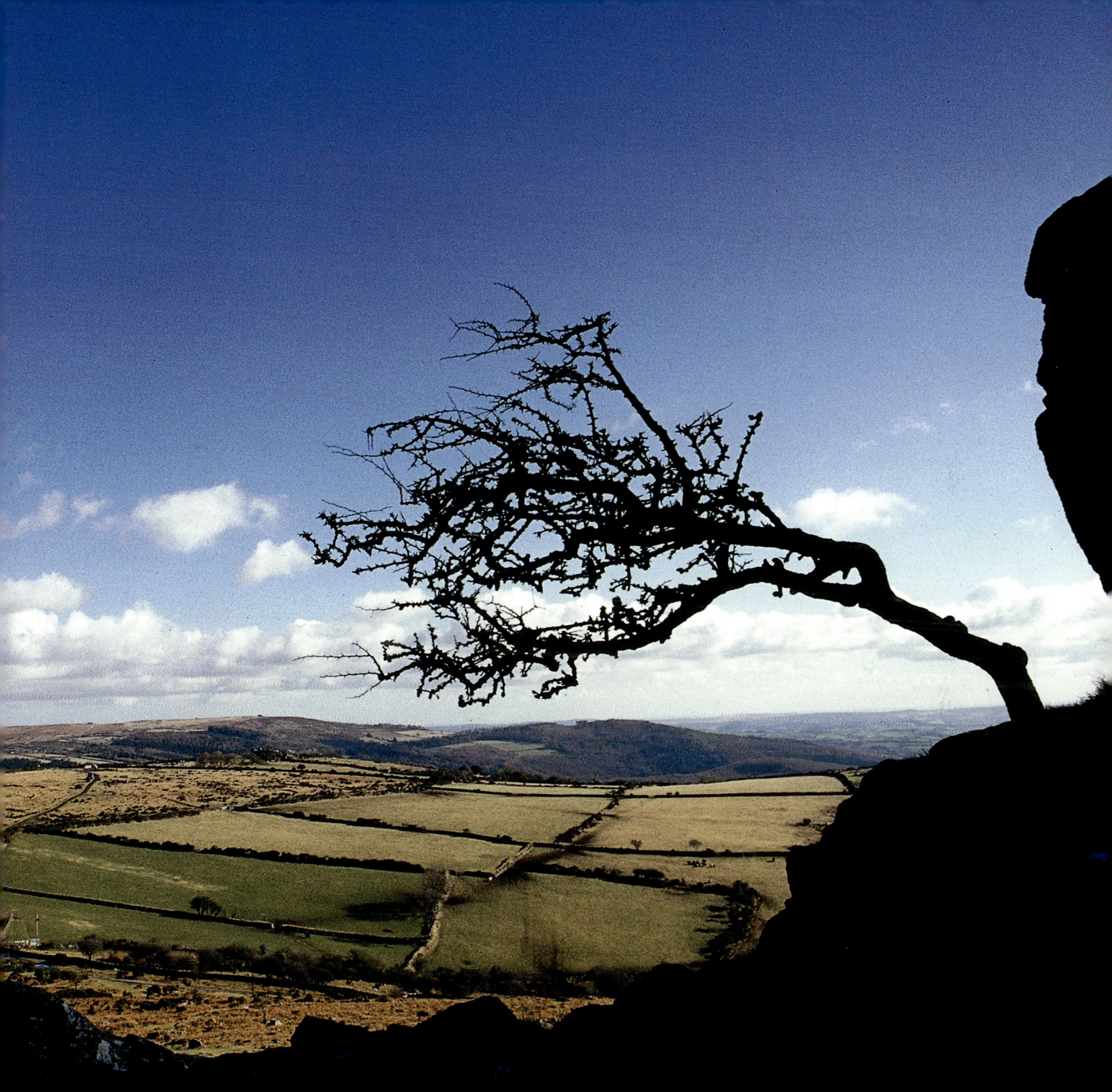

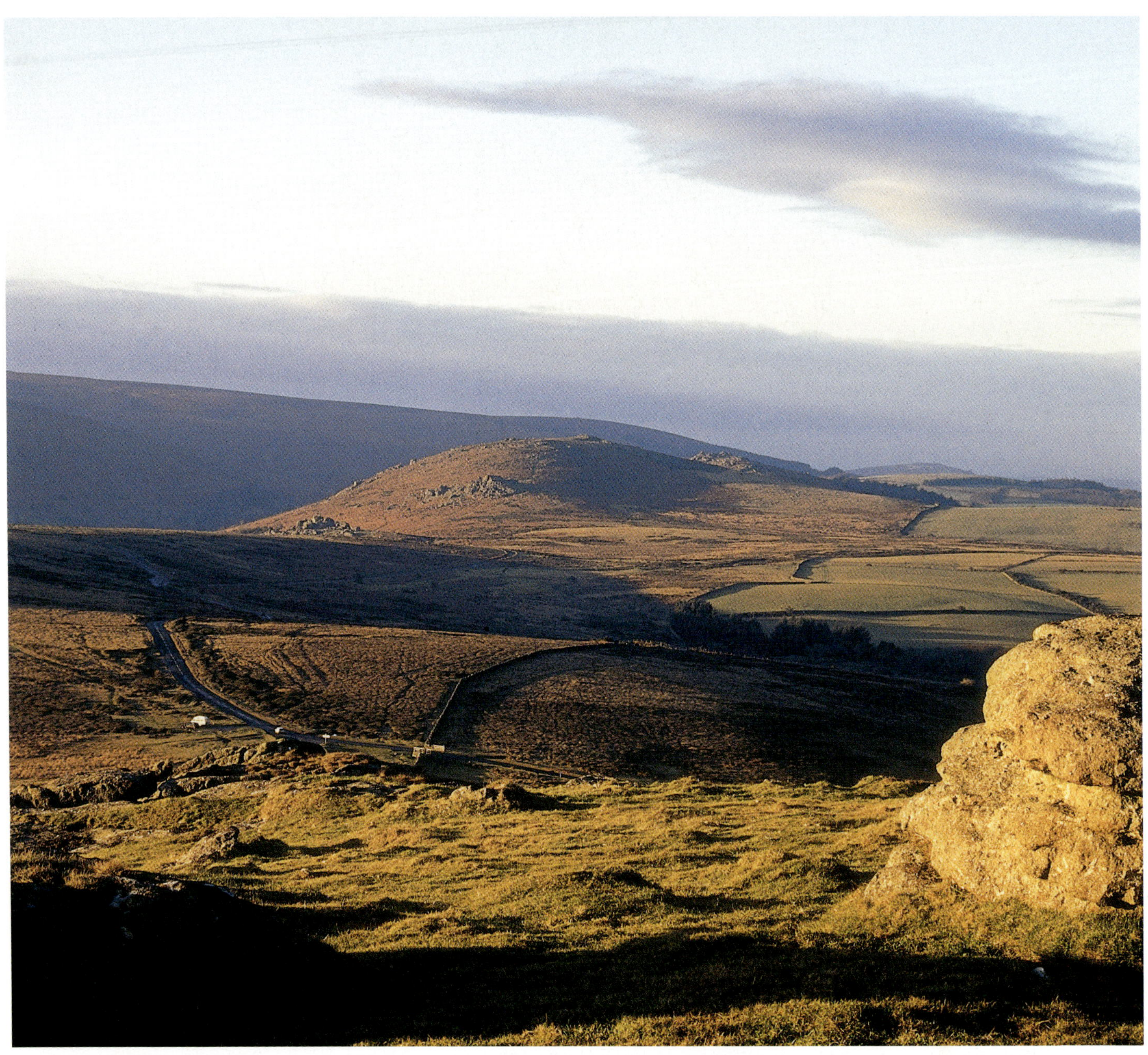

Evening light on Rippon Tor, looking towards Hamel Down

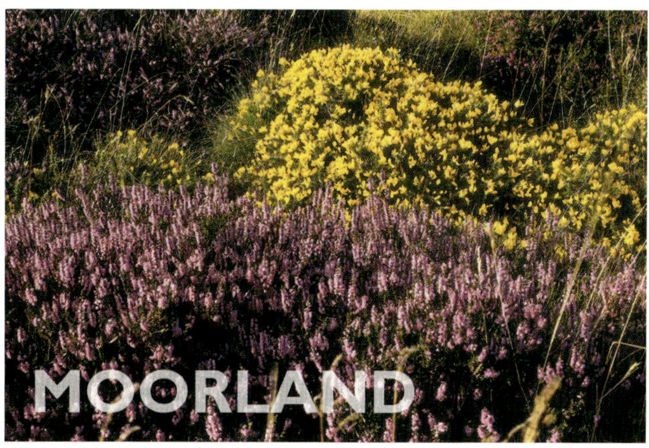

The heart of Dartmoor

Moorland is at the heart of Dartmoor, geographically and spiritually. It gives that all-important sense of space and distance. The two high plateaux have few distinctive features and because of this you cannot easily tell which rounded hill it is on that distant skyline – it could be on the far edge of the moor, or there could be another dozen skylines beyond it. The space appears infinite. The lack of walls, hedges or fences reinforces this impression – you feel that you can walk for ever. And indeed you can walk for a very long way – up to 25 miles north to south without crossing a boundary, taking in the highest point in southern England (High Willhays at just over 2000 feet) and the point which is most remote from a public road. You can wander over all of the unenclosed country, and many of the enclosed areas, or newtakes, are also open to the public.* Join a National Park guided walk, buy a walking guide, or consult the Ordnance Survey Outdoor Leisure Map of Dartmoor.

If you're feeling energetic set out for Yes Tor and High Willhays – the highest points on the moor. If the weather is fine you will get wonderful views over West Devon to Exmoor and into the wild and desolate landscape of the north moor; skylarks will sing, buzzards will soar, wheatears will flit from rock to rock and Dartmoor will seem a friendly place. On a winter's day, rain, wind or snow, you will find a very different experience, requiring navigation skills, proper equipment, and a degree of fitness. Your reward will be exhilaration and a sense of achievement. If the big walks don't appeal there is plenty of moorland close to the road. Try Haytor and Hound Tor; or above Burrator Reservoir, or High Down at Lydford. Here you will often find more detailed interest than in the remoter areas: weird tors and rocks, that wonderful late-August mixture of purple heather and golden gorse, hut circles, stone rows, twisted trees, insect-eating sundew plants, streams, dewponds, ponies – and more. Above all, you will find a sense of freedom and the 'wow' factor that less wild landscapes seldom offer.

* Parts of the northern moor may be closed to the public when military live firing is taking place. Check times in local papers, at Tourist Information Centres, or by phoning the number given on the OS Outdoor Leisure Map.

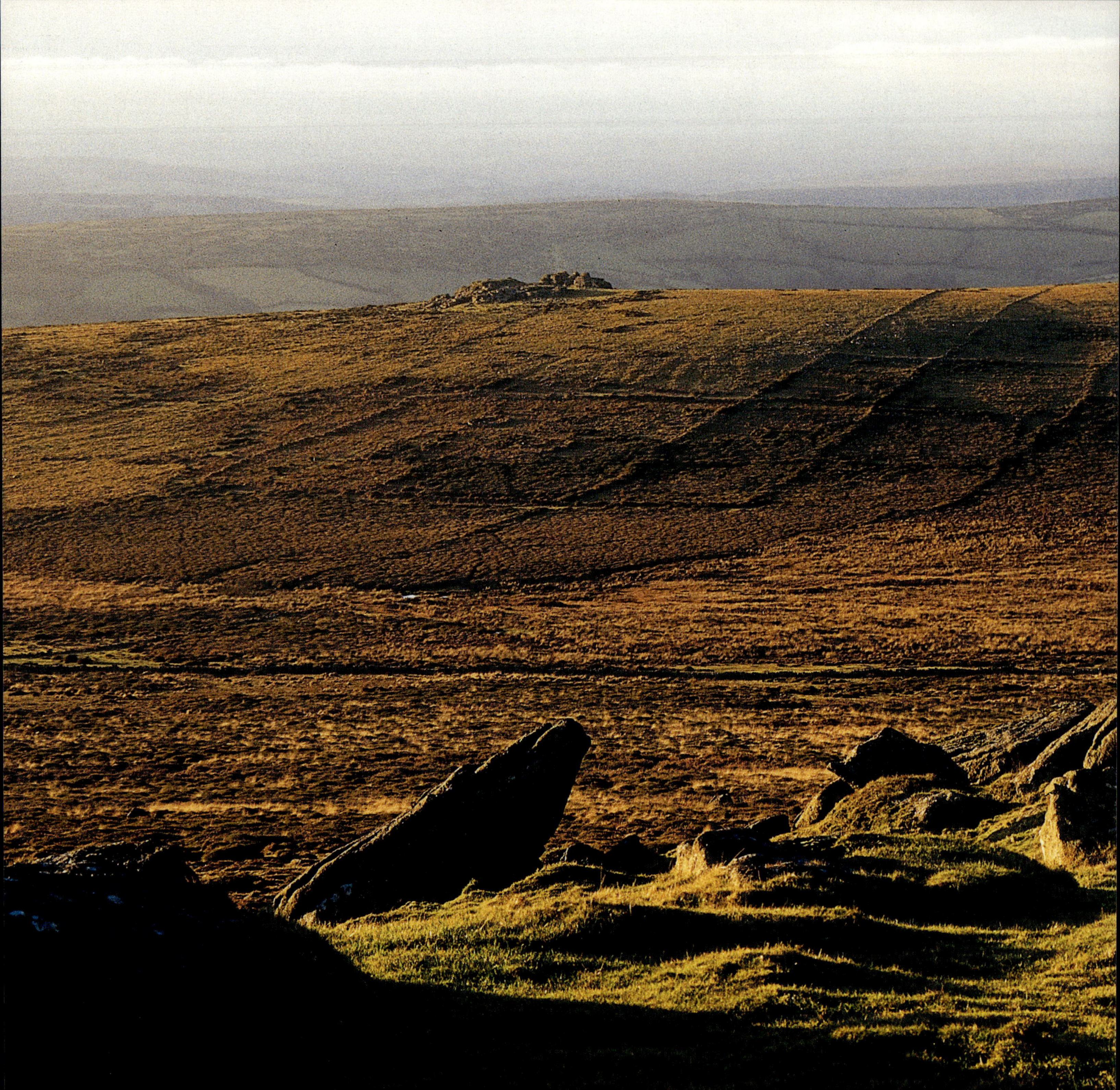

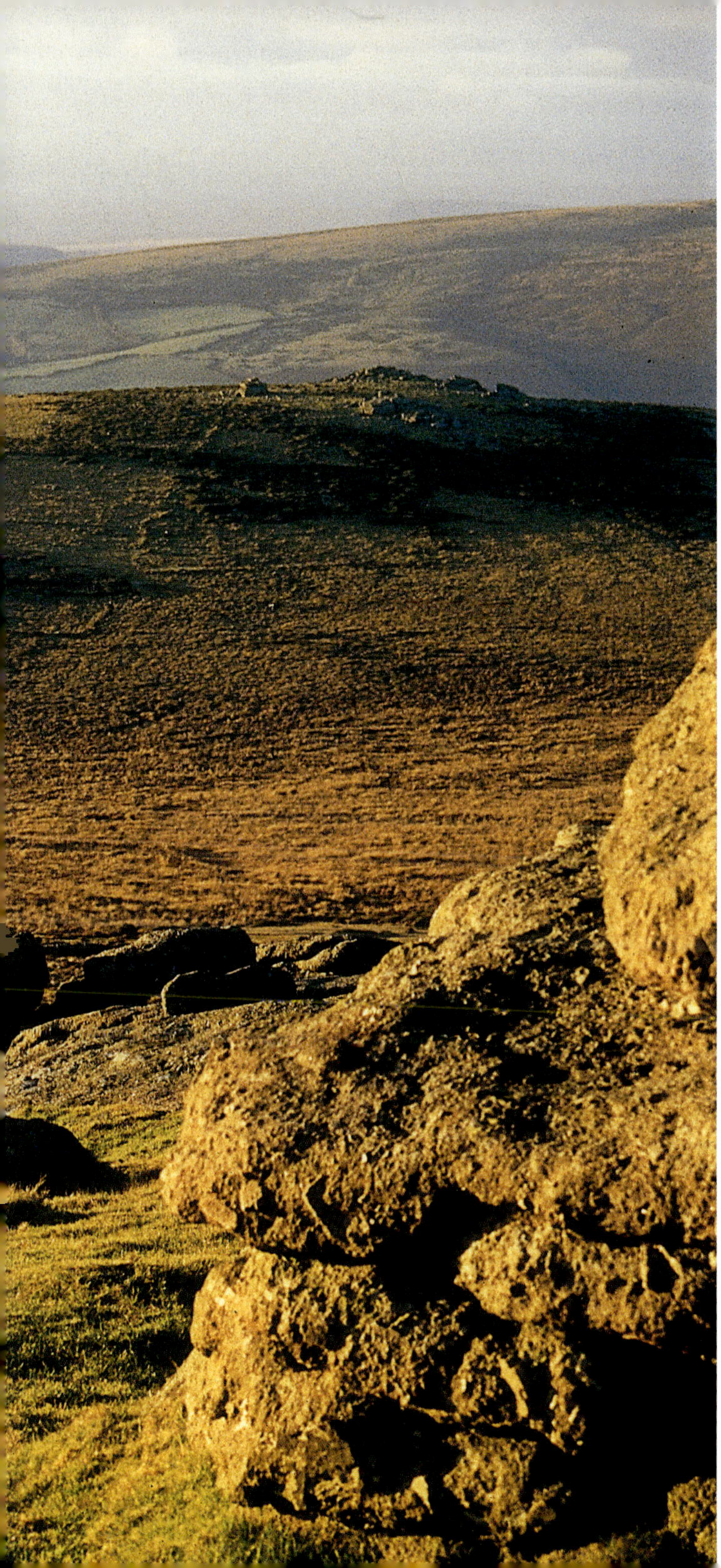

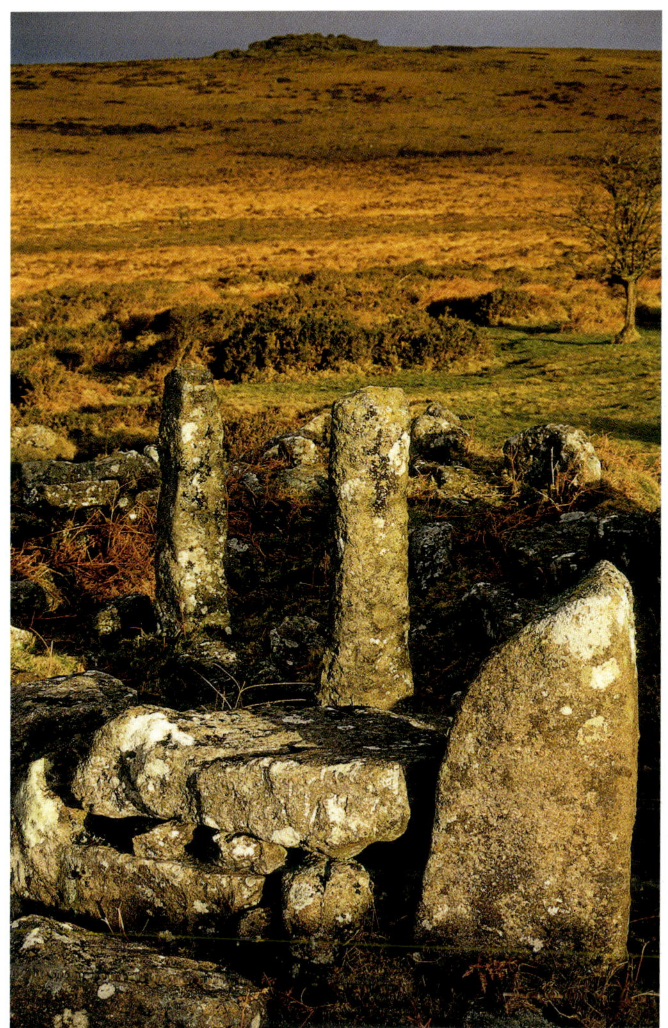

Remains of farm buildings below Pil Tor

Top Tor and Pil Tor from Rippon Tor. Foale's Arrishes on the hillside is an abandoned Iron Age field system

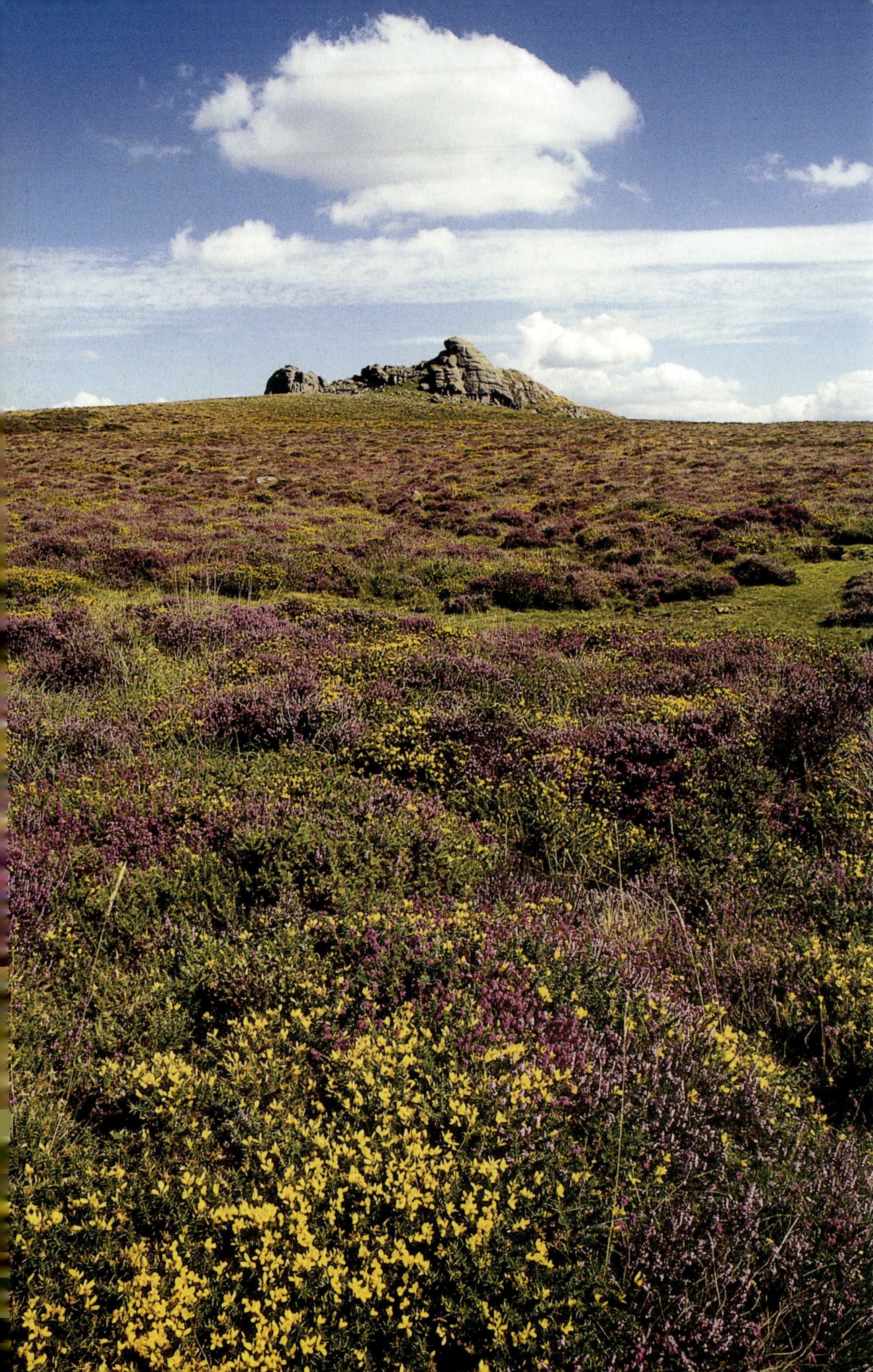

Haytor Down in late summer. The friendly face of Dartmoor moorland

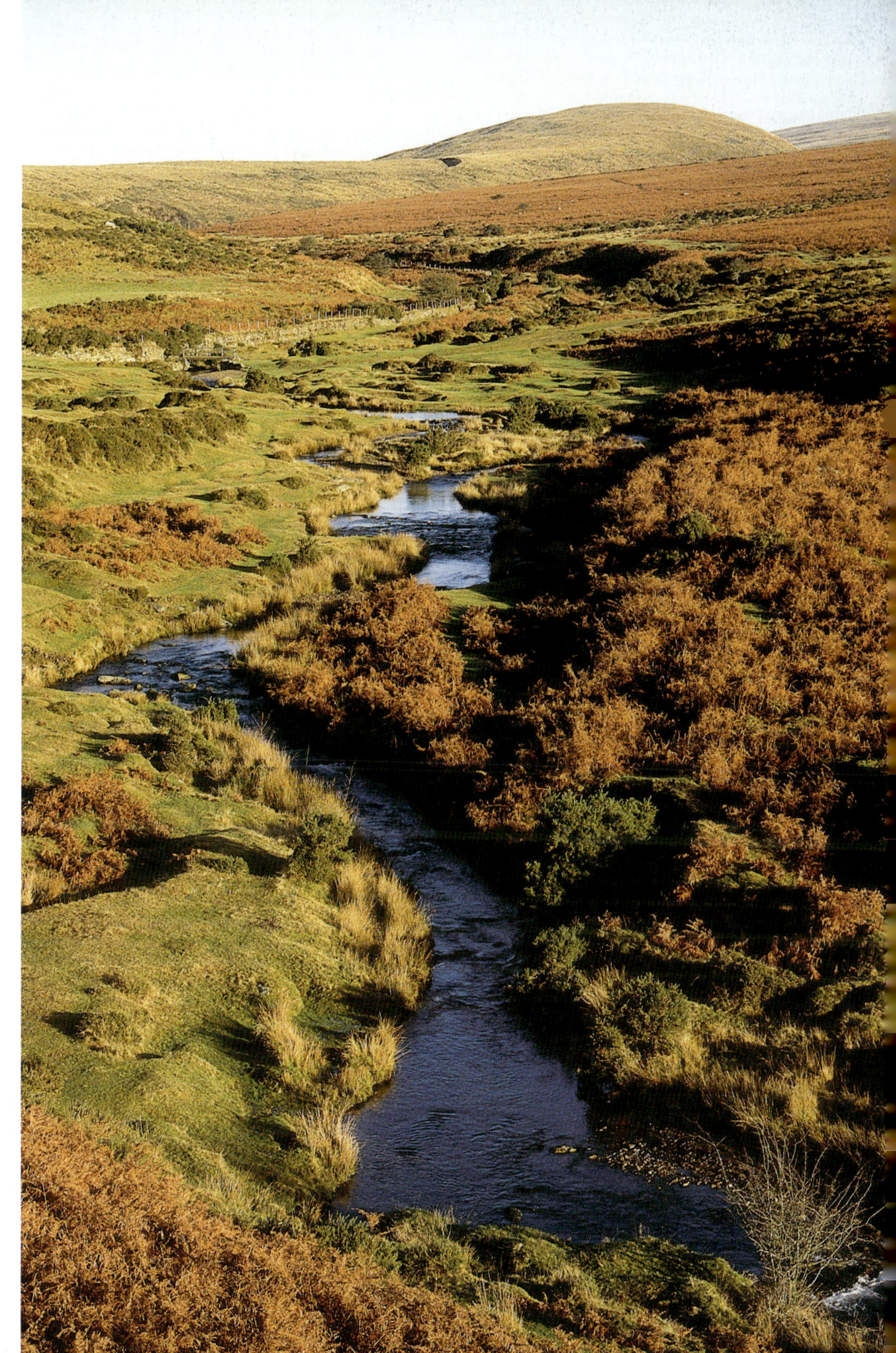

The River Lyd on Lydford High Down

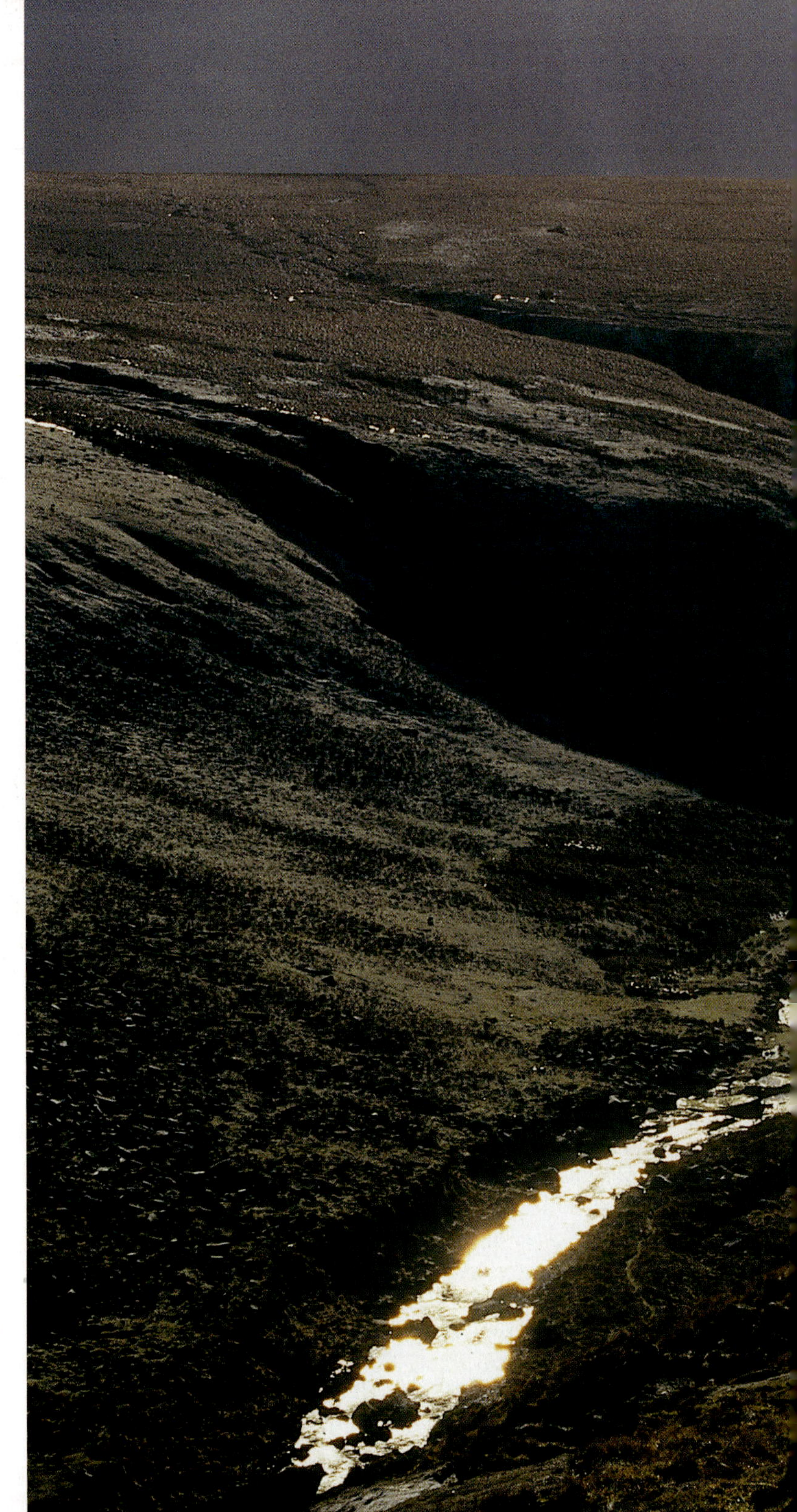

Tavy Cleave and Ger Tor on a frosty morning. This is perhaps the most dramatic moorland scenery on Dartmoor

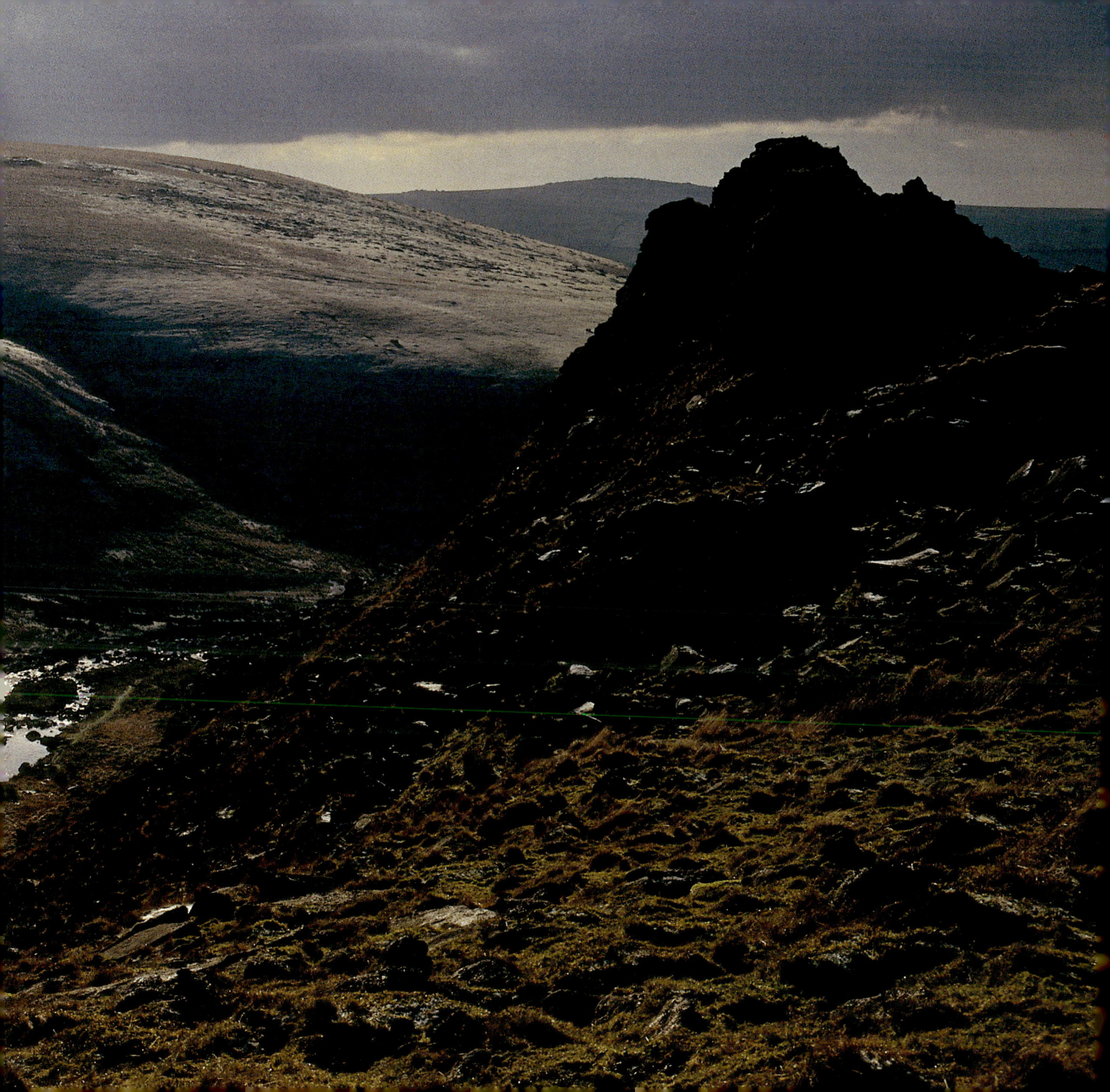

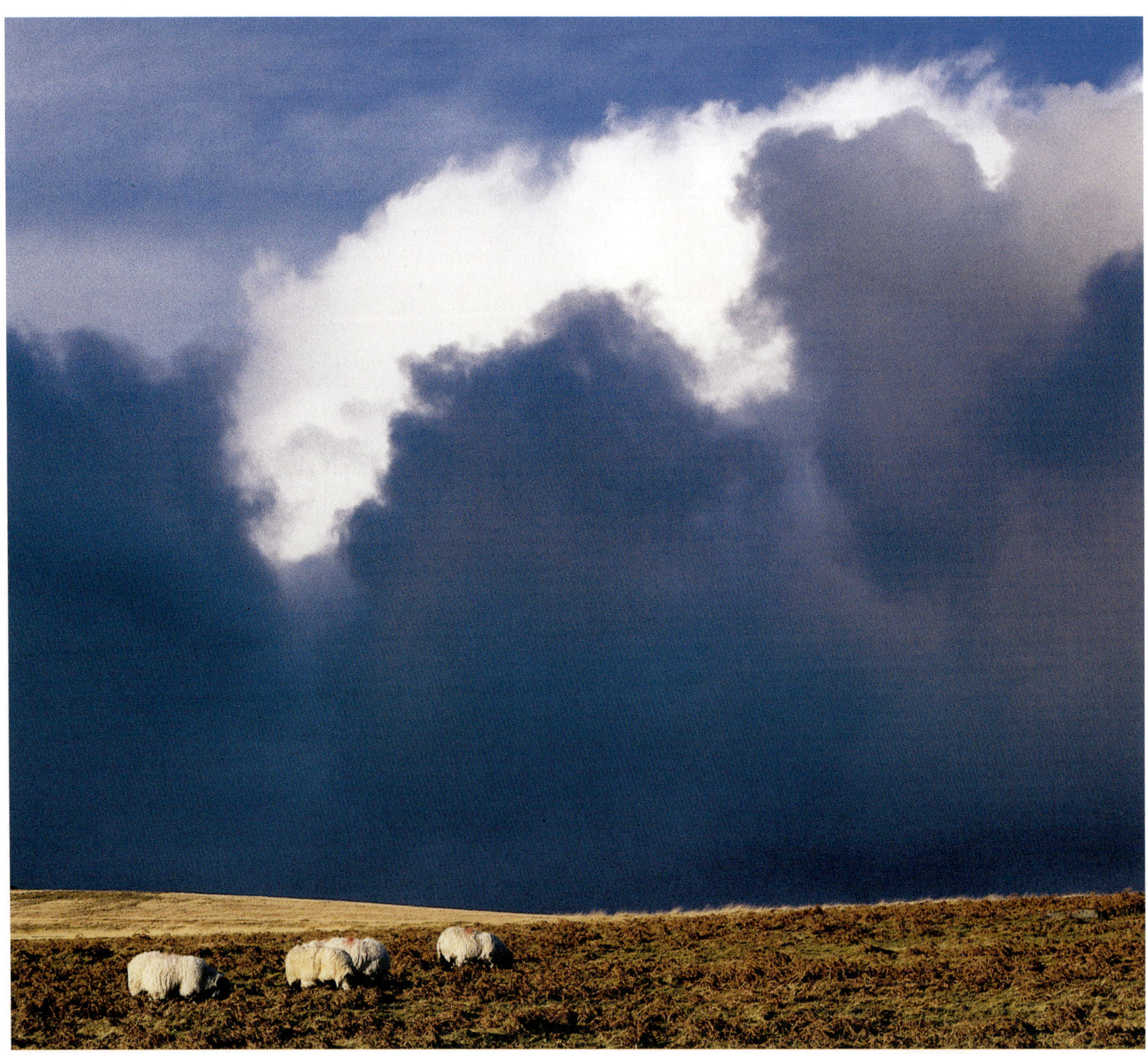

Changeable weather over Brent Moor

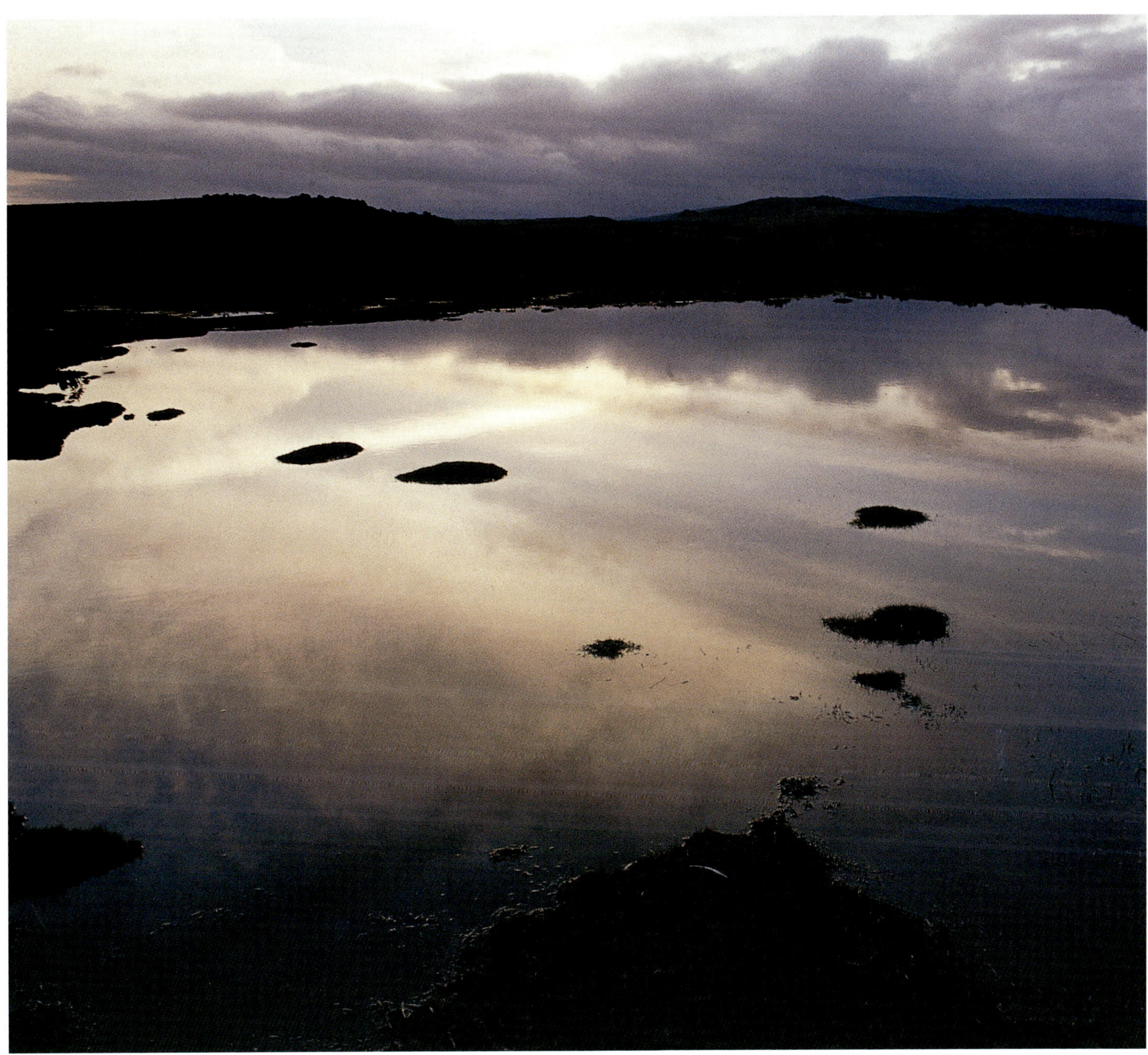

A dewpond on Haytor Down adds to the lonely feel of the moorland

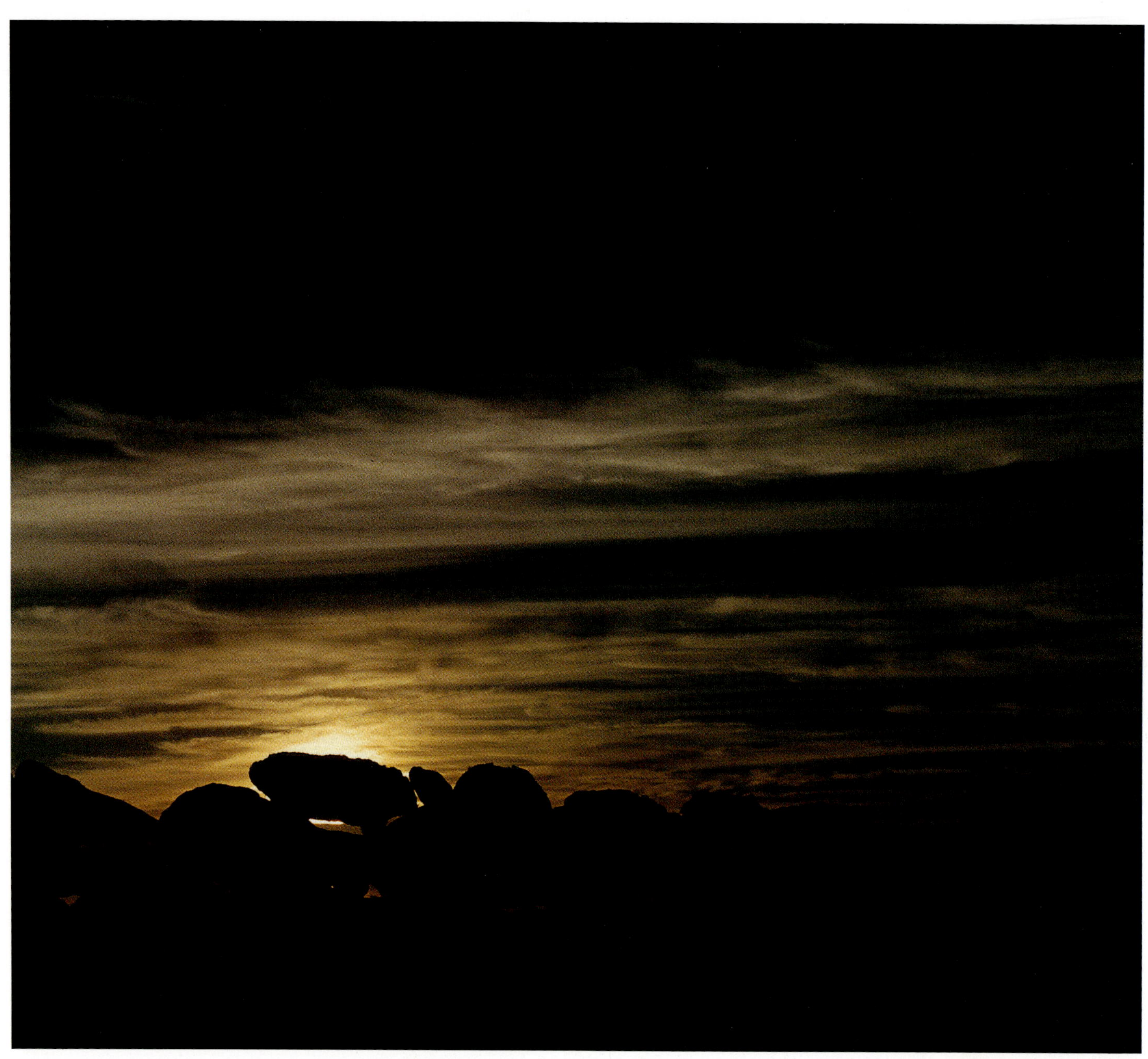

A winter sunset through the drystone wall enclosing Rippon Tor Newtake

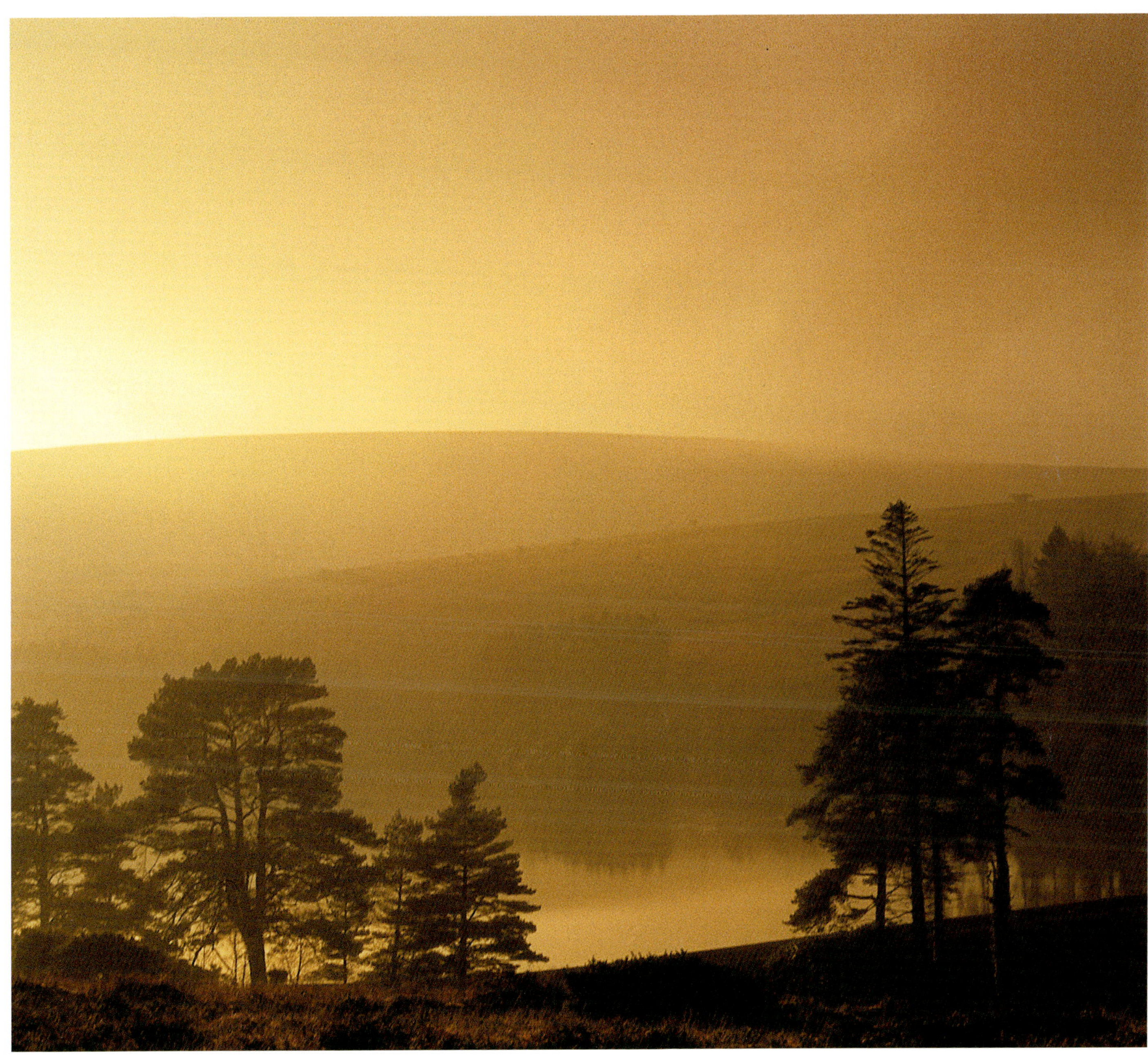

Mist clearing from Venford Reservoir on Holne Moor

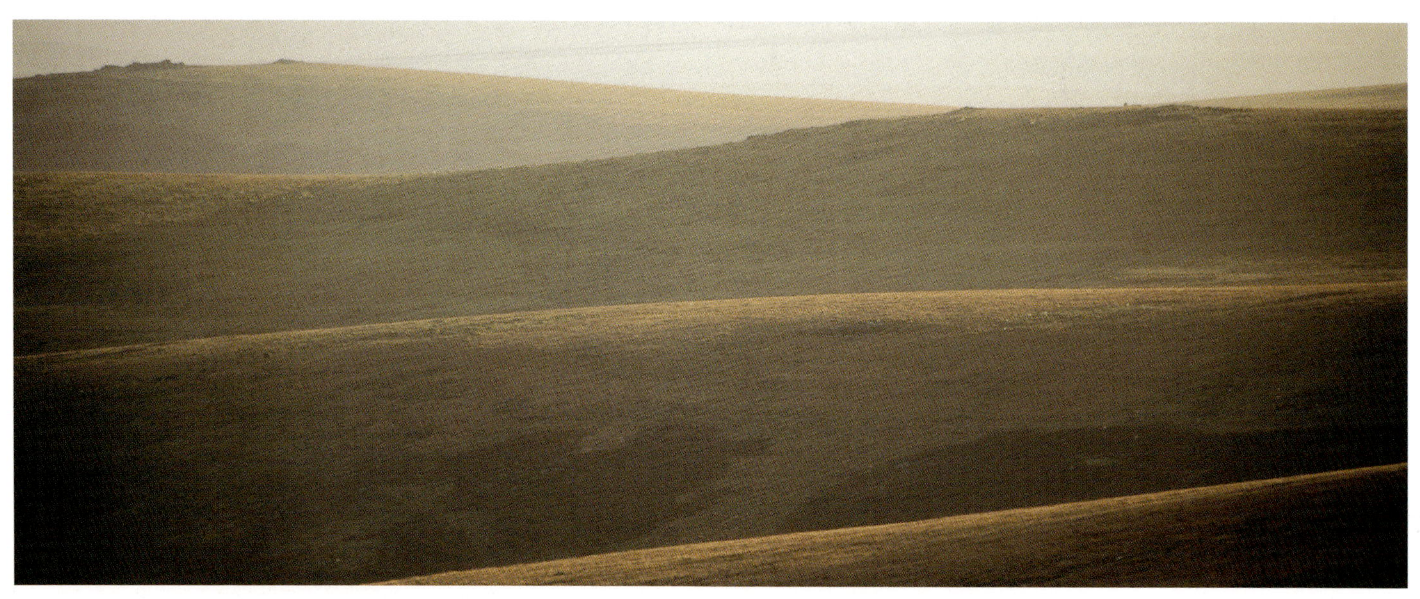

Endless horizons from Petre's Cross on Brent Moor (above) *and from Great Links Tor* (below)

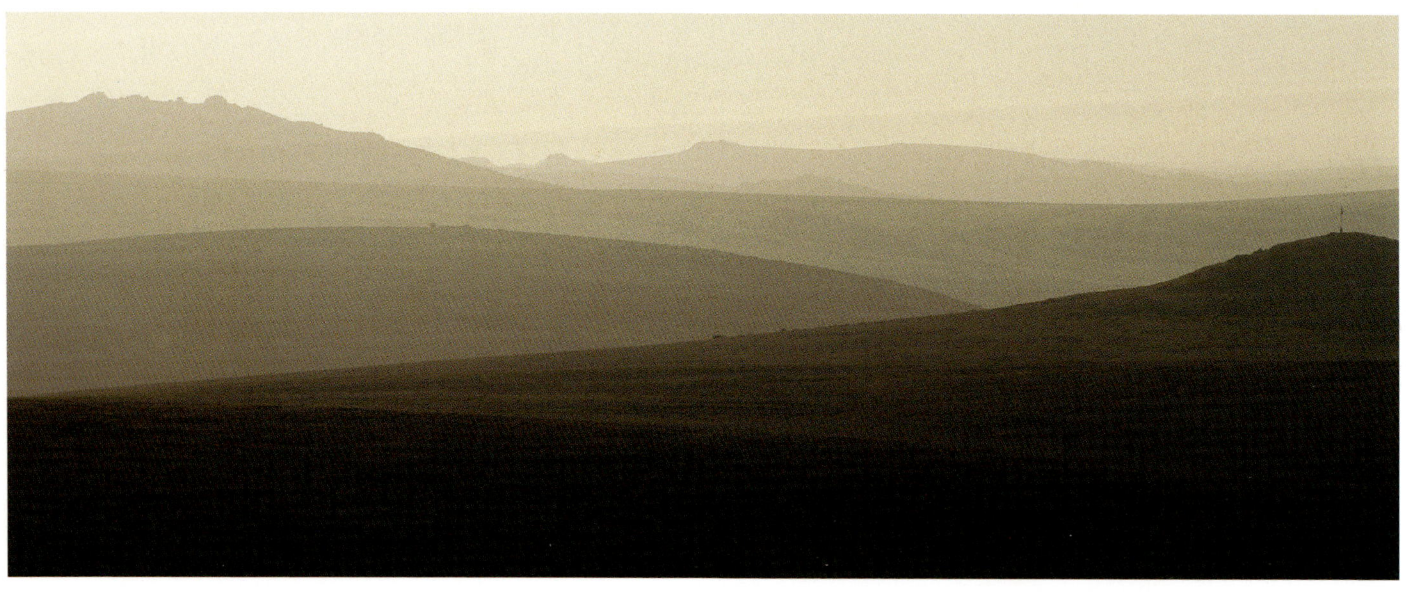

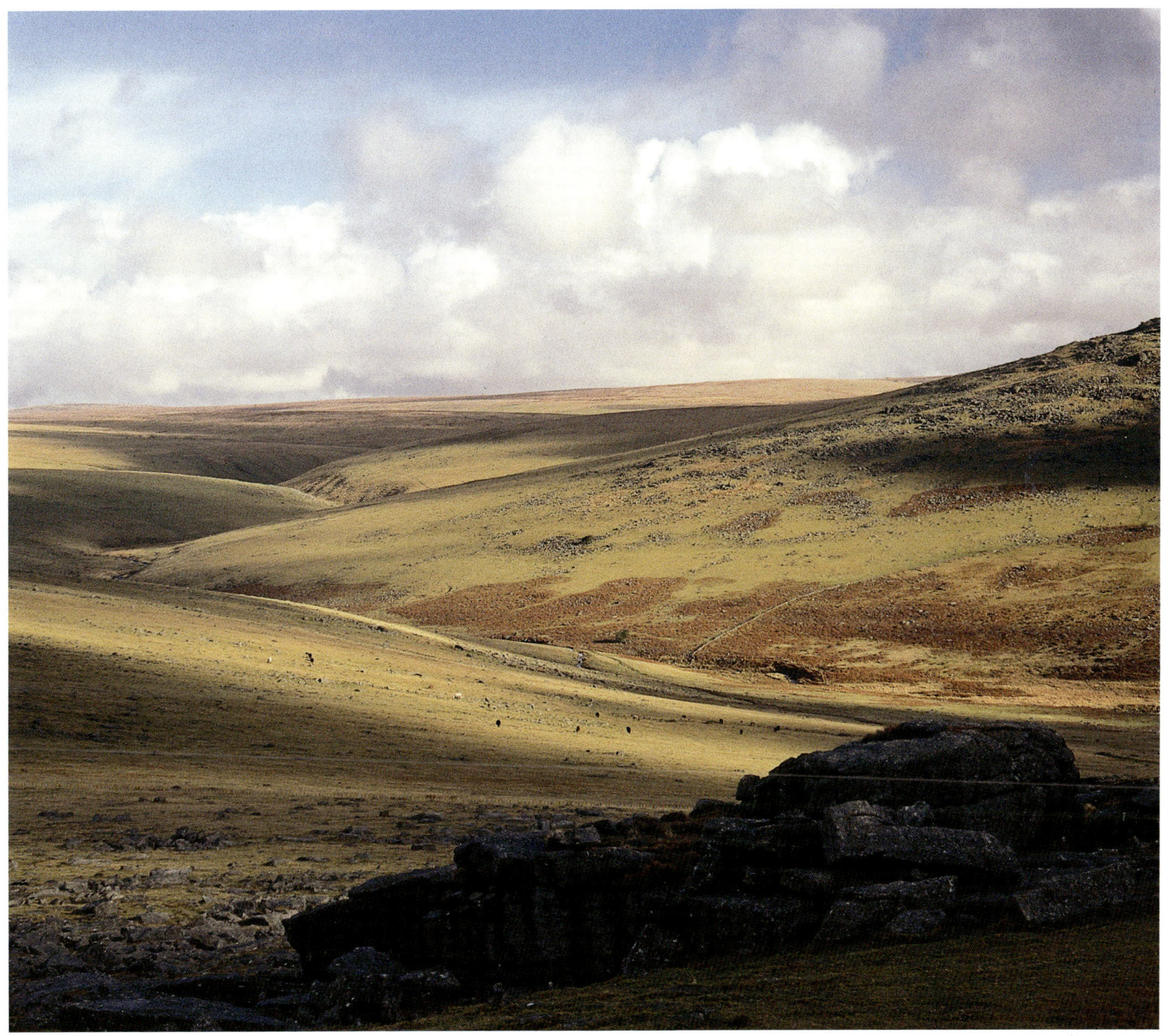

The Walkham valley above Merrivale

Overleaf: *Tor Royal Newtake at Whiteworks. The walls in the central Dartmoor newtakes march across the moorland for miles*

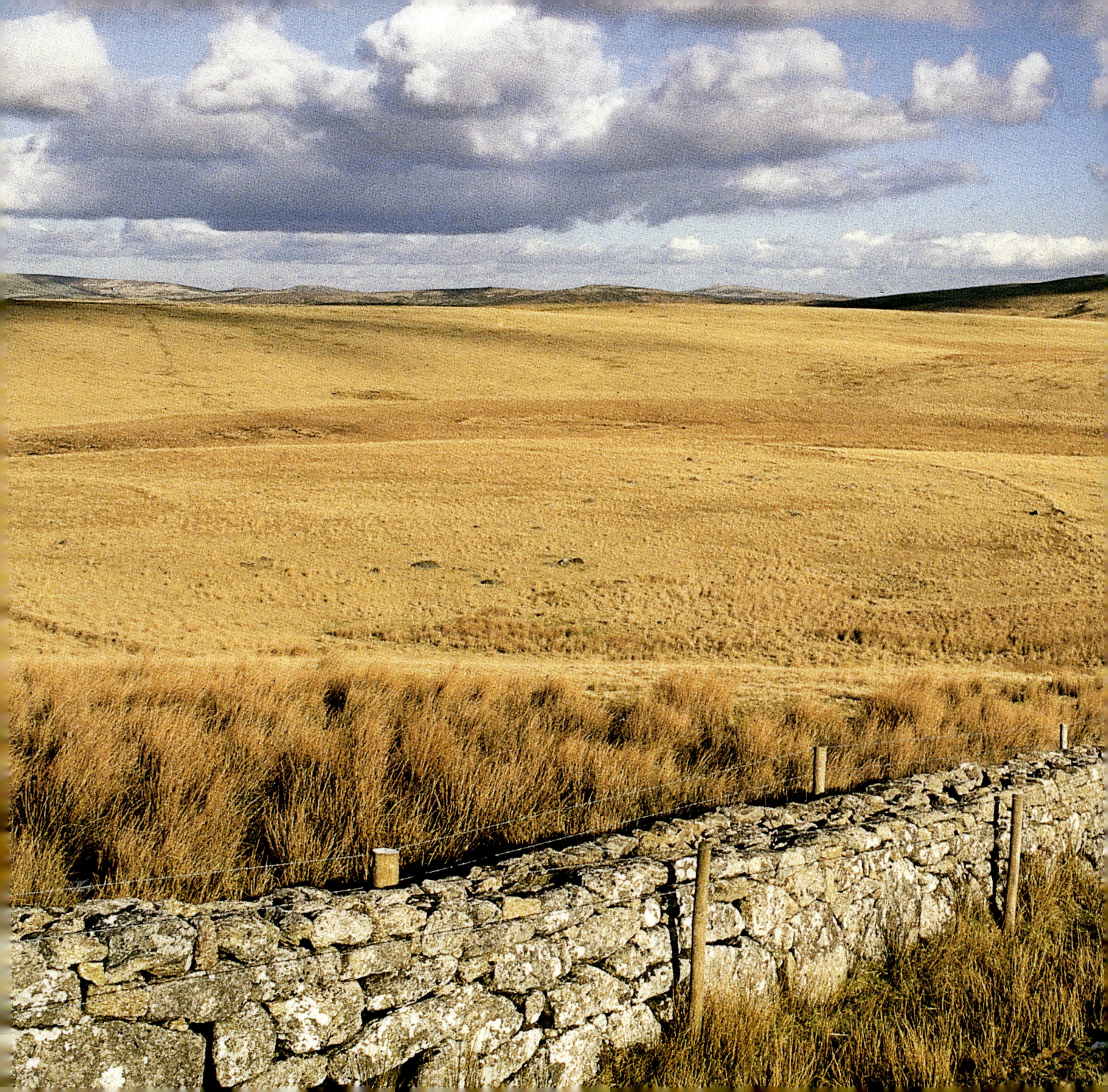

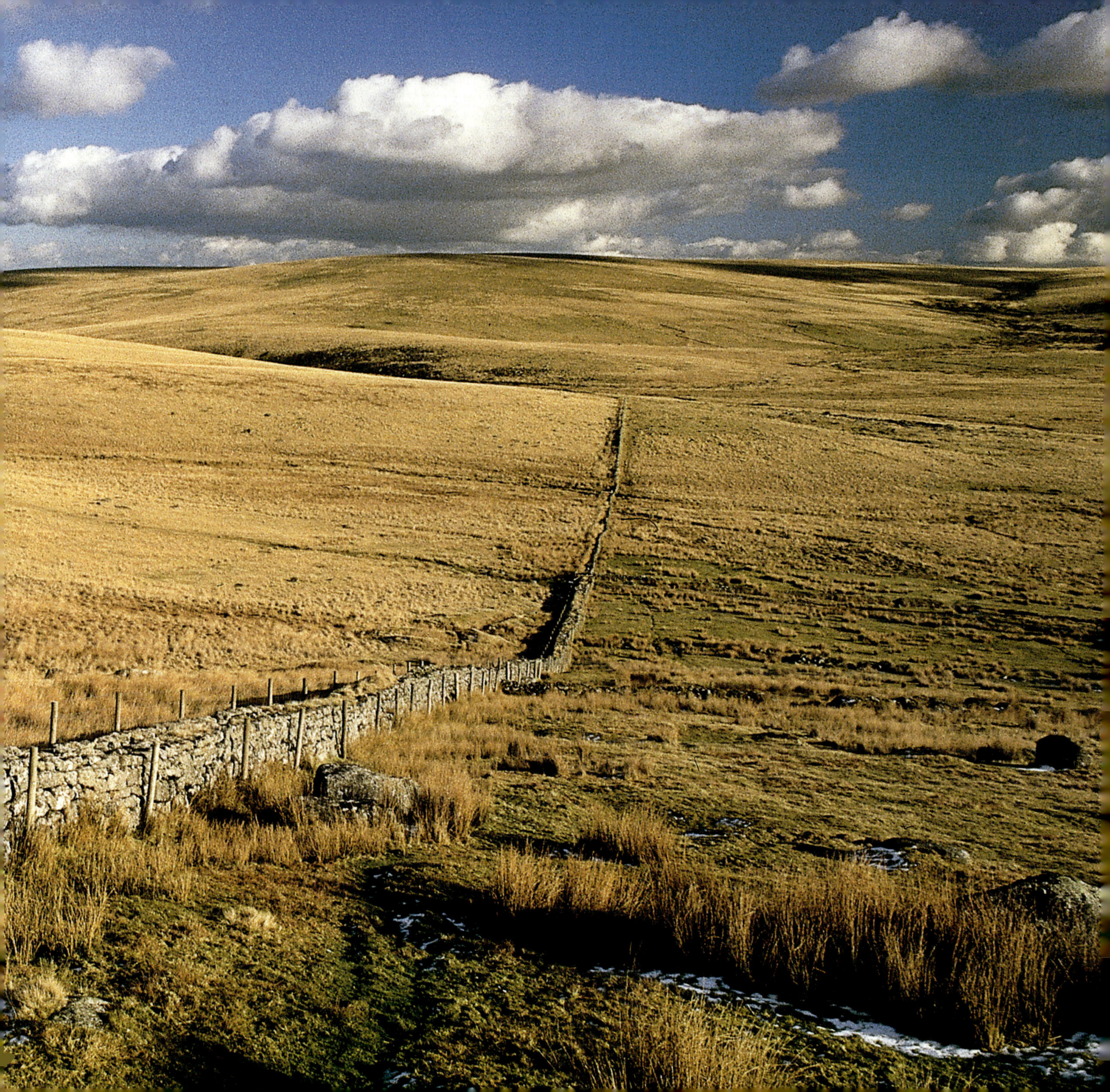

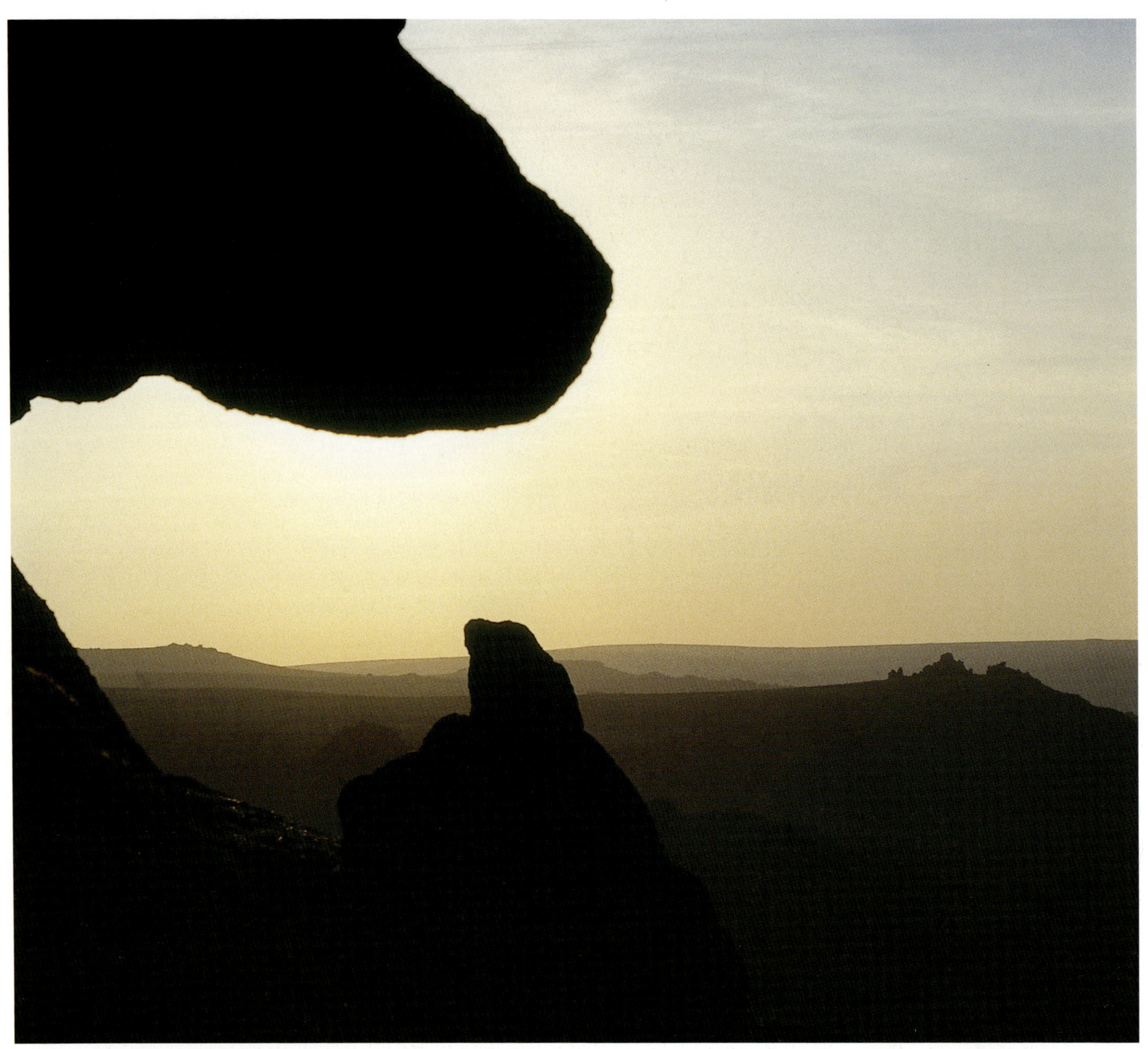

Sunset, with Hound Tor in the middle distance

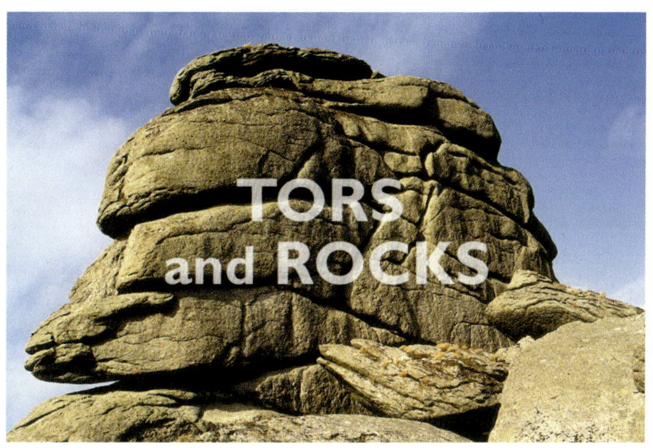

Drama in the landscape

Most people, when they think about Dartmoor, not surprisingly, think of tors. They are the exposed bones of the landscape: the bits that have withstood the ravages of time and weather. They punctuate the skyline, provide a target for your walk, that 'on-top-of-the-world' feeling when you get there, and views which often extend into Cornwall, Somerset, even Dorset. But they are more than just viewpoints; as natural sculptures they can provide the foreground or dramatic feature which transforms a nice view into an artistic composition.

Tors vary enormously. Many stand like sentinels guarding the inner sanctuaries of the northern and southern plateaux. Others crown steep hills detached from the main moorland blocks. Some have enough bare rock to attract rock-climbers; others are just piles of boulders.

Some of the best tors do not stand on a hilltop at all. The Dewerstone rises out of the woods of the Plym valley with its base almost literally in the river; and Vixen Tor, one of my favourites, sits atop a very minor bump in the landscape. Walk out towards Bench Tor from Venford Reservoir and it looks insignificant, but when you get there the ground drops away beneath your feet into the gorge of the Dart below and you find yourself standing on one of the most airy perches in the Park. Some of the rocks in Lustleigh Cleave or in the woodlands of the Wray valley only just clear the treetops and give you that wonderful feeling of sitting in the canopy with the birds.

Tors offer viewpoints, scrambling, shelter, picnic spots and eyries from which to contemplate the world below. They also have amazing and very varied architecture. Contrast the huge monolith of Haytor with the weirdly weathered, precariously perched, blocks of Great Staple Tor. Compare the soaring pinnacles of the Dewerstone with the massive bulbous shapes of Great Links Tor or the totally insignificant rounded excrescence that is High Willhays – Dartmoor's highest point. They are all interesting places to explore and enjoy; places that bring a touch of drama to the Dartmoor landscape.

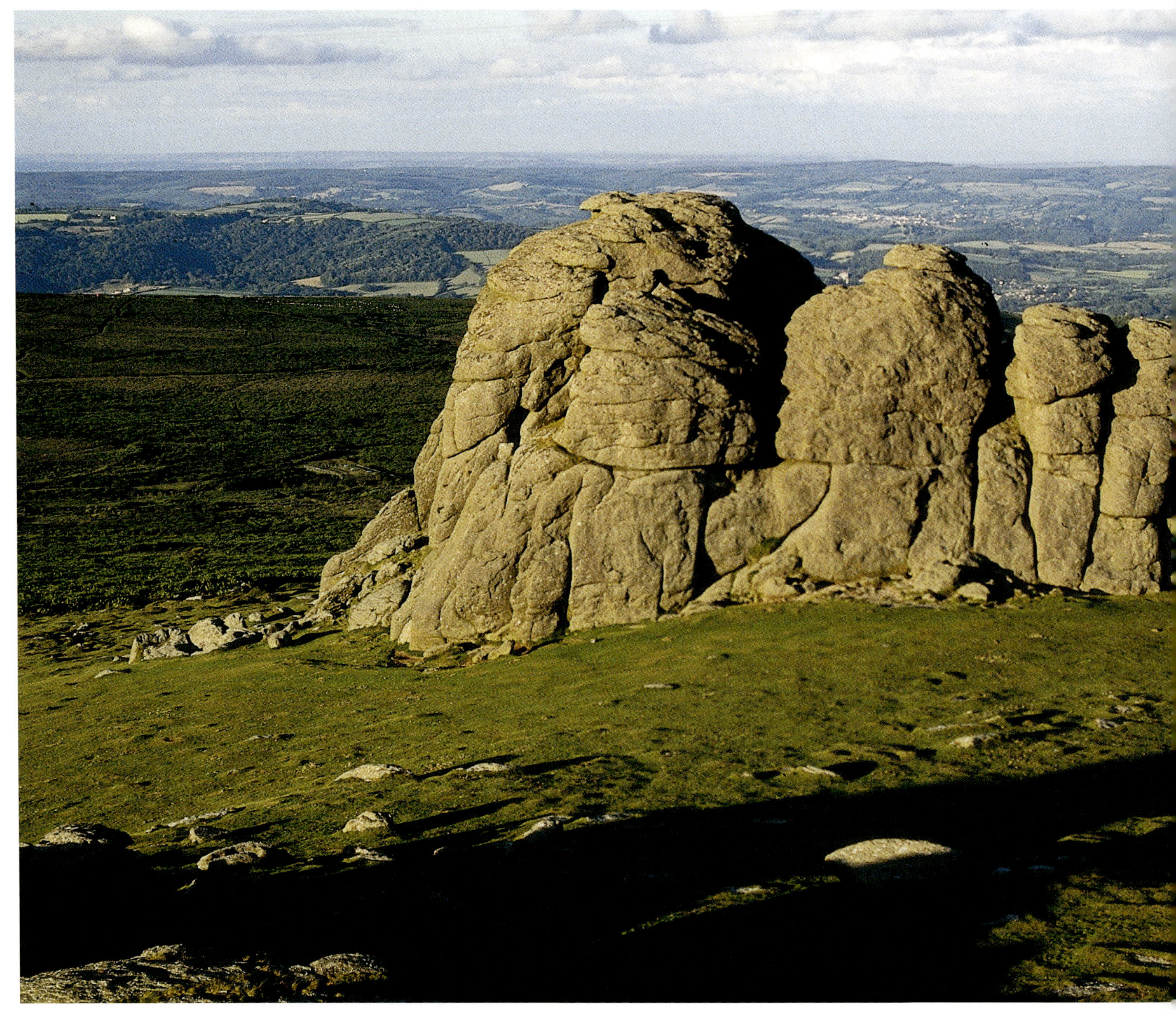

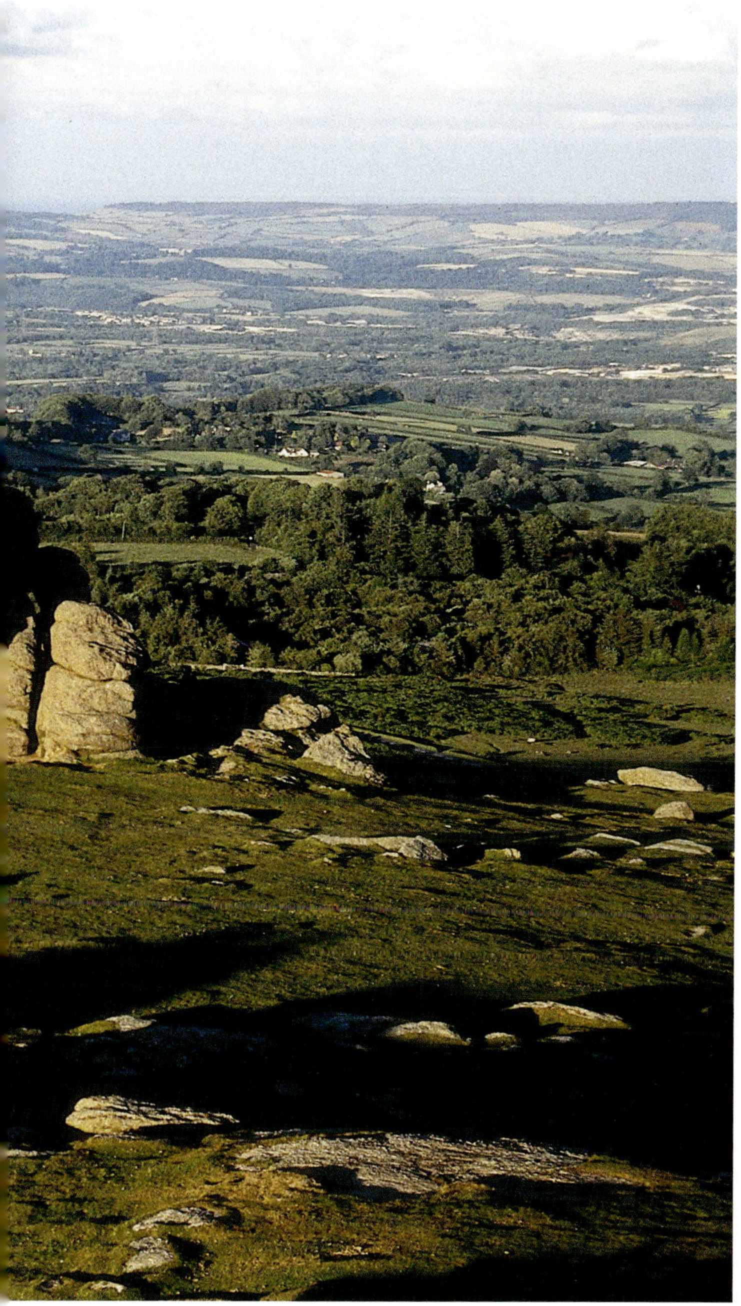

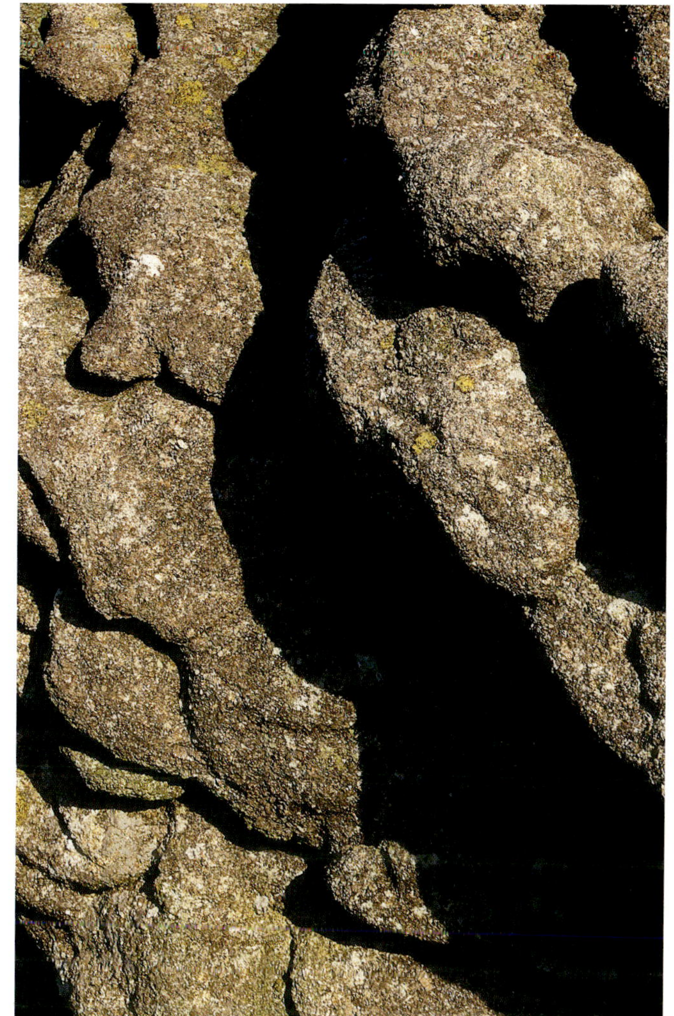

Granite comes in many shapes and forms

Overleaf: Widgery Cross on Brat Tor, near Lydford

Haytor Rocks are prominent from miles around and are a grand viewpoint over South and East Devon

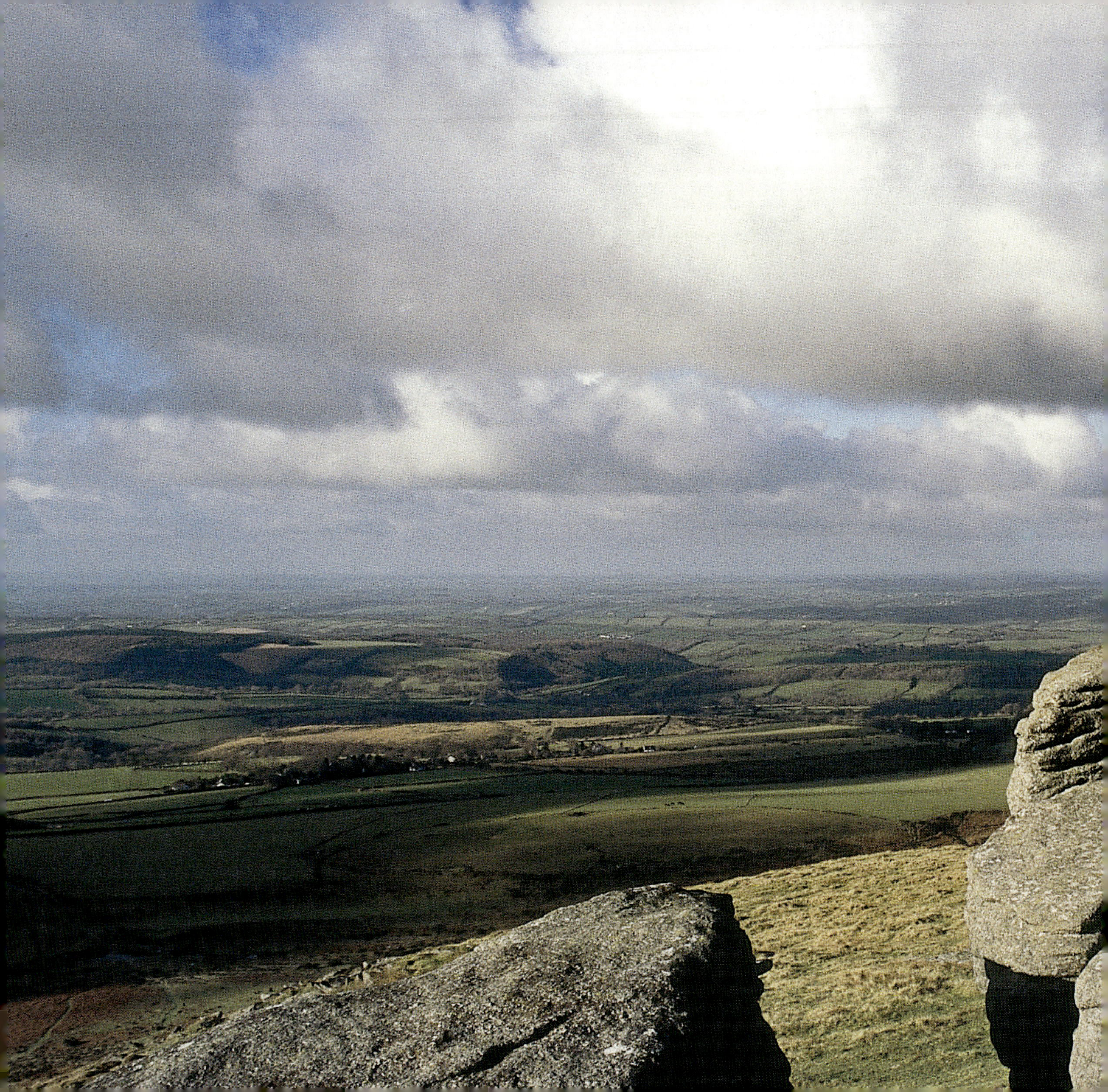

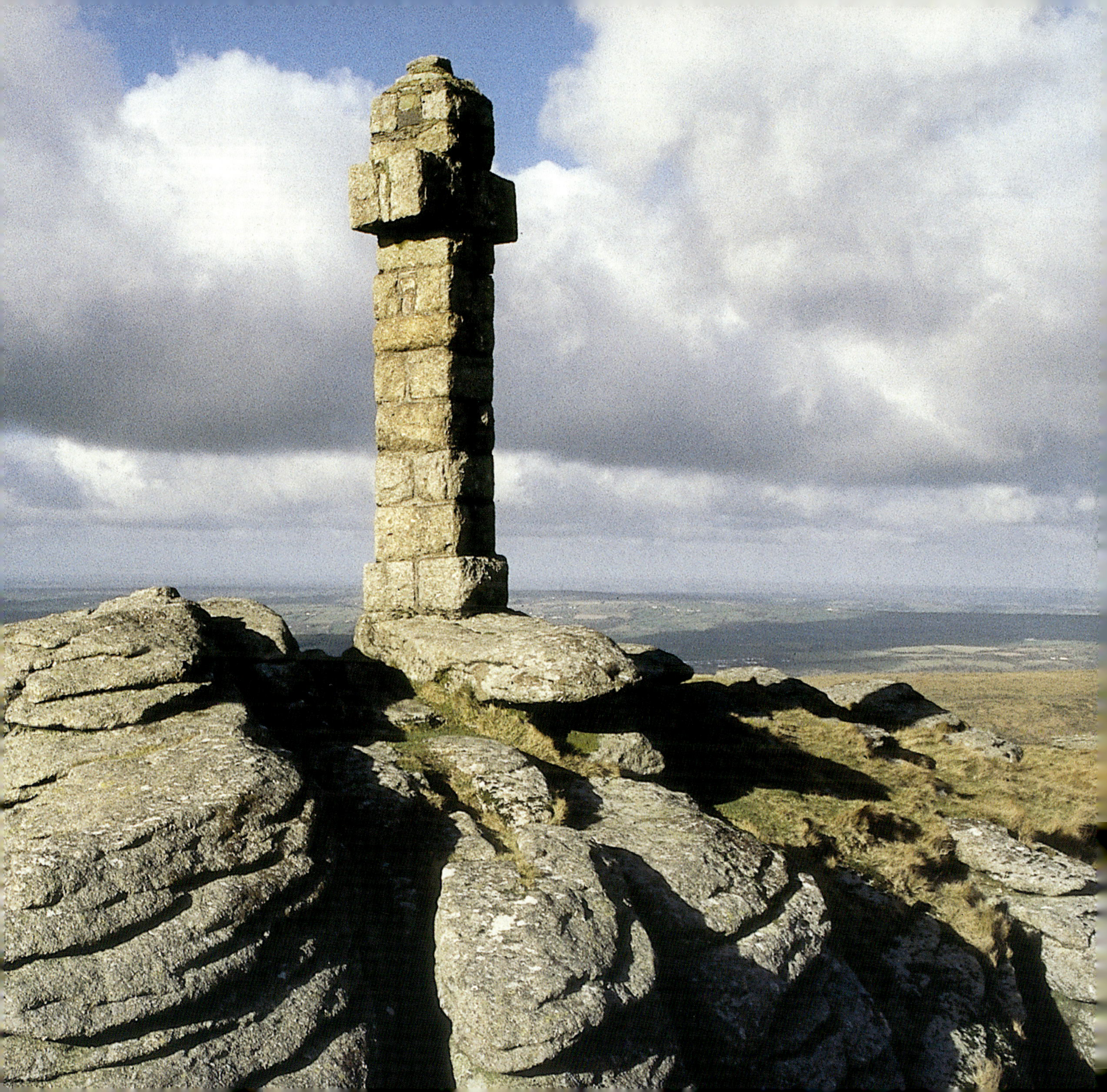

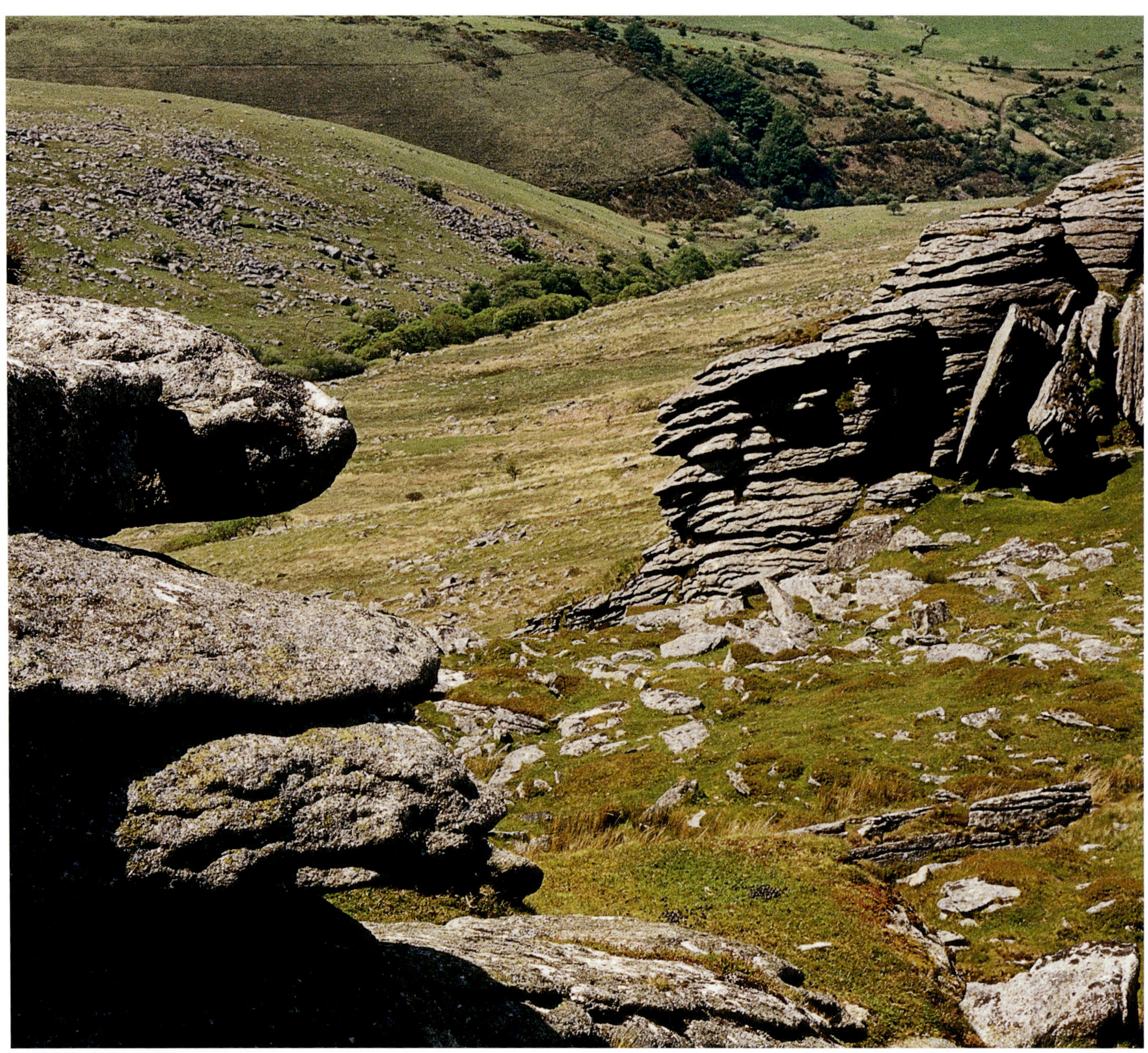

Black Tor, looking across the West Okement valley

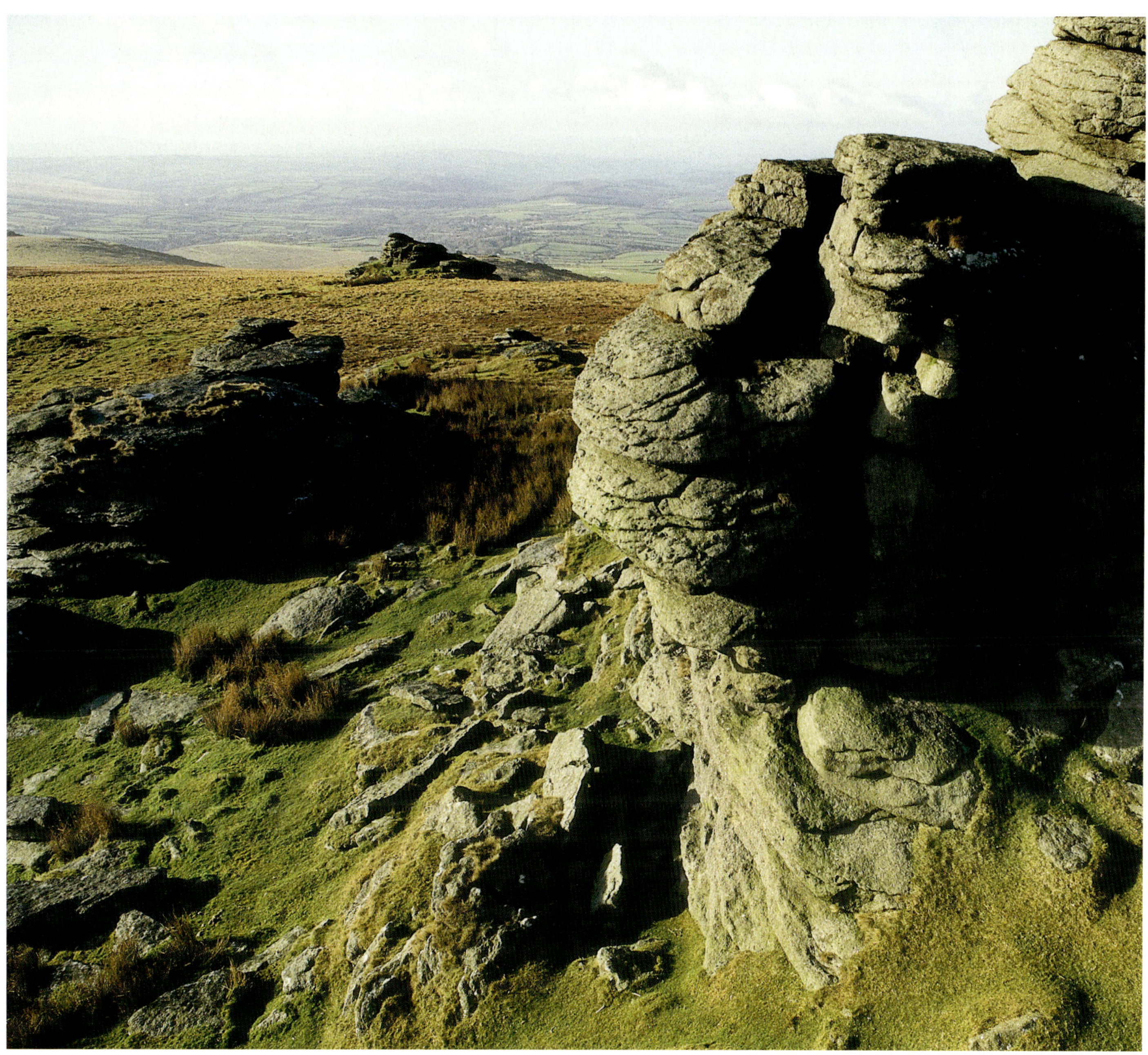

The bulbous shapes of Great Links Tor, looking out over West Devon into Cornwall

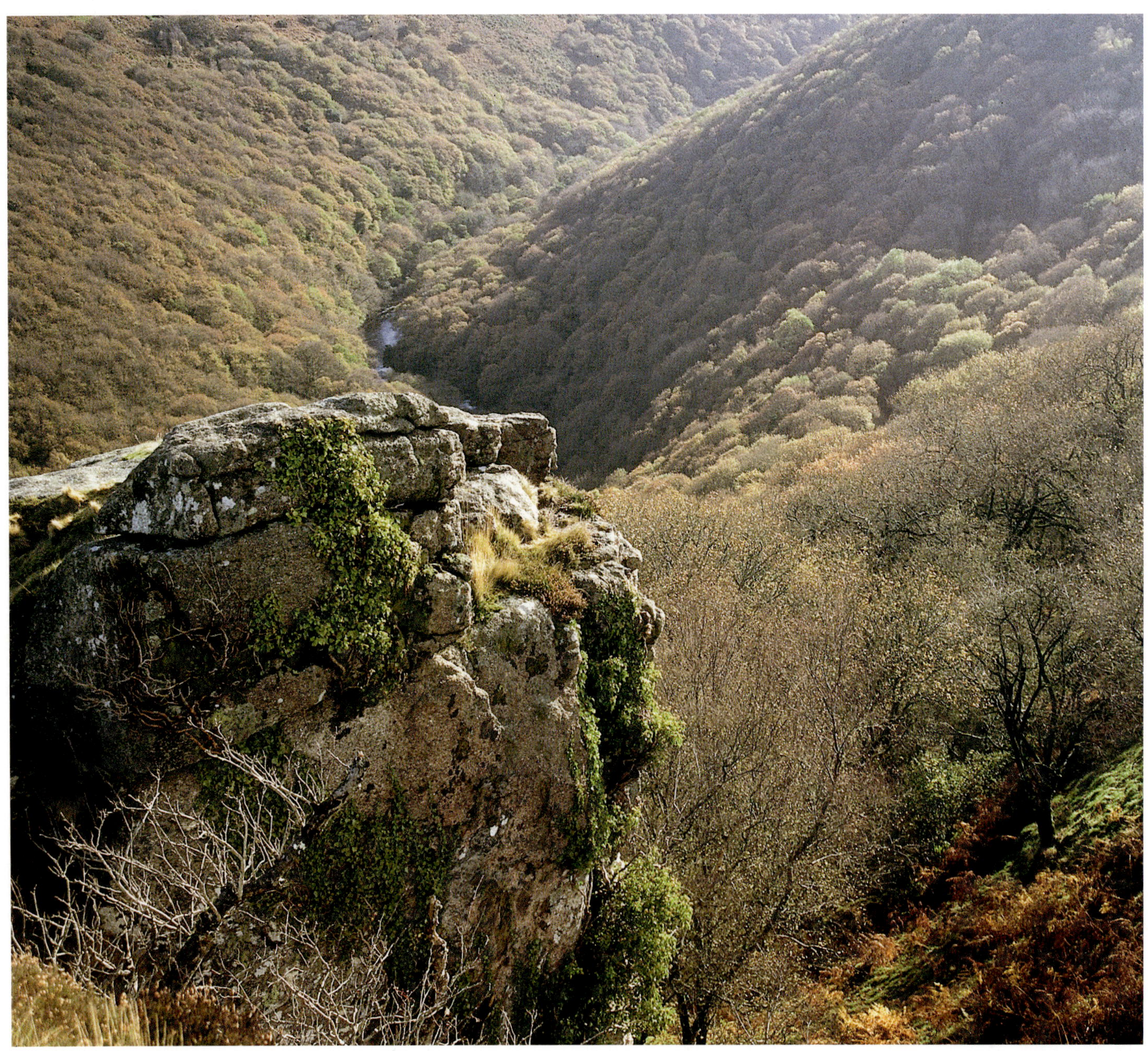

Bench Tor gives an airy perch over the Dart valley

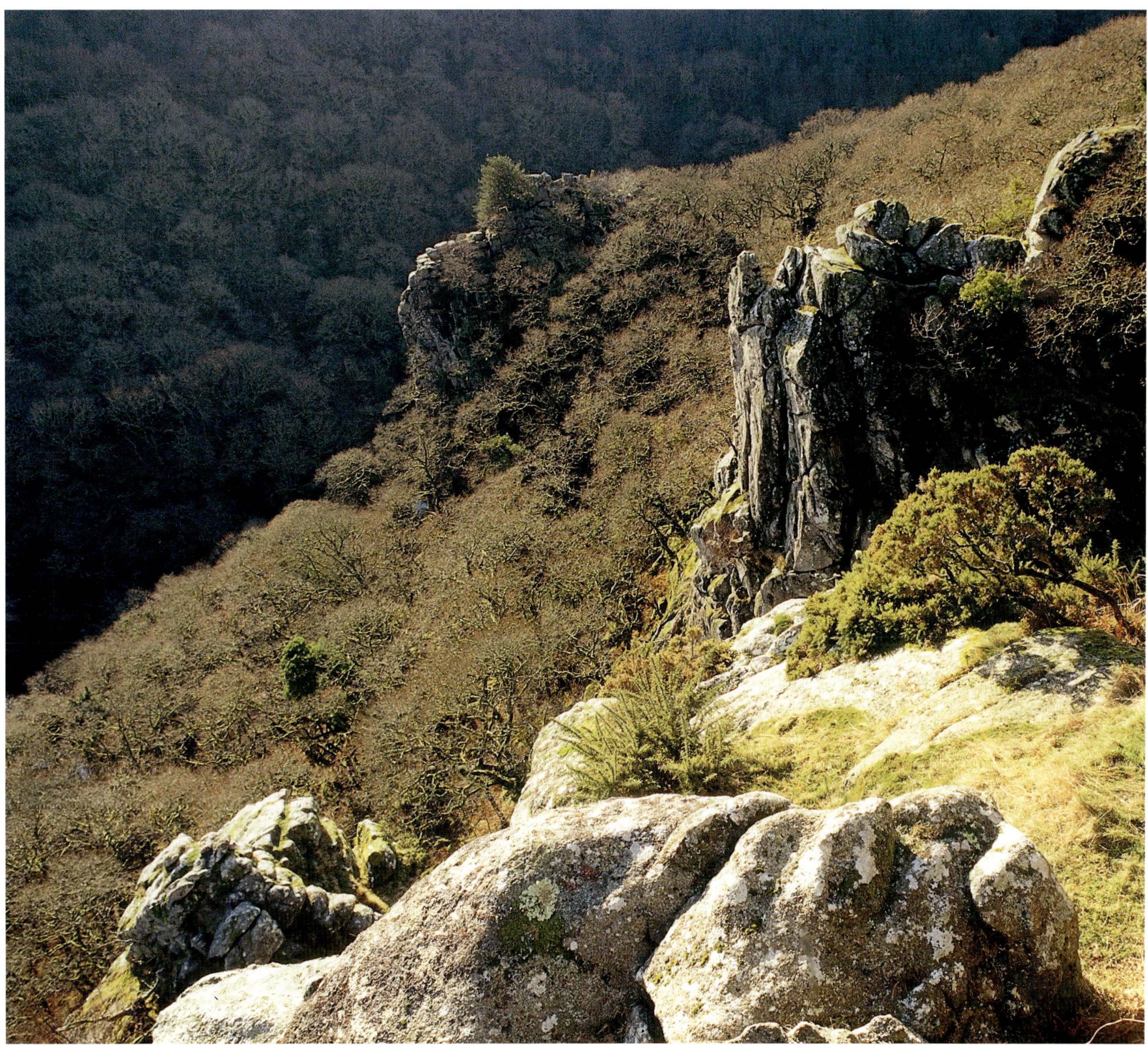

The Dewerstone rises above the River Plym, and offers the best rock-climbing on Dartmoor

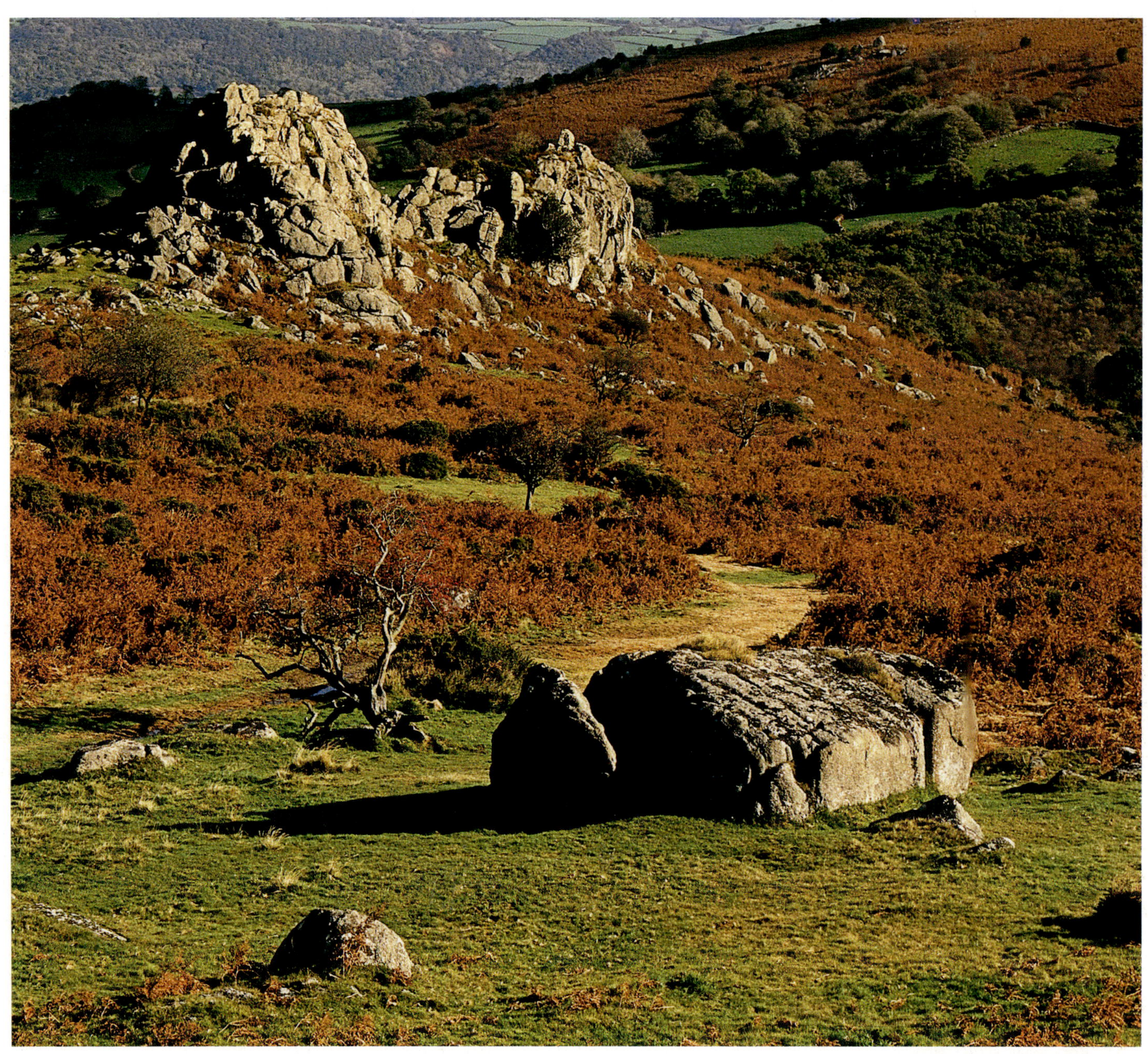

Greator Rocks on Houndtor Down have an almost mountainous feel about them

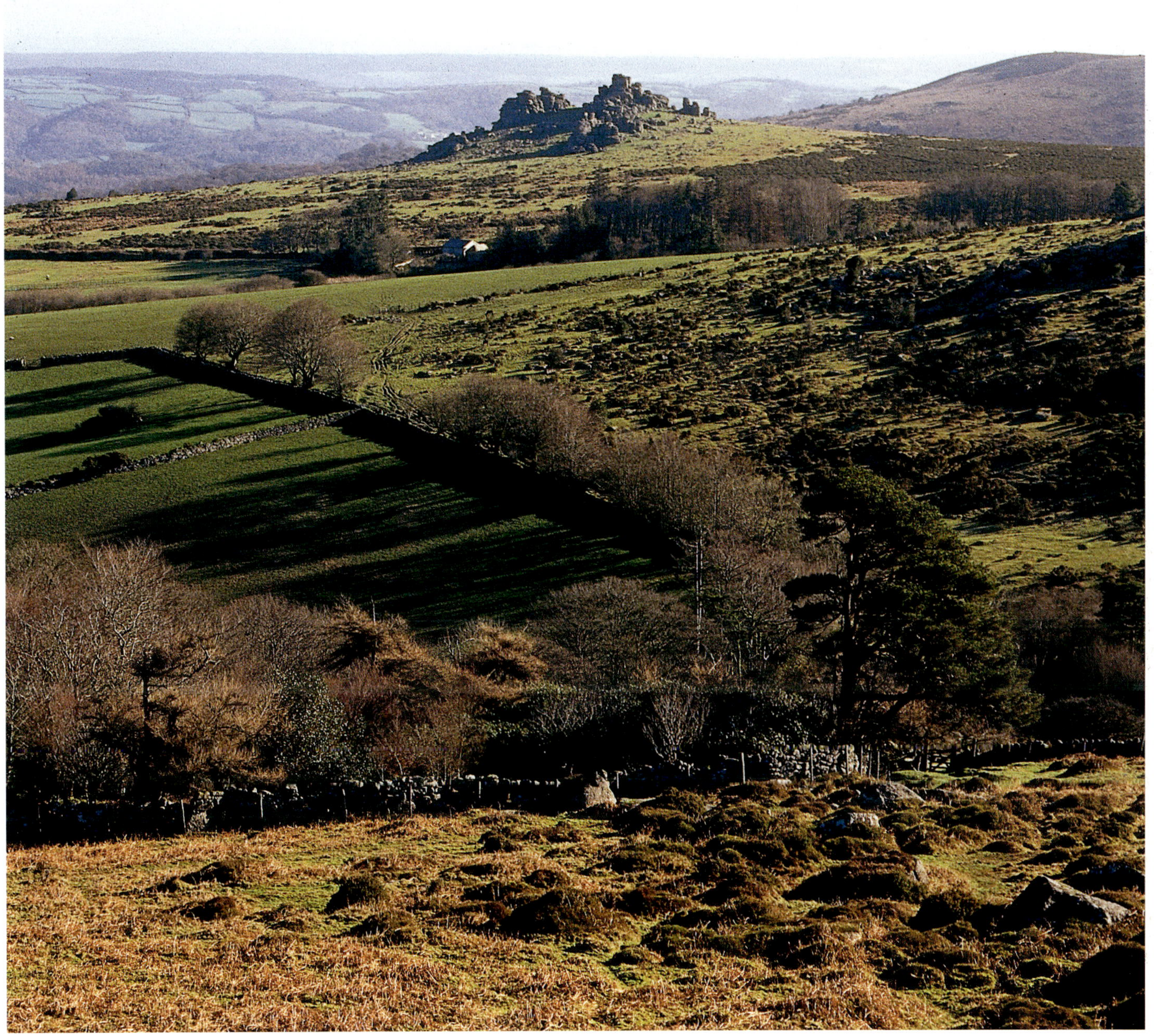

Hound Tor seen from Honeybag Tor

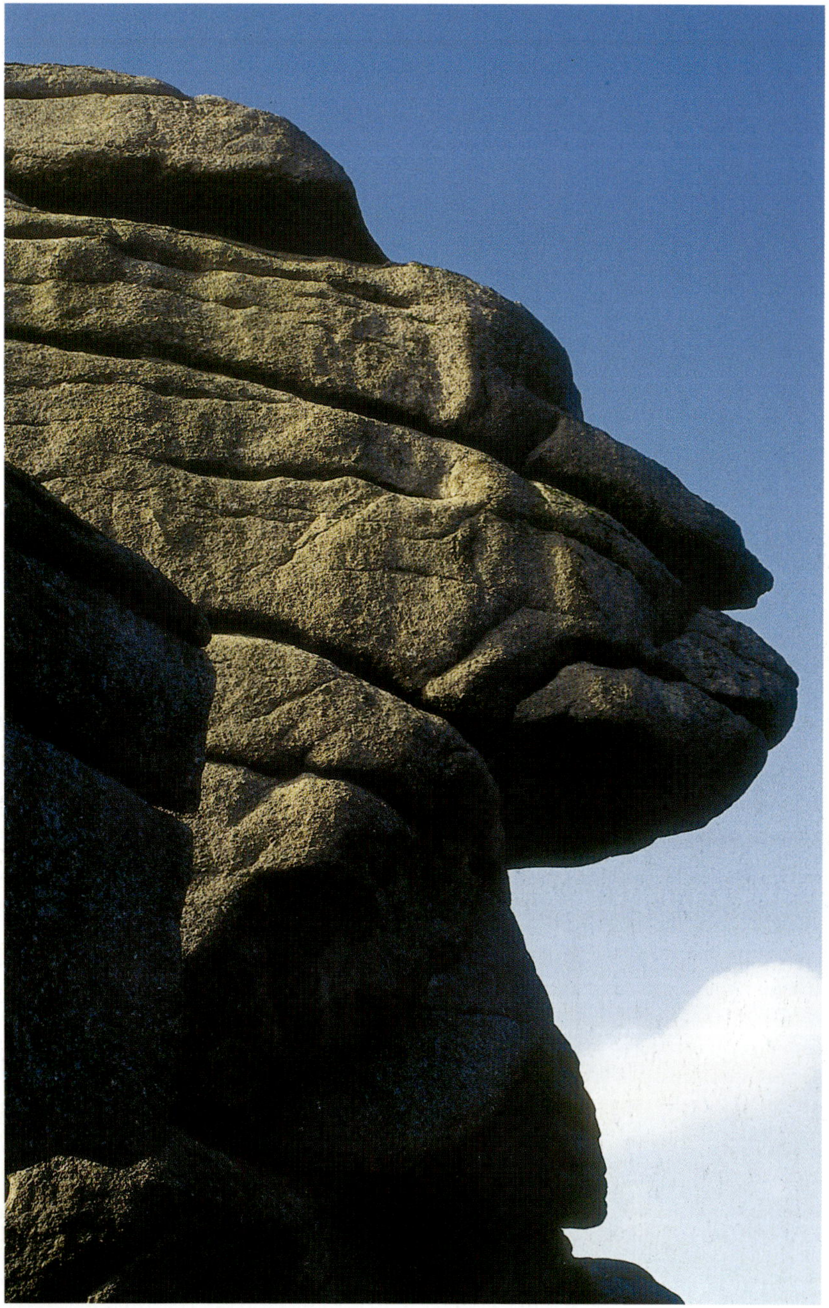

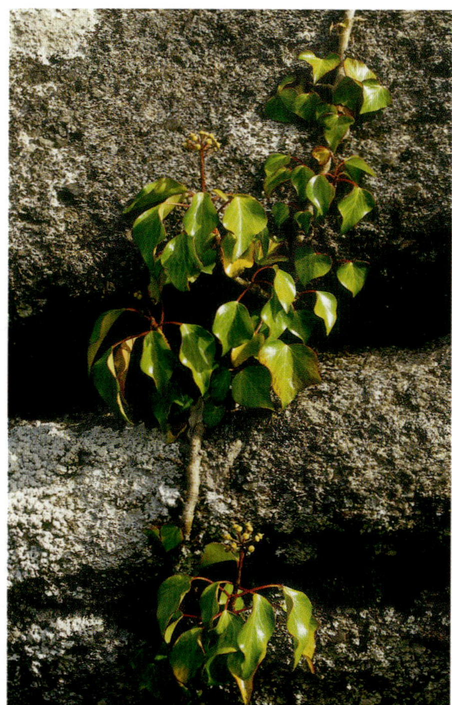

Ivy clinging to granite

Vixen Tor, looking rather like a grumpy Indian chief

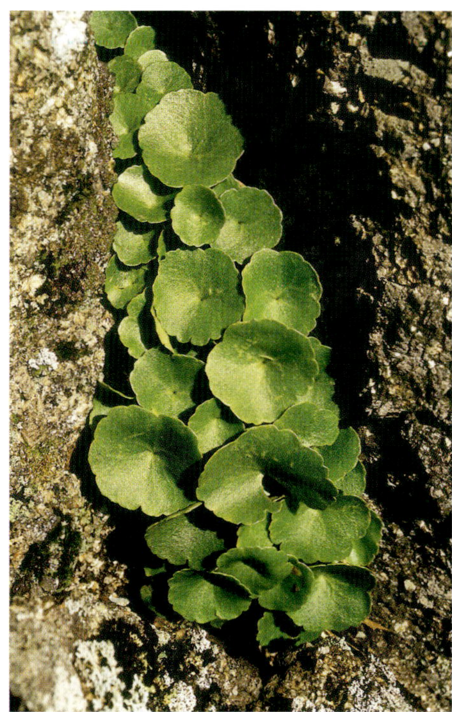

Pennywort nestles in the cracks

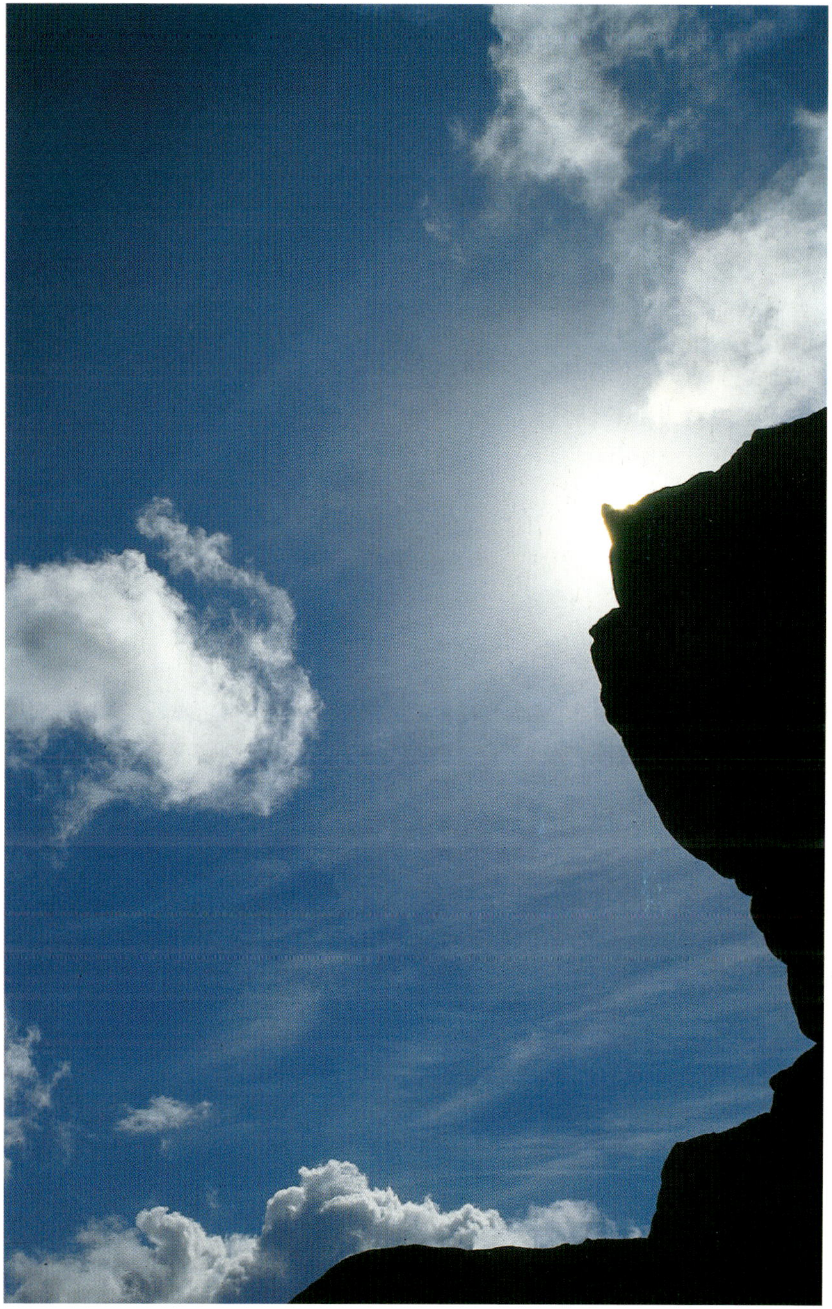

Vixen Tor, now dramatic against the sky

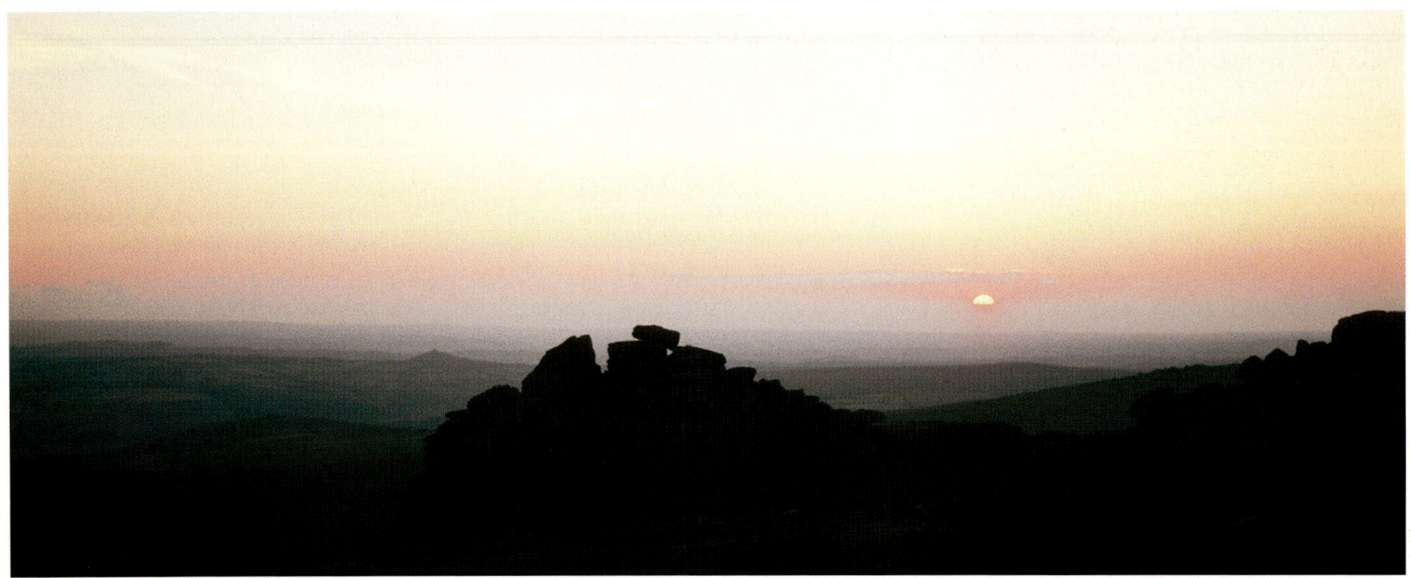

Sunset over Great Mis Tor

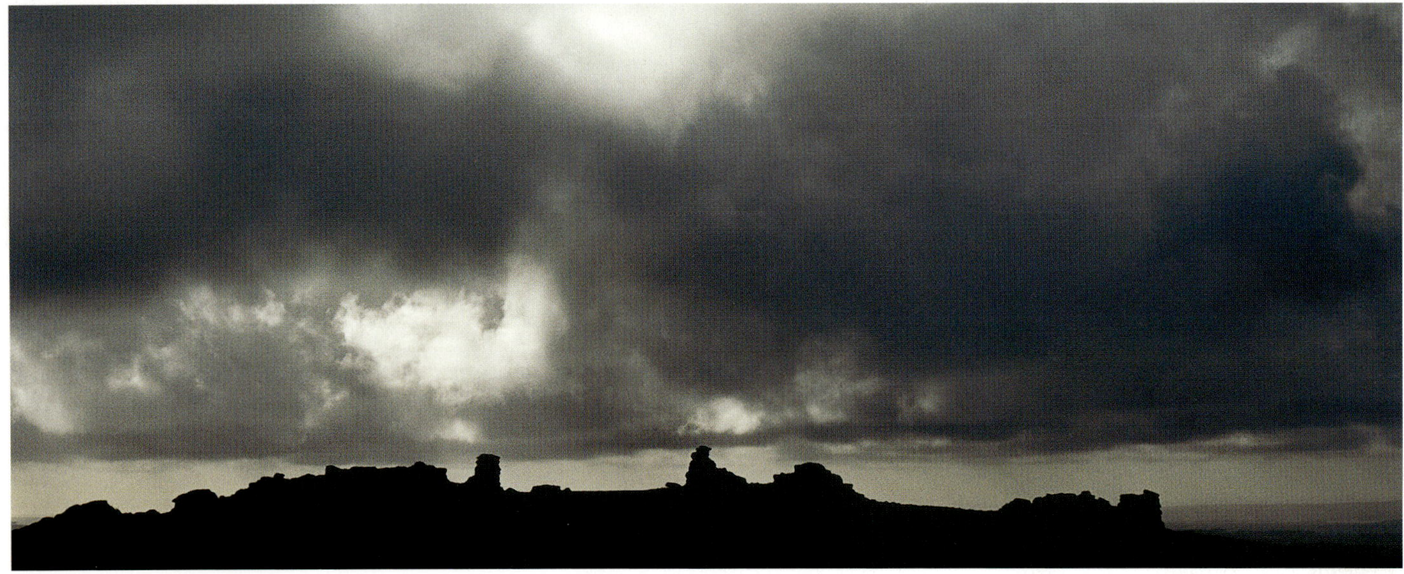

Great Staple Tor from Roos Tor

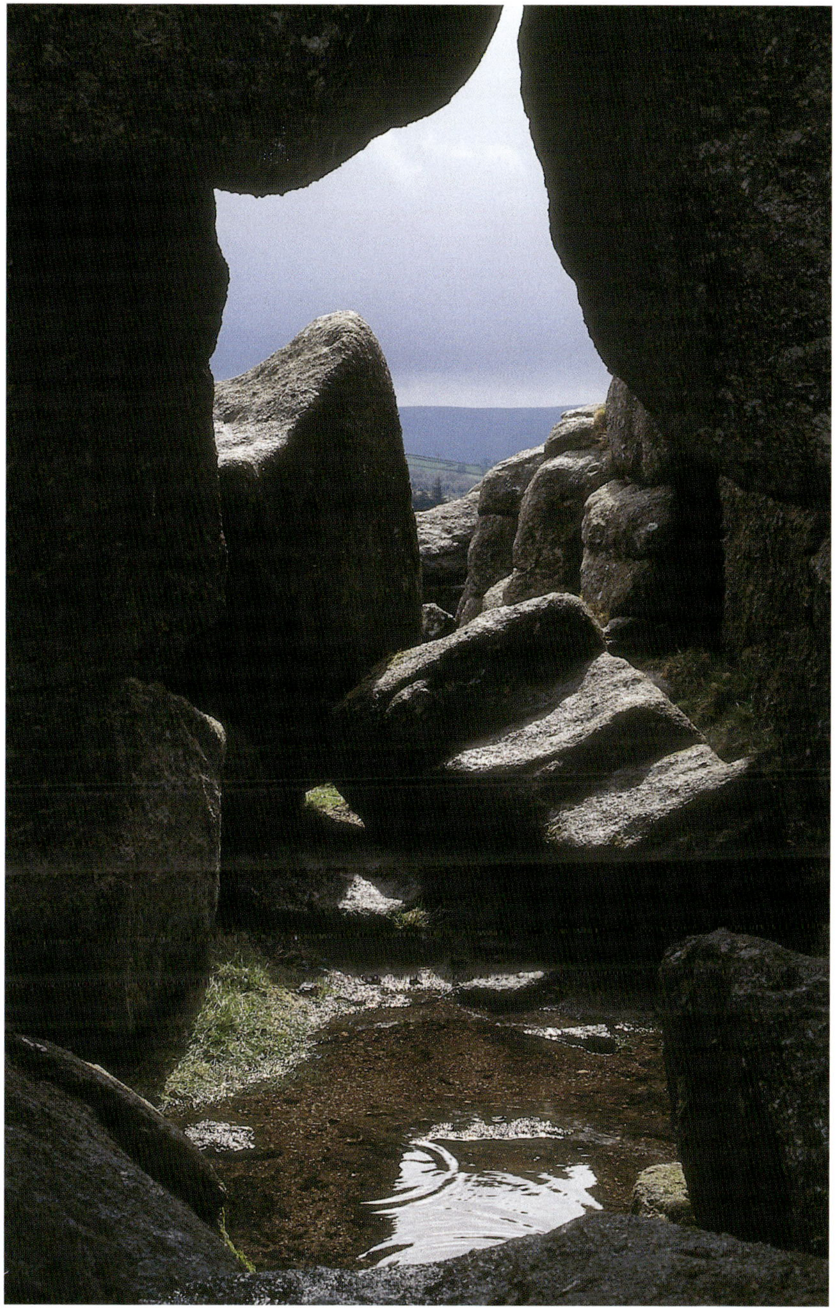

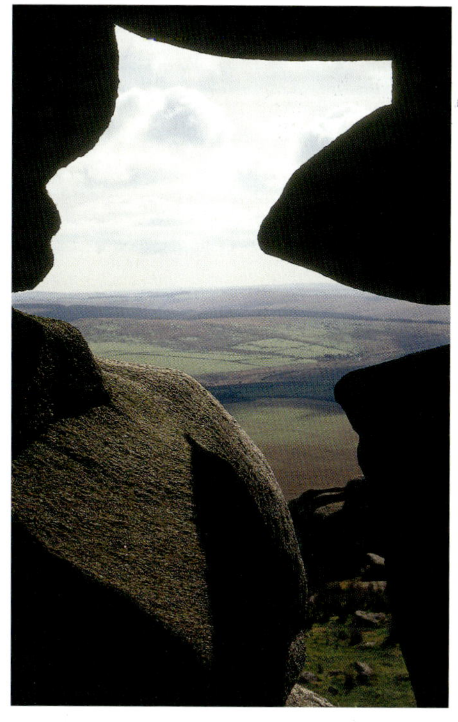

Explore the nooks and crannies in tors. The children will love it!

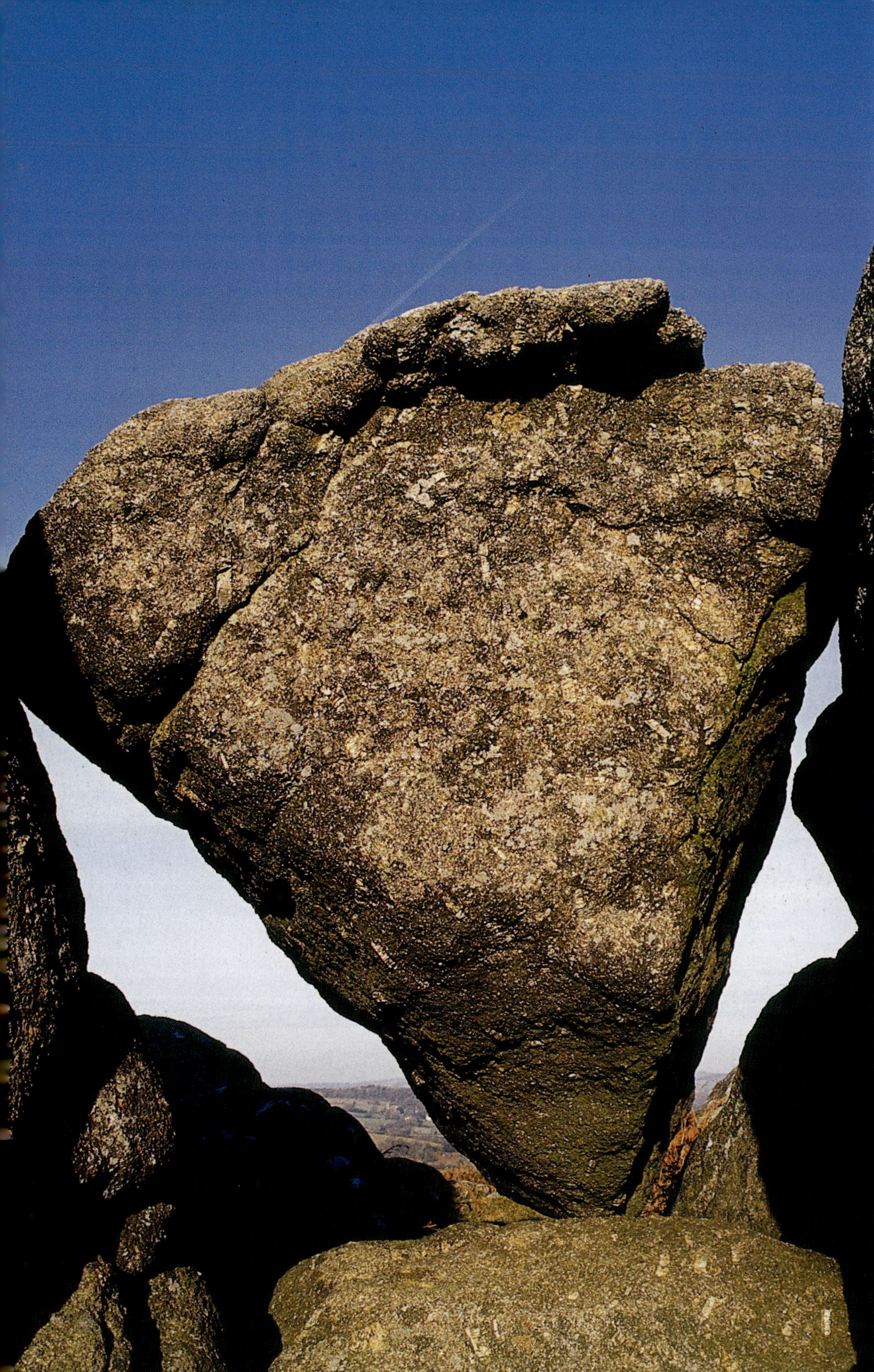

Well balanced!

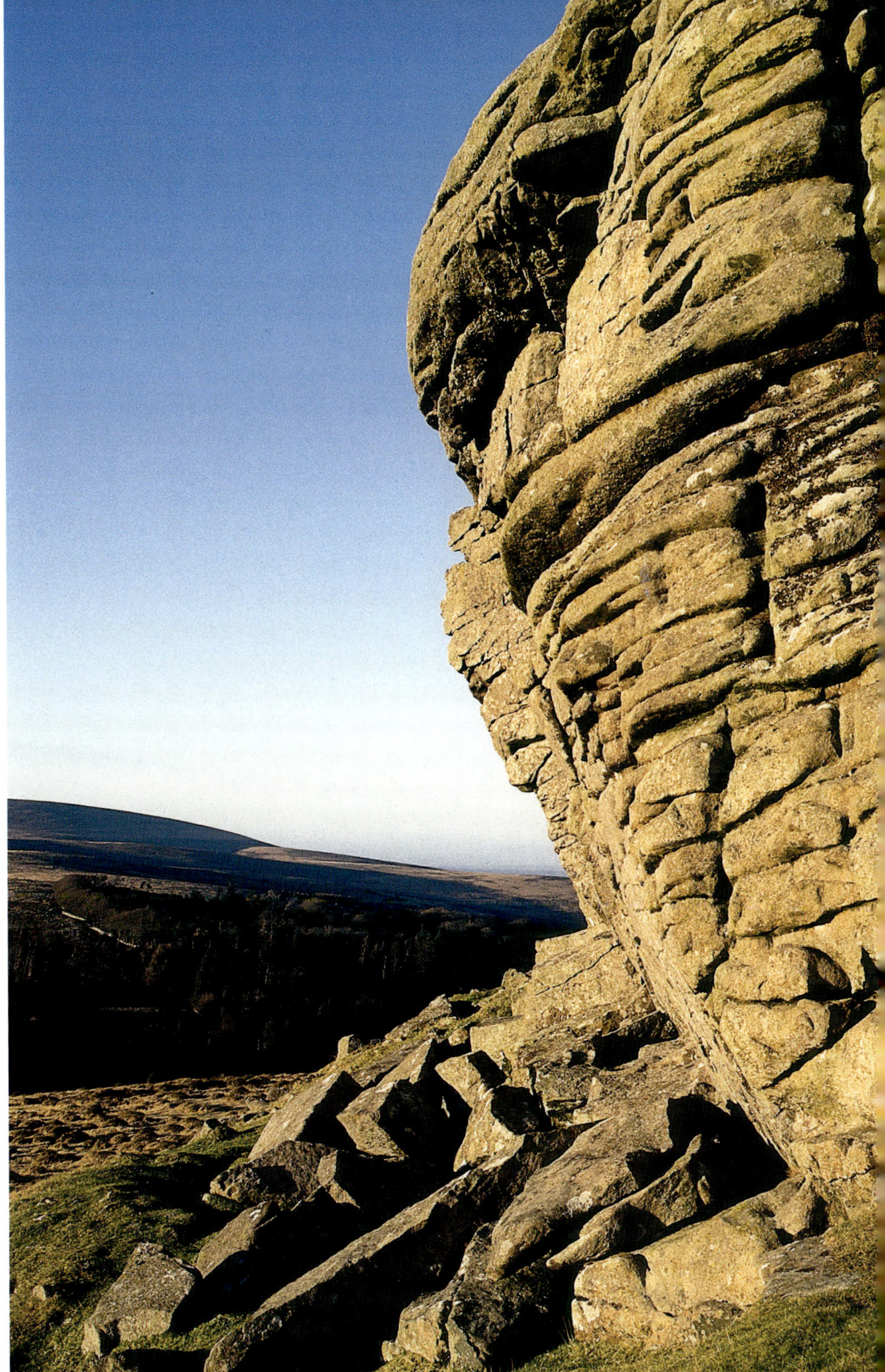

Kestor, near Chagford

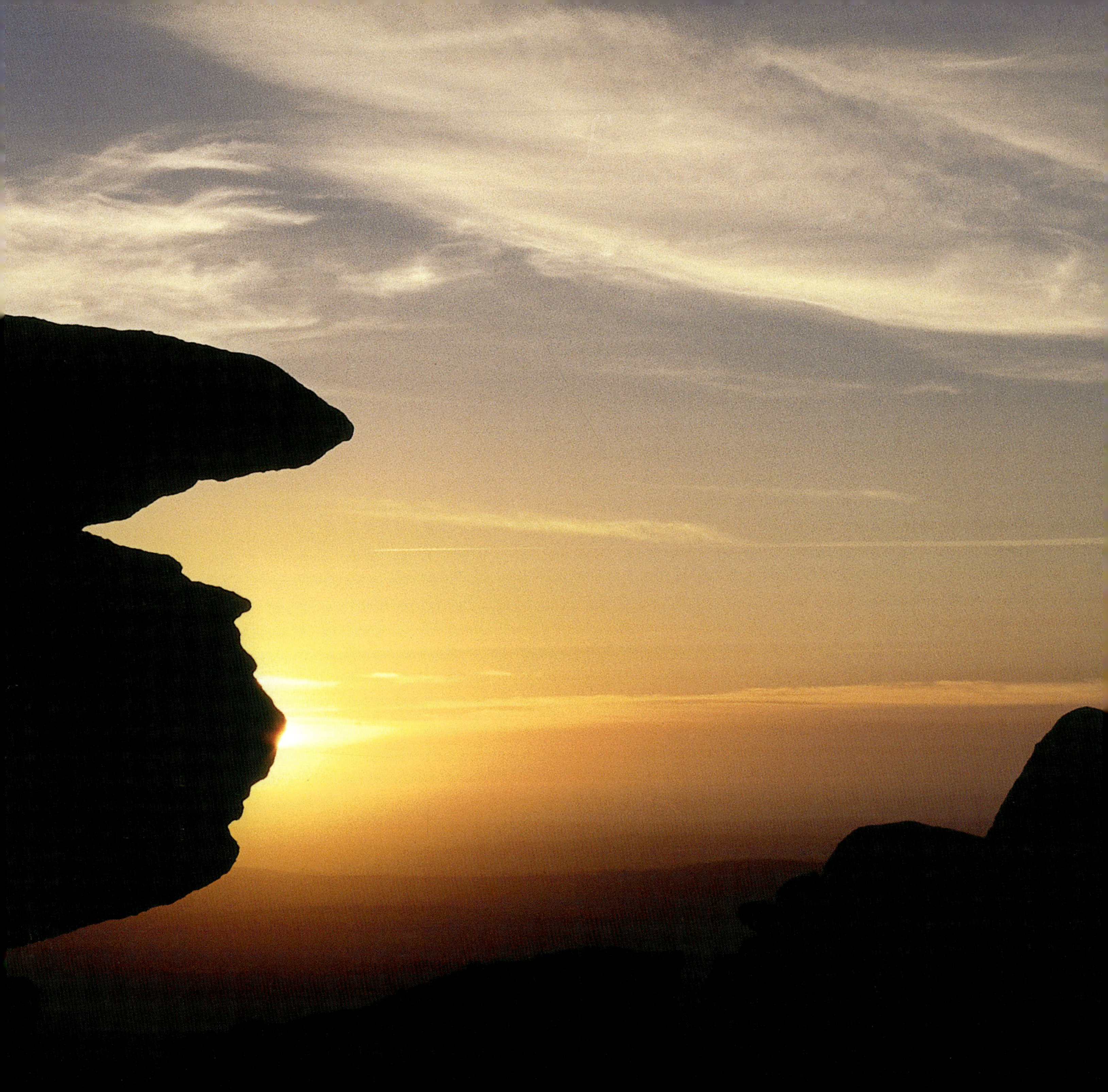

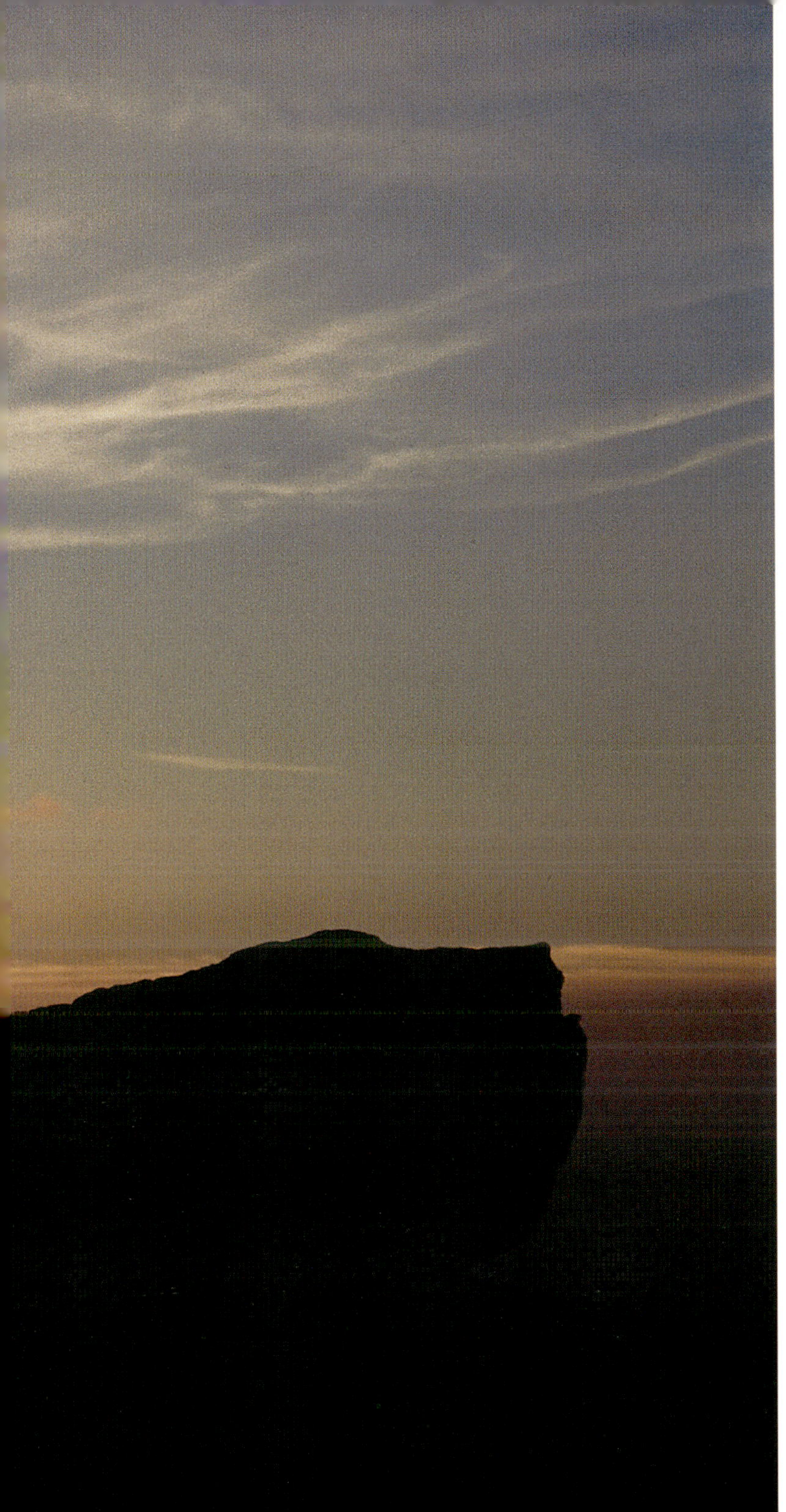

Sunset from Middle Staple Tor

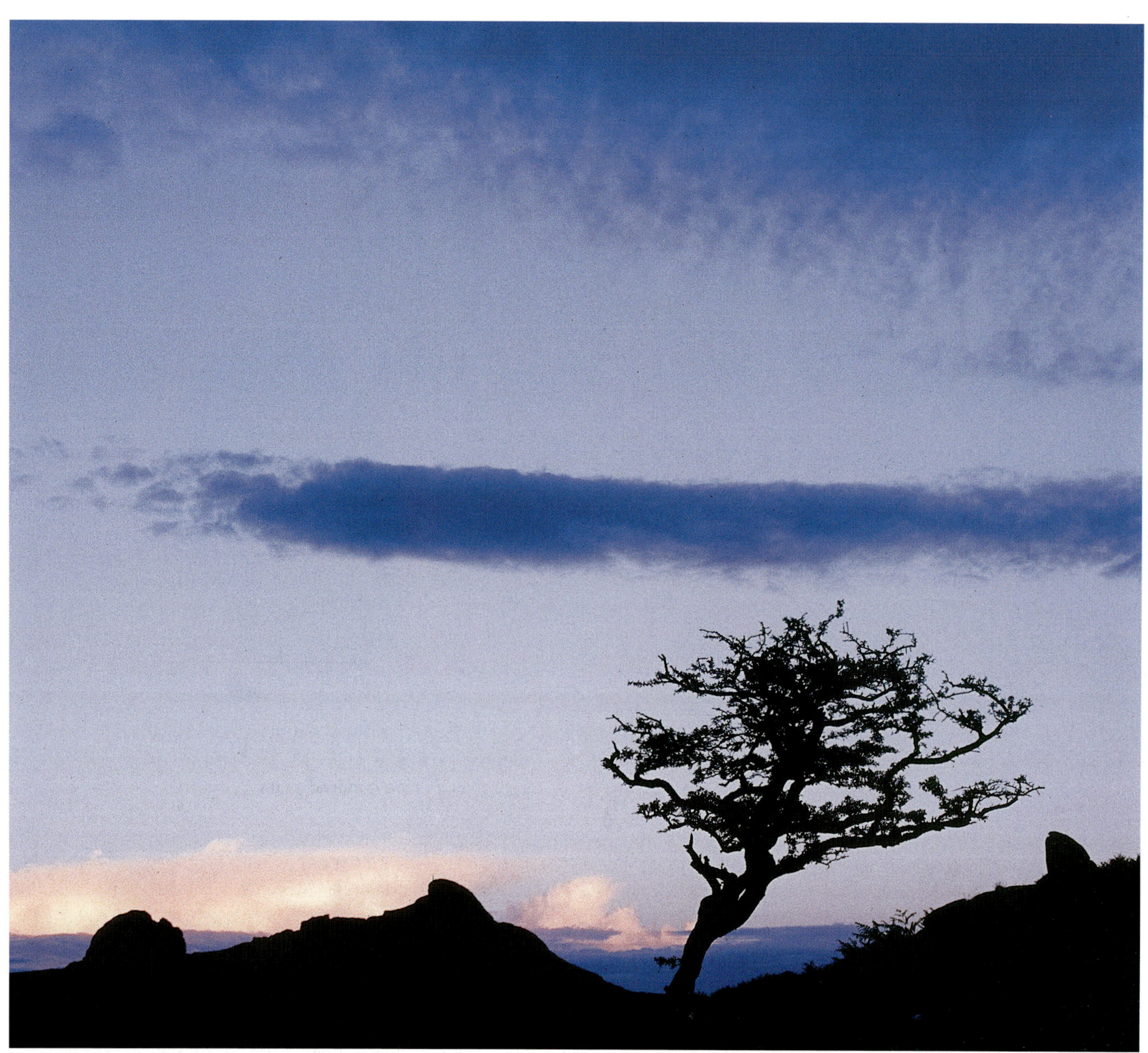

A lone tree against the evening sky with Haytor in the distance

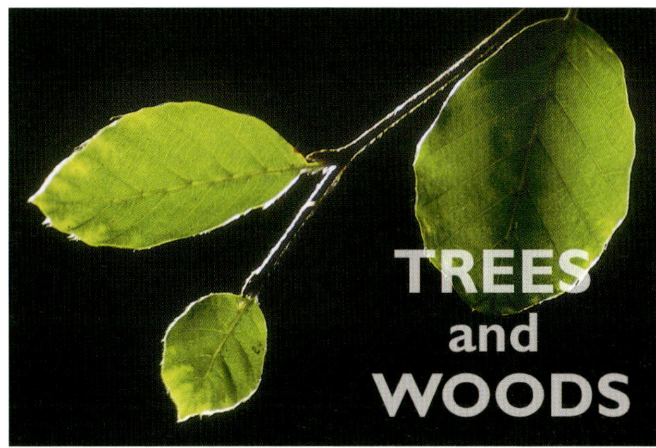

A touch of softness

Dartmoor may be best known for its moorland and its tors, but trees and woodlands are vital elements in its character. In a way, trees both complement and contrast with the wild open spaces of the moor. The single, stunted, wind-blown thorn, rooted in a crack in the rock, emphasises the exposed and harsh nature of the high ground. The three little upland oak woods of Piles Copse, Wistman's Wood and Black-a-tor Copse, remnants of the ancient woodland which once covered most of the moor, are likewise fashioned to reflect and survive their environment. They turn in on themselves, the trees huddling together for shelter, roots grasping the mossy boulders, branches twisted and gnarled as though struggling to stay alive, hung with mosses and lichens which grow rampant in the pure, moist, air.

But at lower altitudes, in the middle reaches of most rivers, the softness of the valley woodlands provides a contrast to the moorland above and a relief from its spartan nature. The canopy of oaks is often of a more or less uniform age, having grown up since coppicing ceased some eighty or one hundred years ago.

Further down the valleys, the woodland becomes interwoven with farmland. The trees are more stately, wild daffodils add colour to a winter walk, wild garlic spreads its heady aroma, and bluebells provide a spectacular show in May. Outside the main valleys, beech hedges left to grow big mark old field boundaries, shelterbelts march across high windswept farmland, and conifer plantations add variety.

The annual cycle from leaf bud to leaf fall marks the passing of each year, and the longer cycle from seedling to decaying stump somehow emphasises the timelessness of the landscape. In between, trees provide shelter and food for wildlife, sculptural forms of great beauty, and sheltered places to walk where you are actually less likely to meet anyone than on the open moor. Trees add variety, subtlety and a sort of friendliness to the landscape. They make great foregrounds for photographs and are often works of art in themselves.

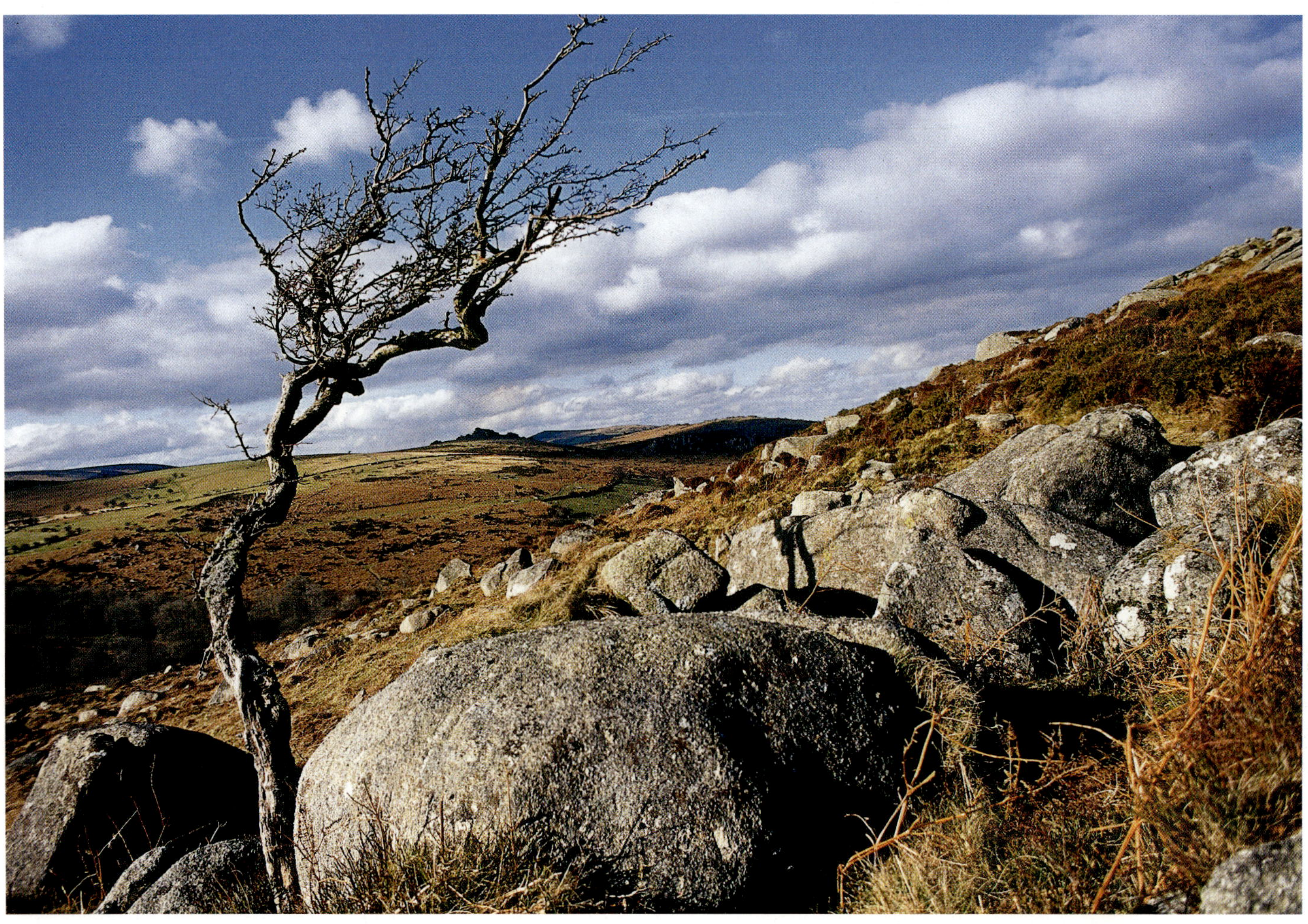
A thorn tree surviving above the Becka Brook valley

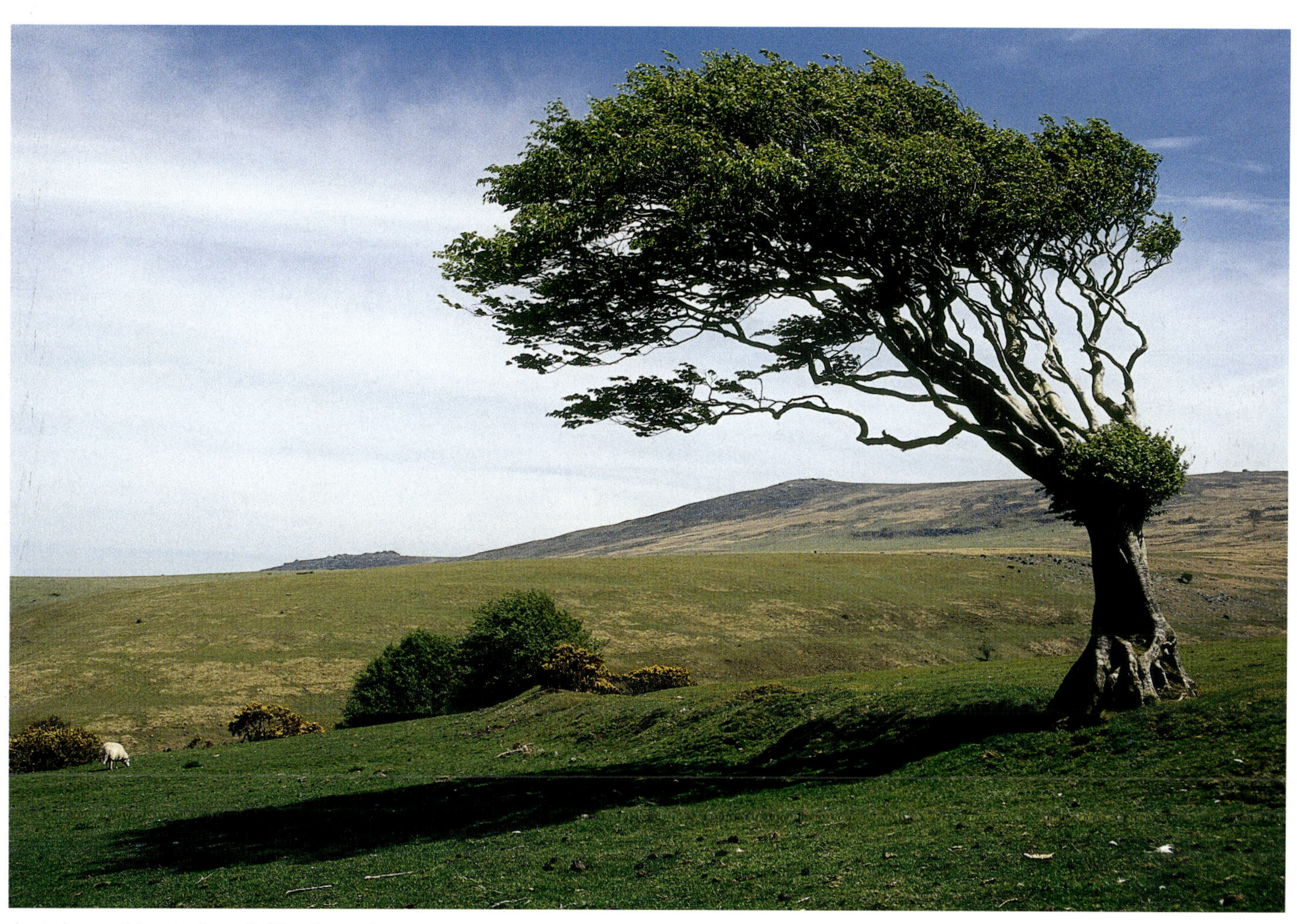

A wind-pruned beech above Meldon Reservoir

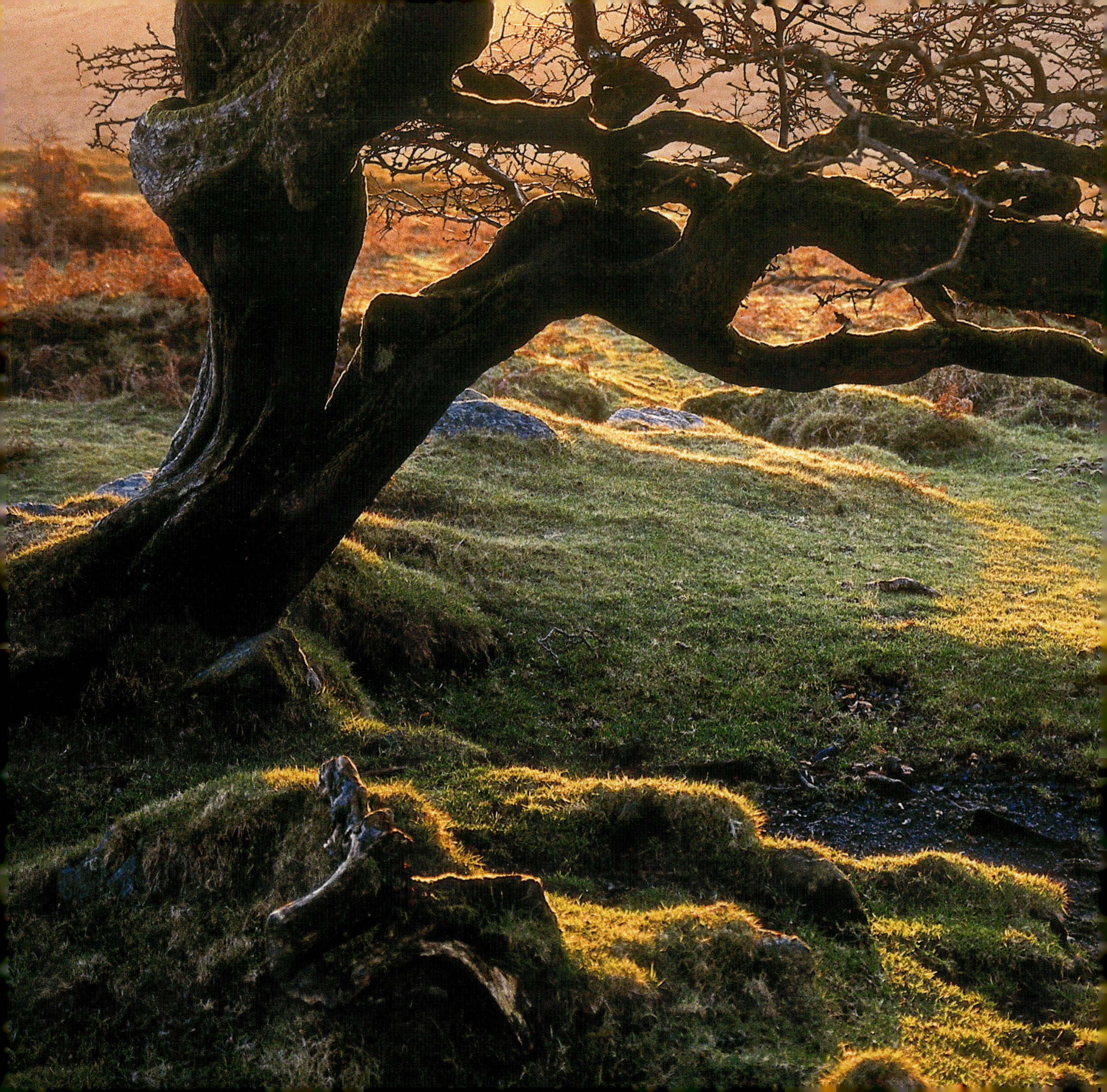

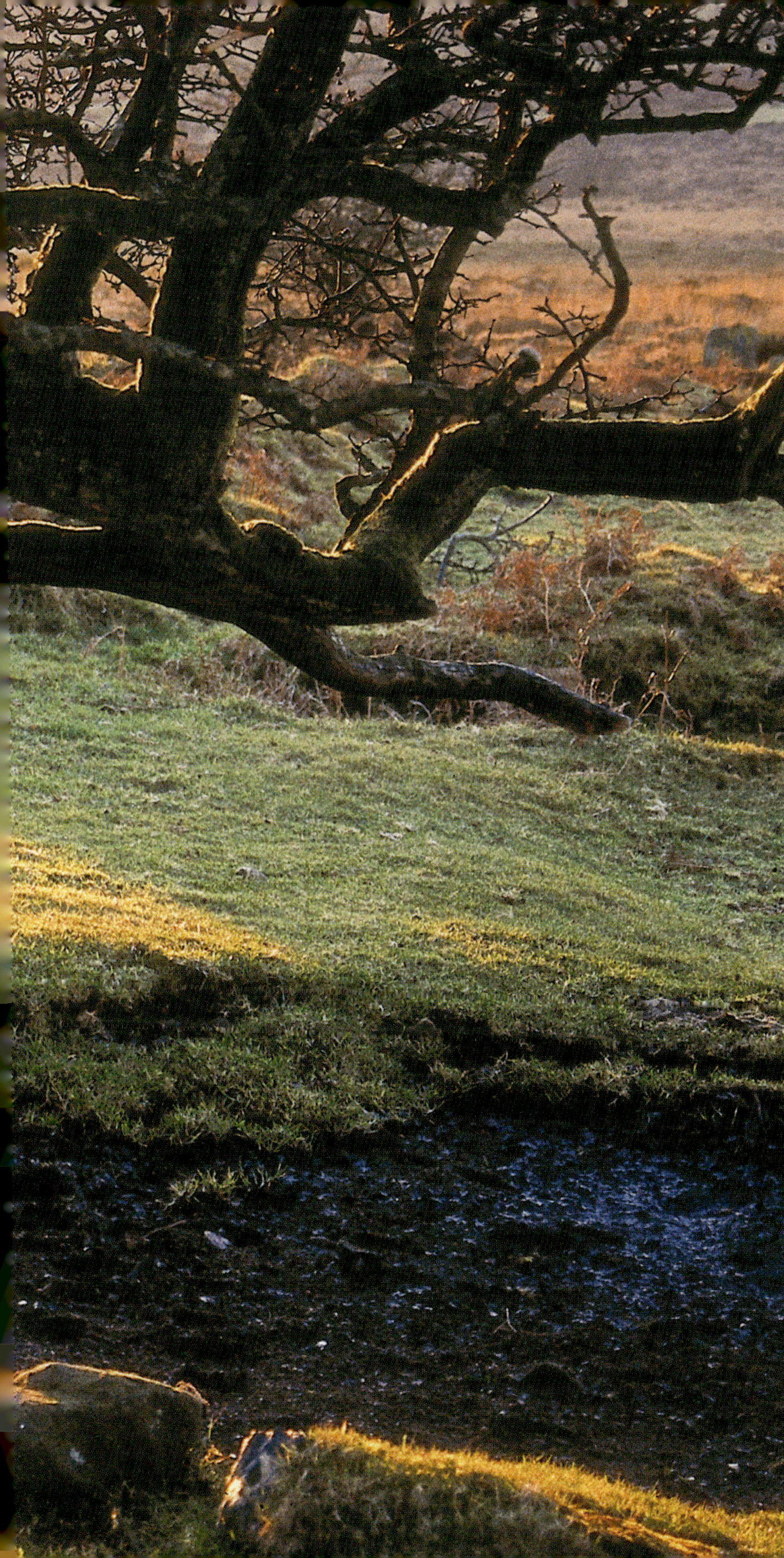

Evening sun lights up a horizontal thorn tree above Blackslade Mire

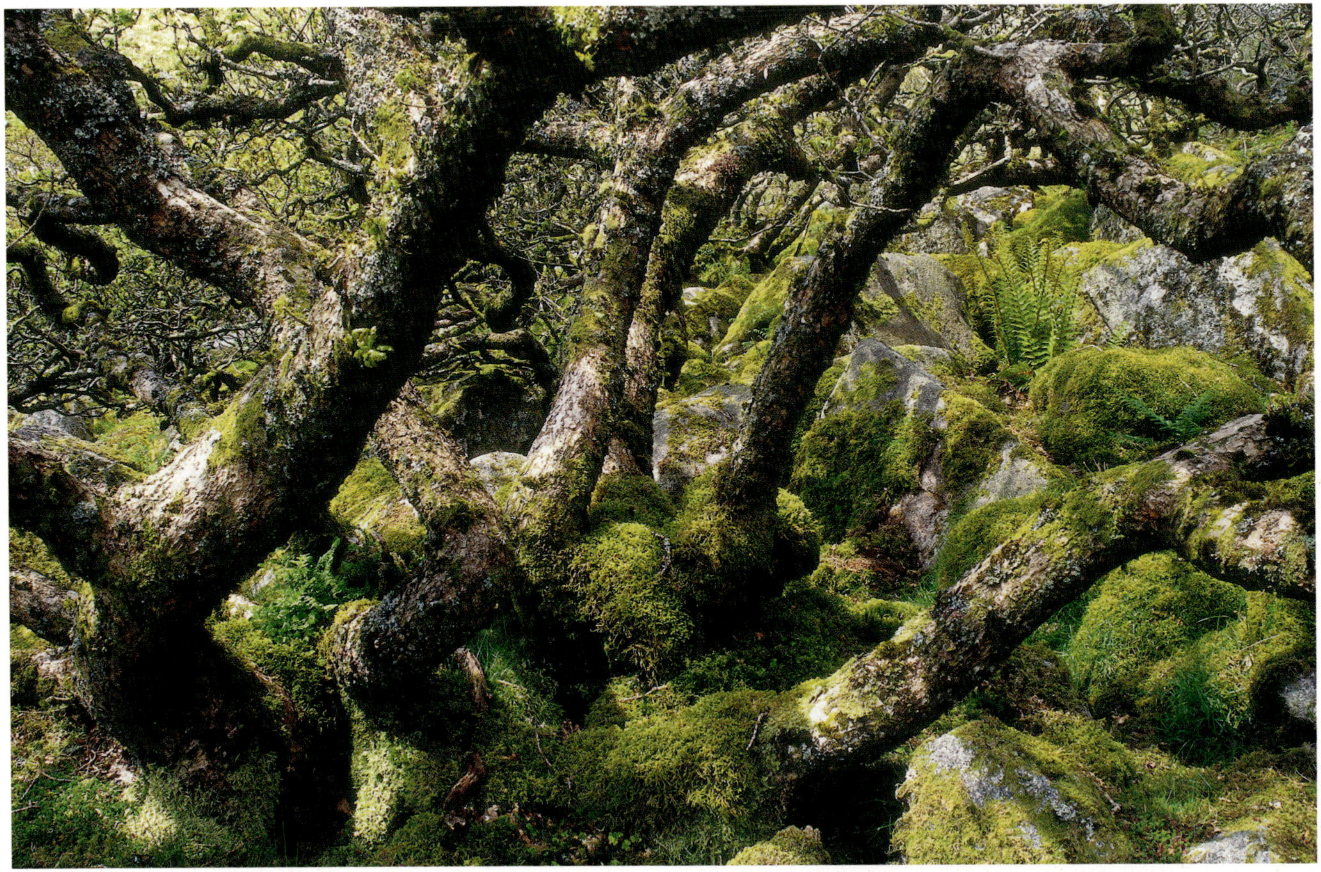

Wistman's Wood. One of the three remaining ancient upland oak woods high on the moor – a jungle of stunted trees, hung with mosses and lichens

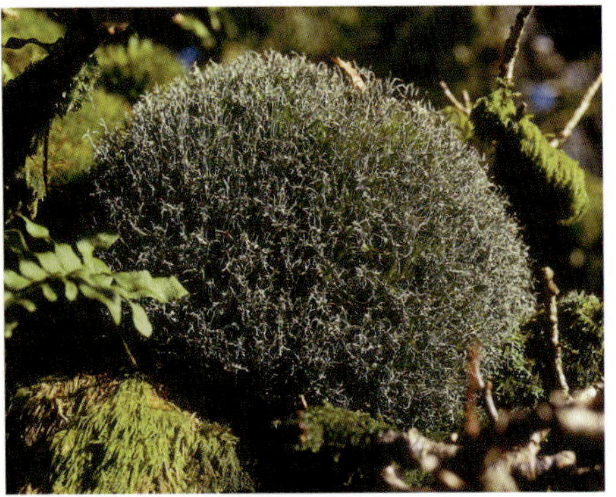

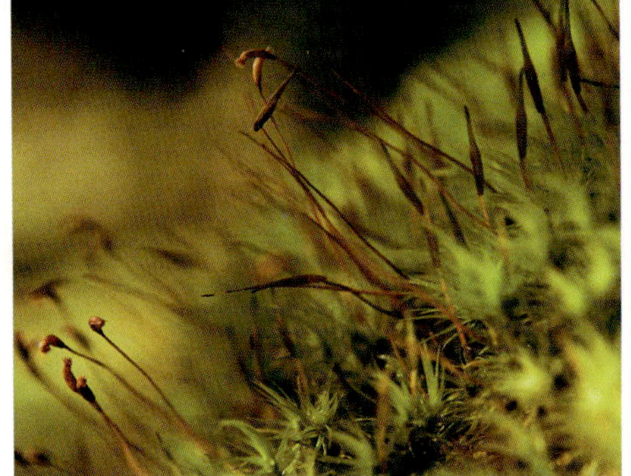

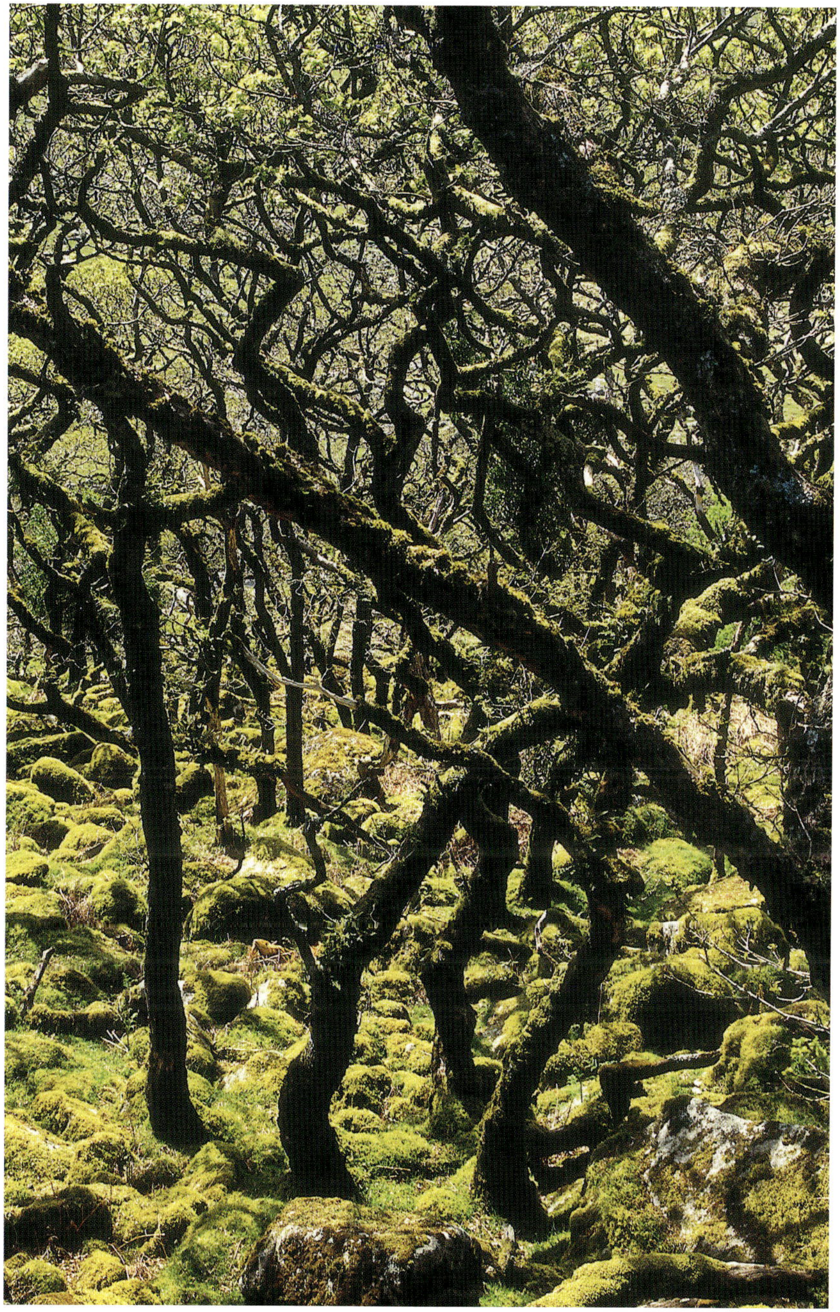

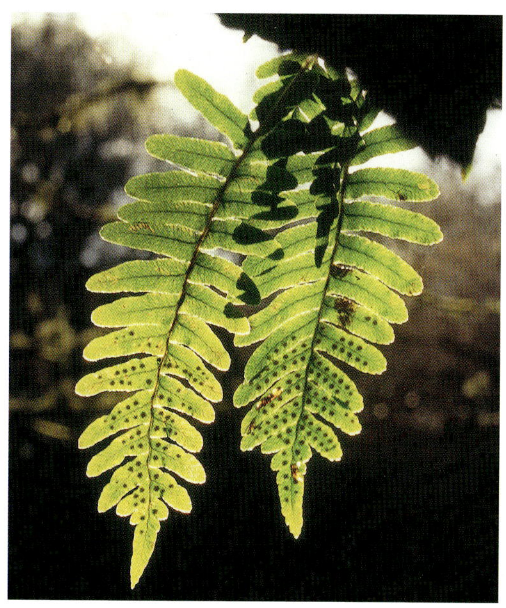

Black-a-tor Copse. Another of the relict woodlands,
with gnarled and twisted oaks sheltering
a wonderful collection of ferns

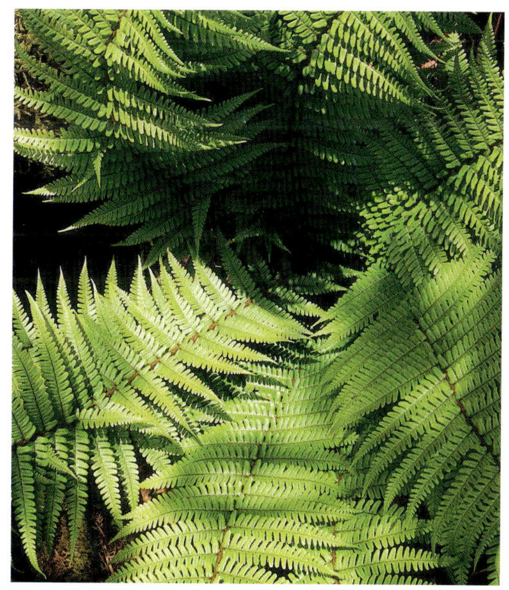

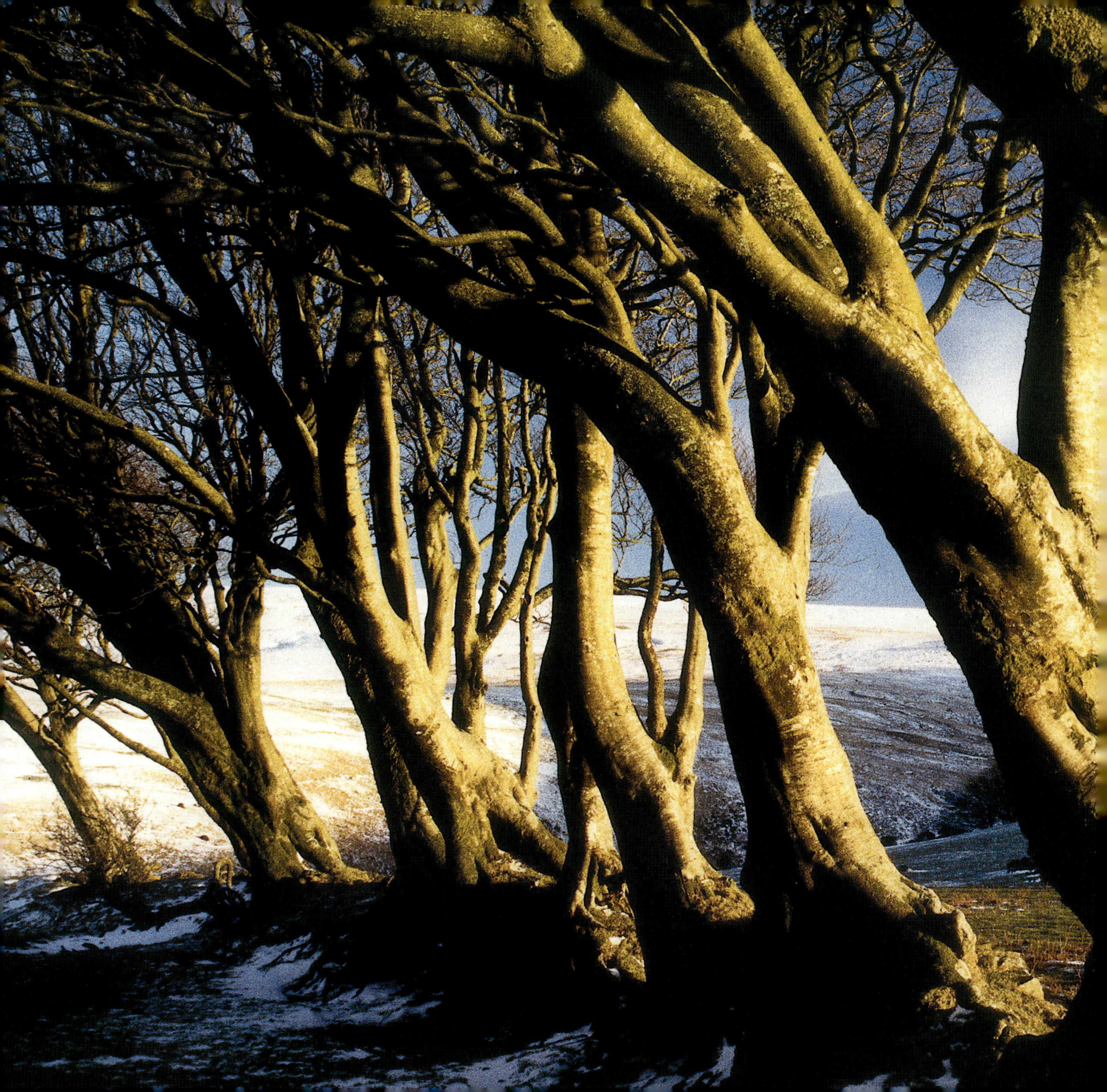

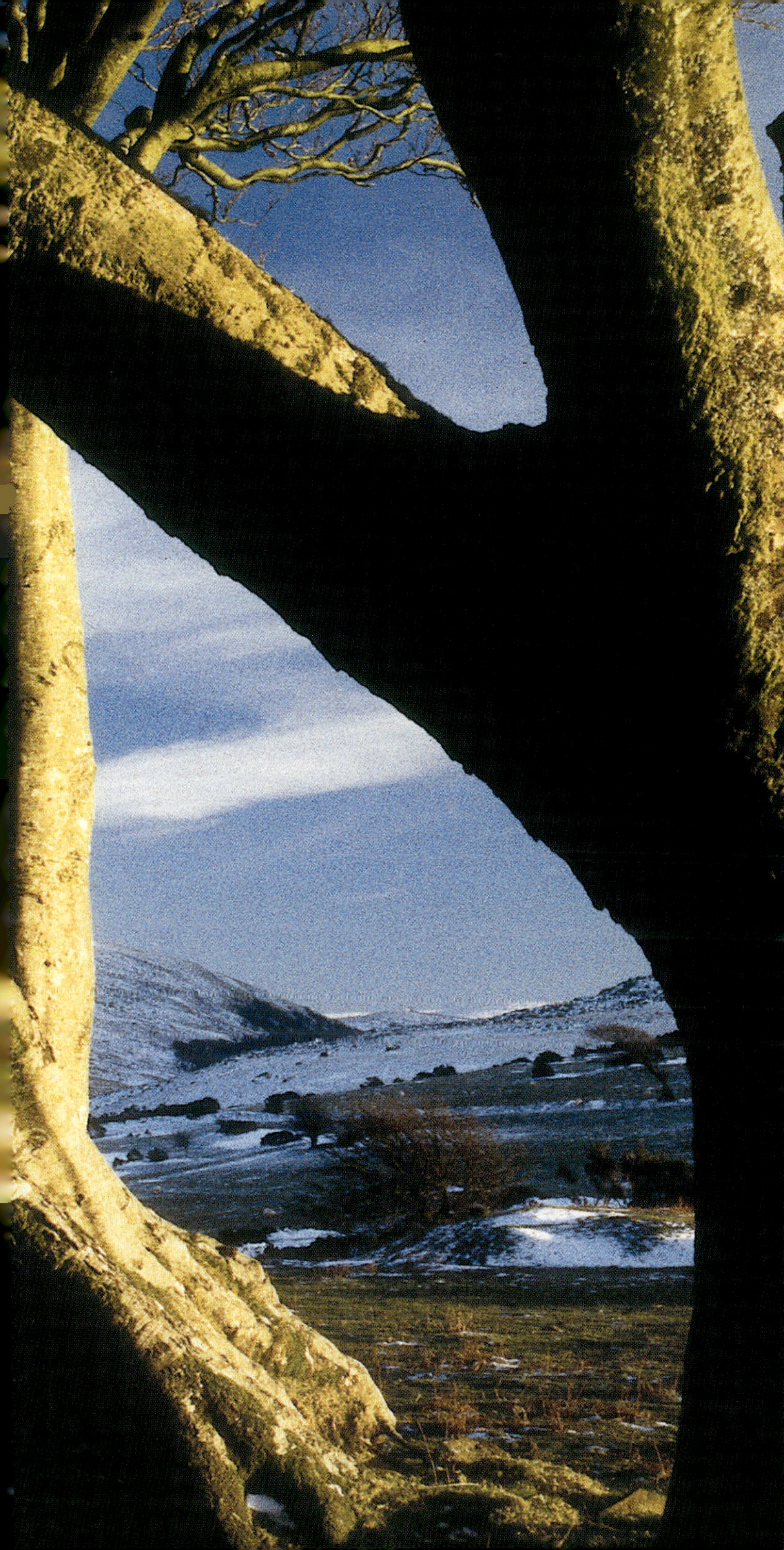

Beeches above Prewley Moor, lit by the evening sun

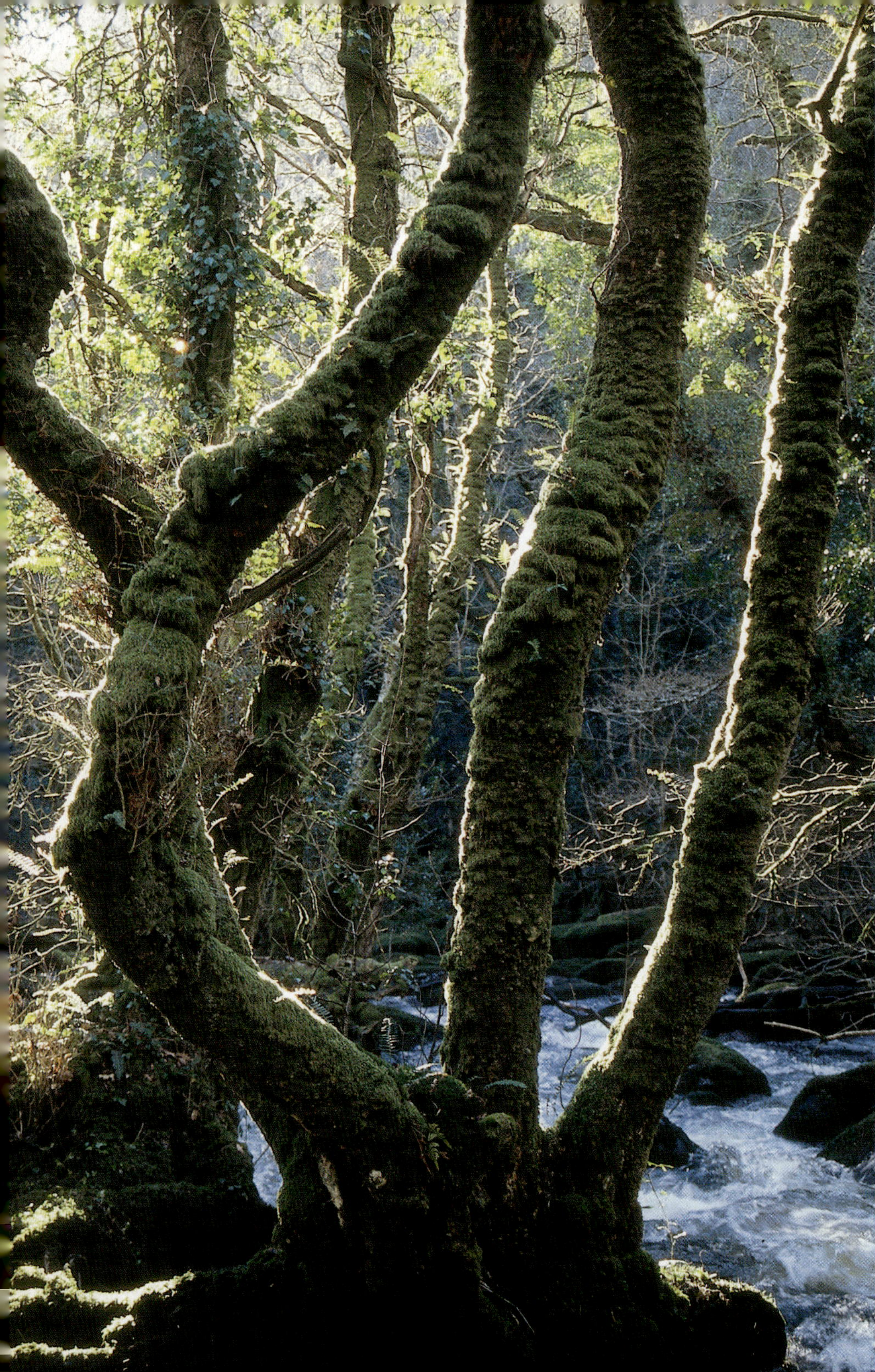

A twisted oak by the River Bovey at Horsham Steps

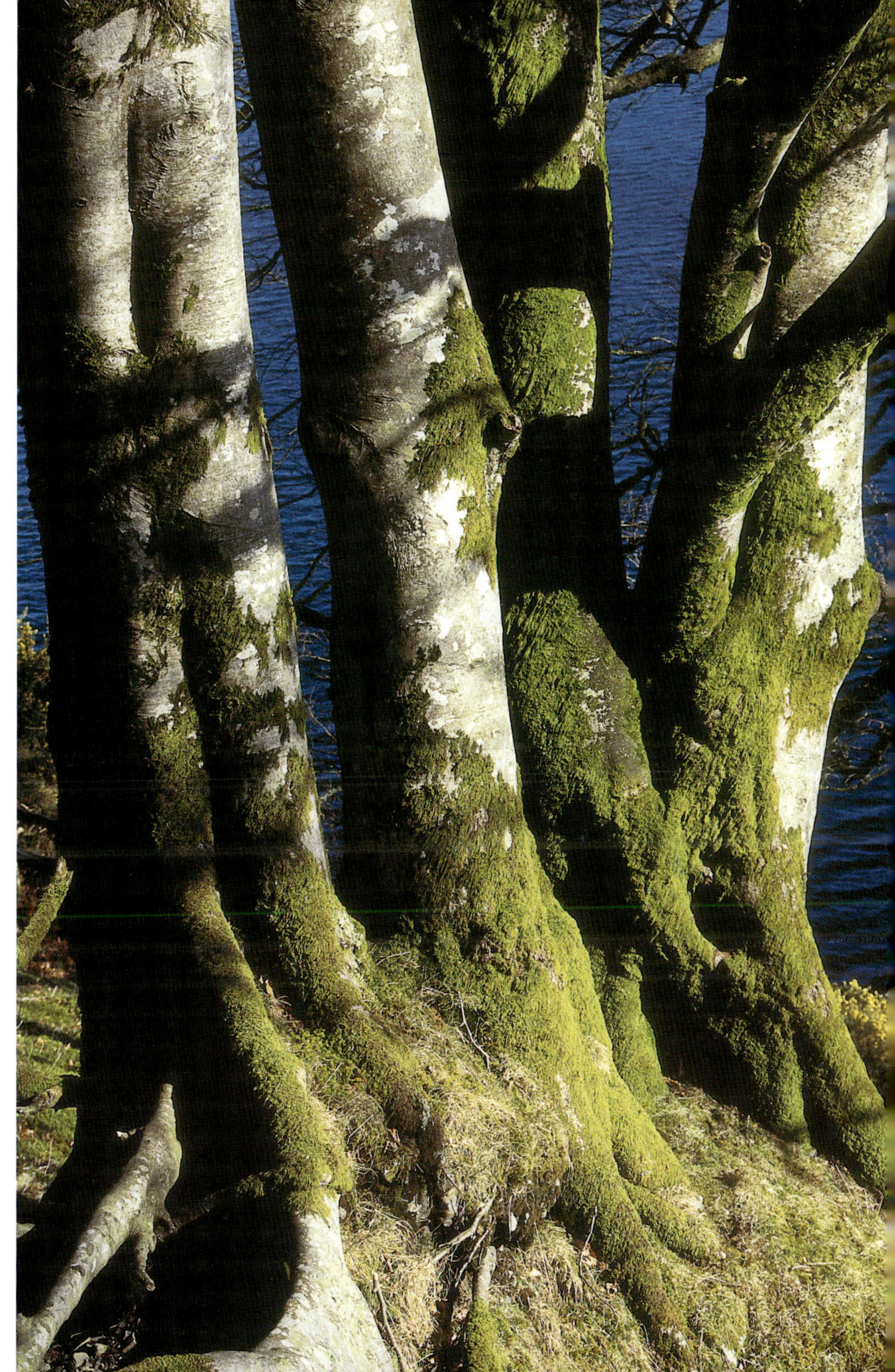

Beeches by Meldon Reservoir

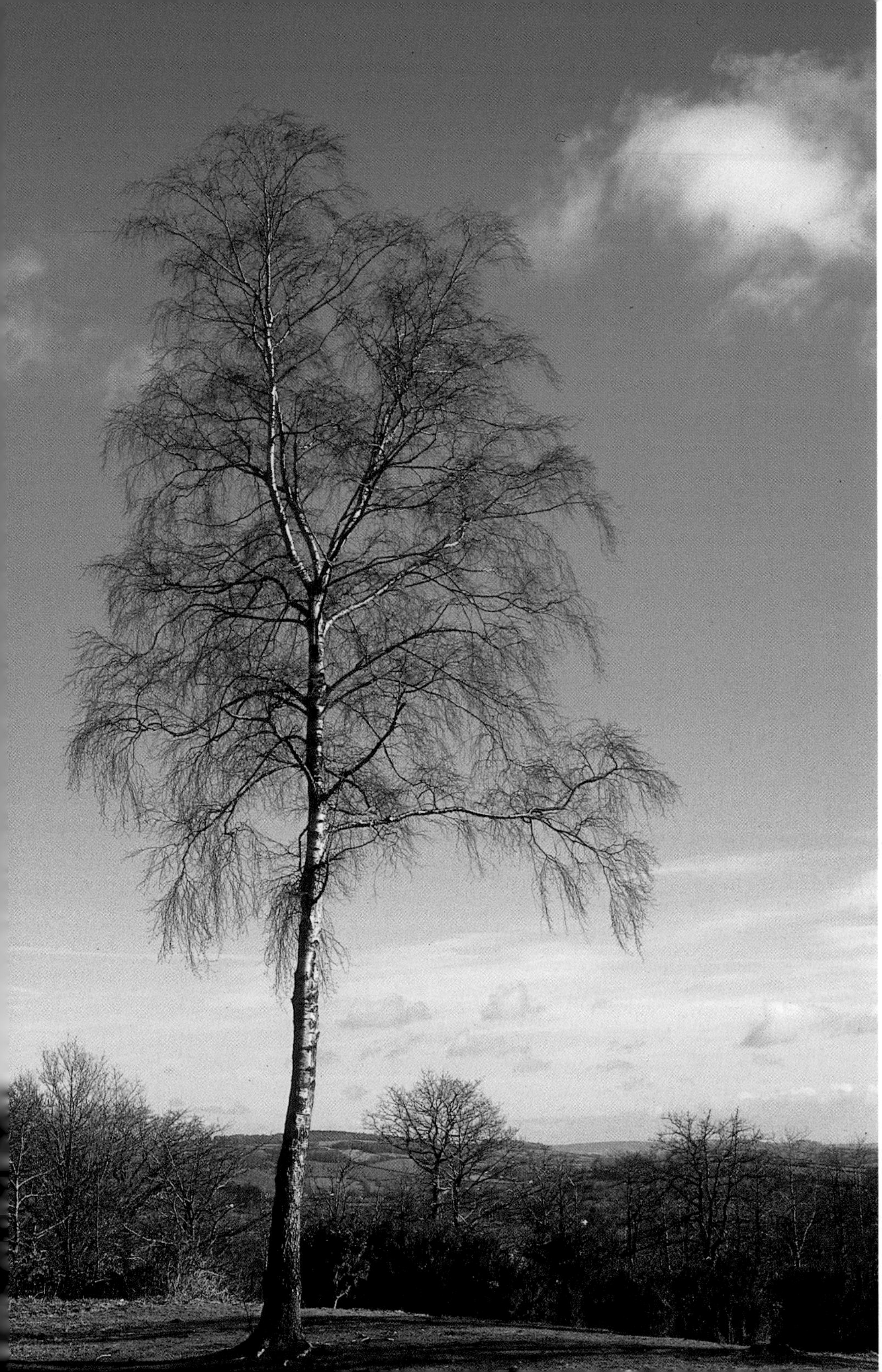

The delicate tracery of a silver birch at Hembury
Iron Age hill-fort

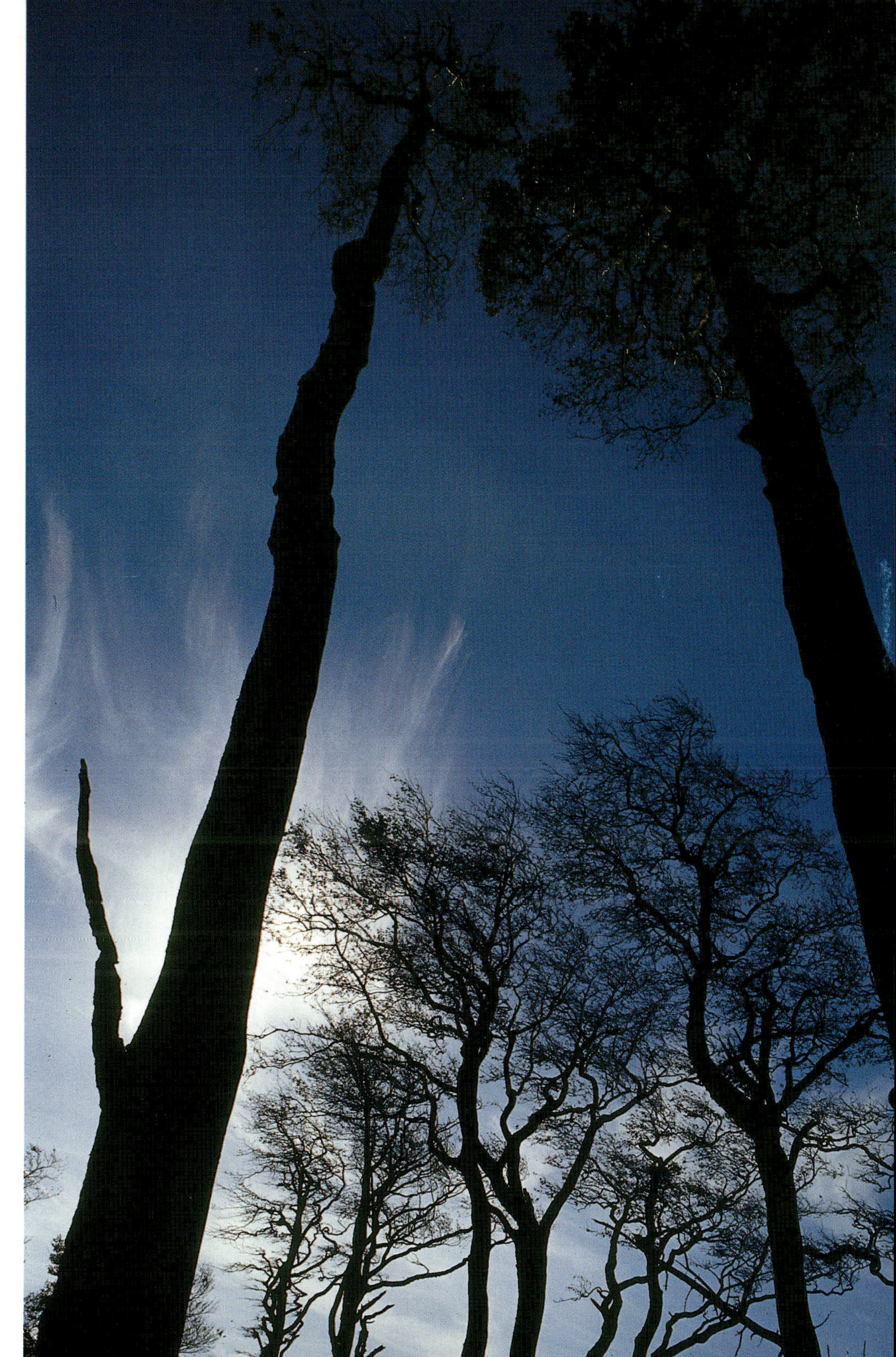

*Silhouettes against the sky in a shelterbelt above
Bagtor Down*

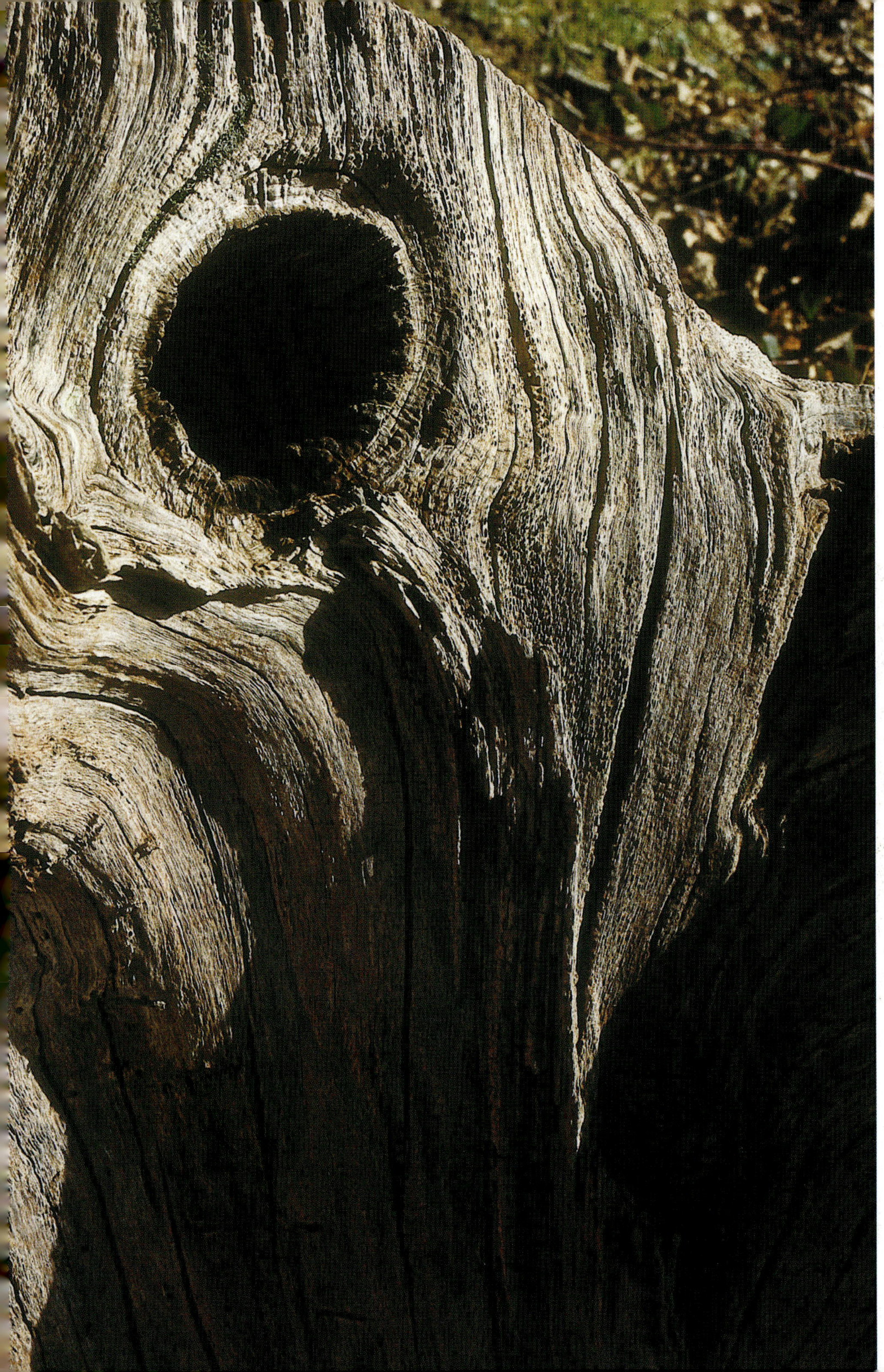

A stump with character on Hembury Iron Age hill-fort

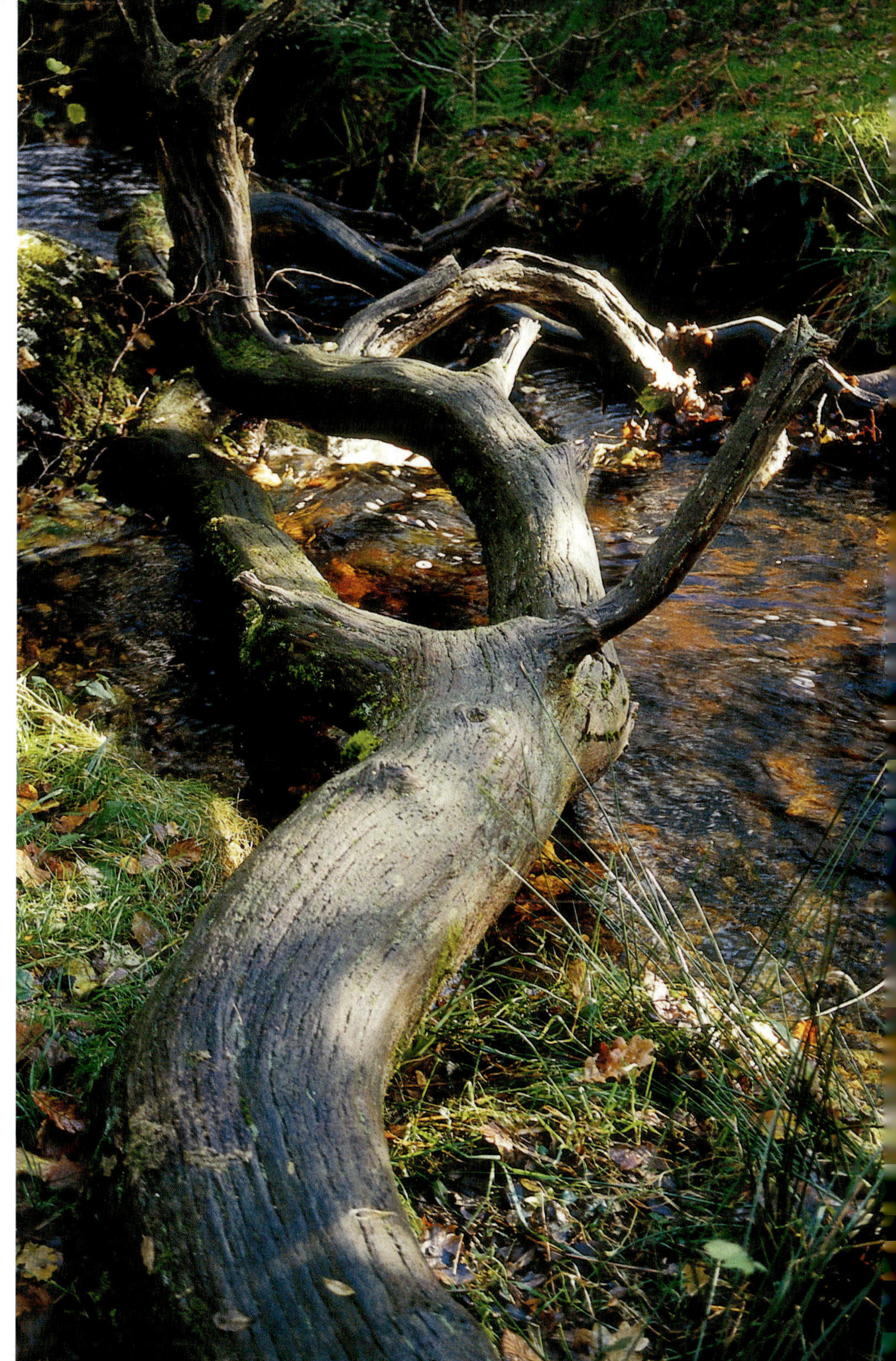

A fallen tree provides a bridge over the Becka Brook

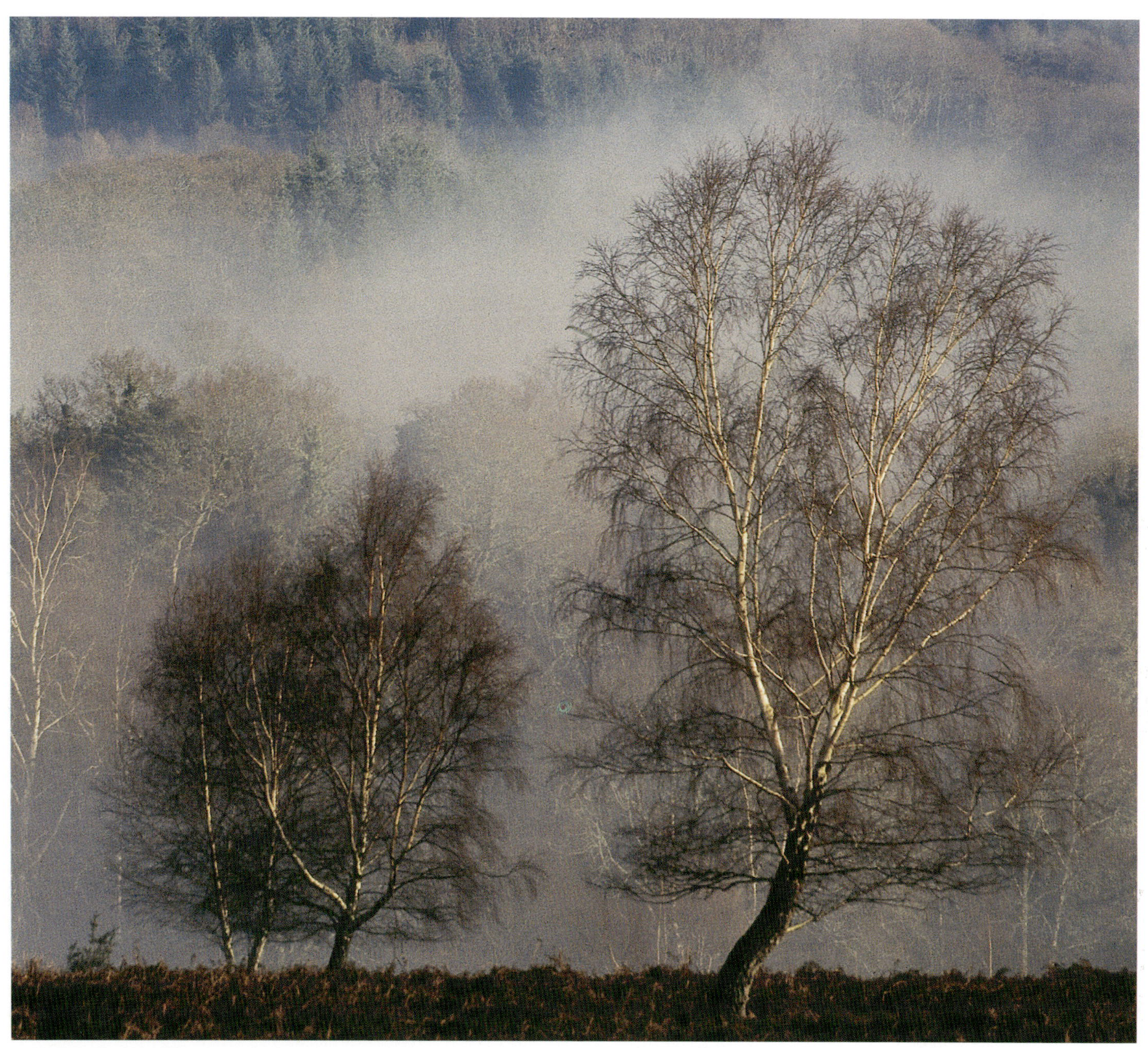

Misty woods in the Dart valley, seen from near Leigh Tor

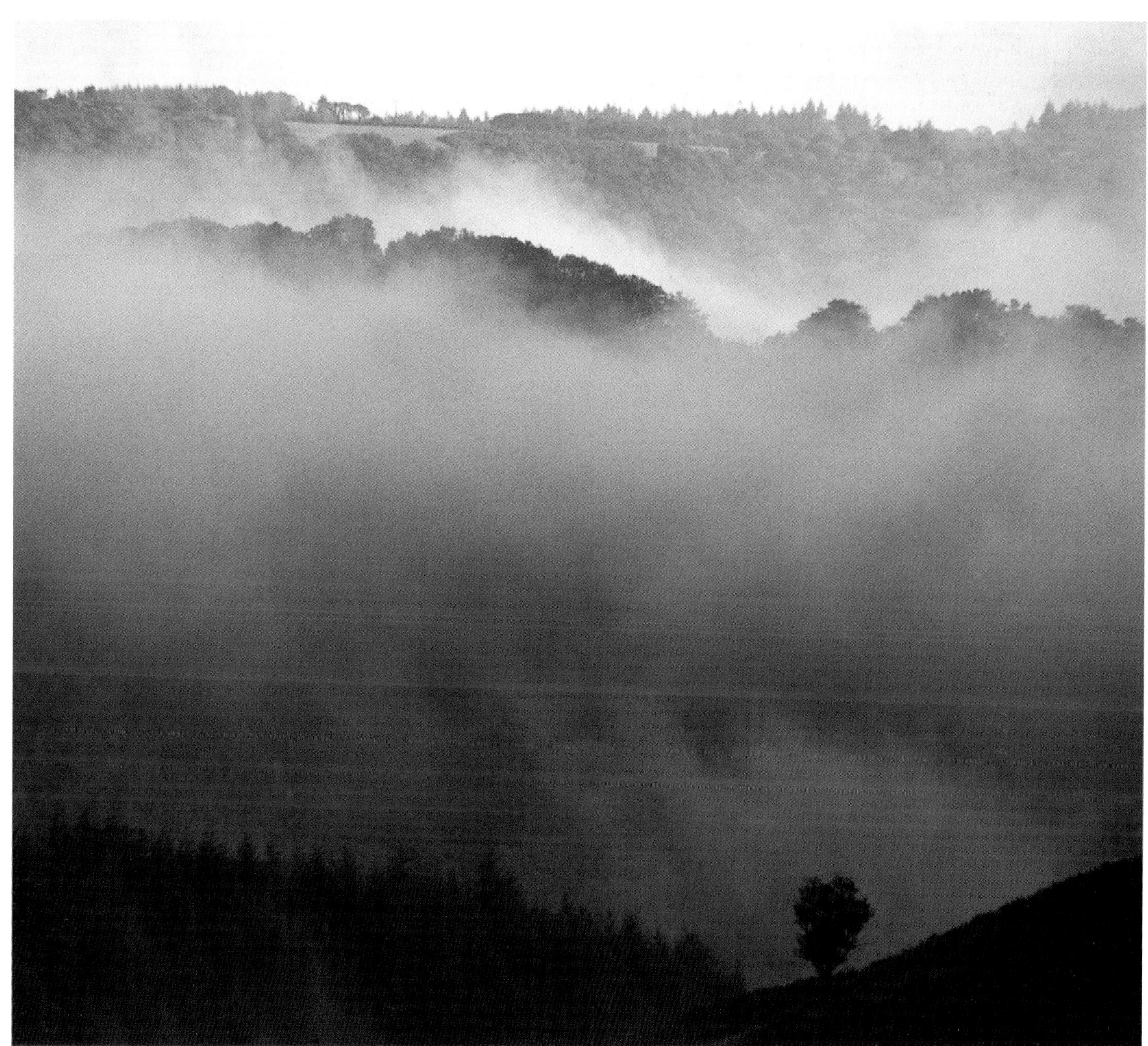

Morning mist clearing from Trendlebere Down, looking towards Lustleigh Cleave

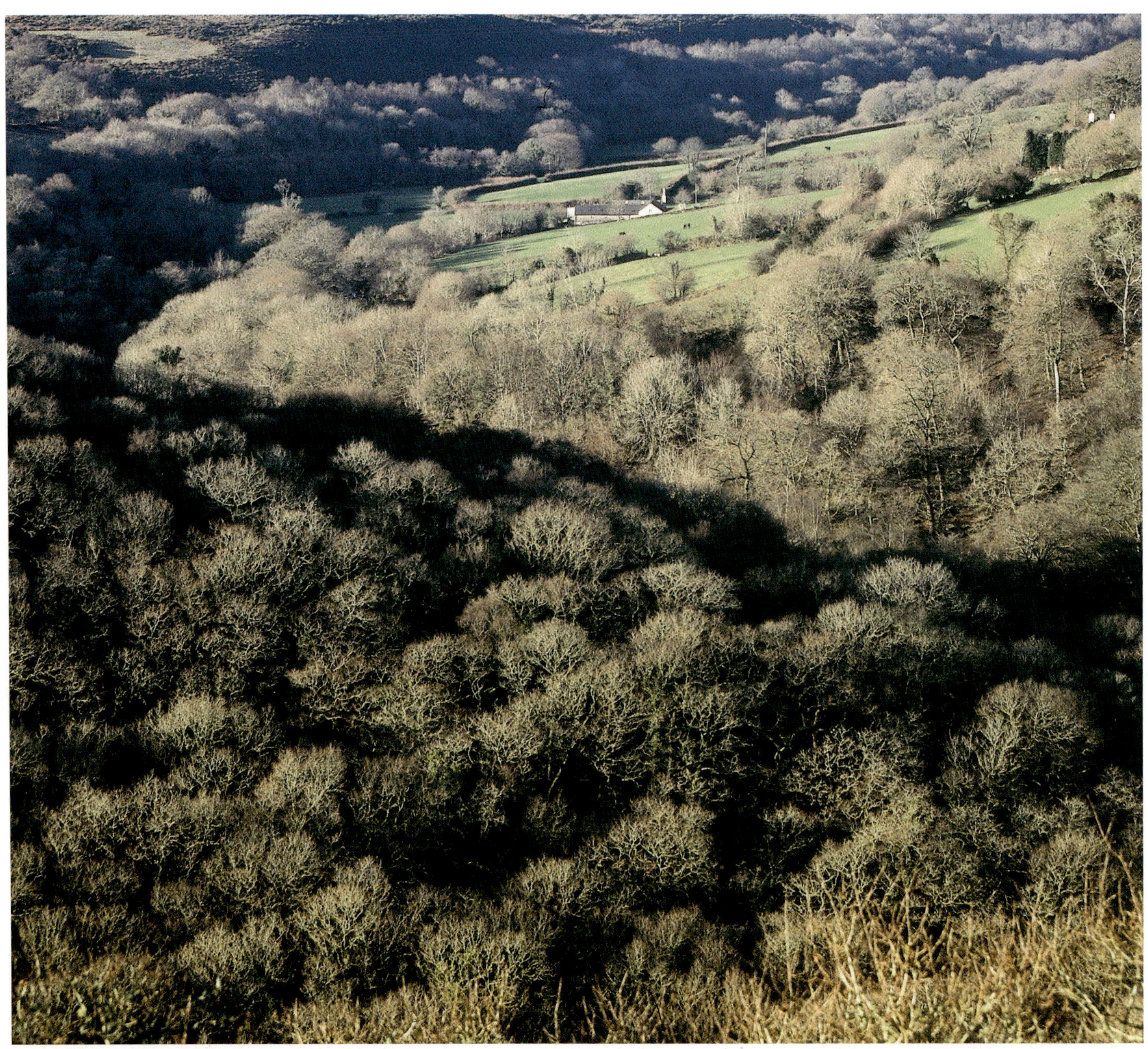

Soft woods in the Meavy valley, seen from near the Dewerstone

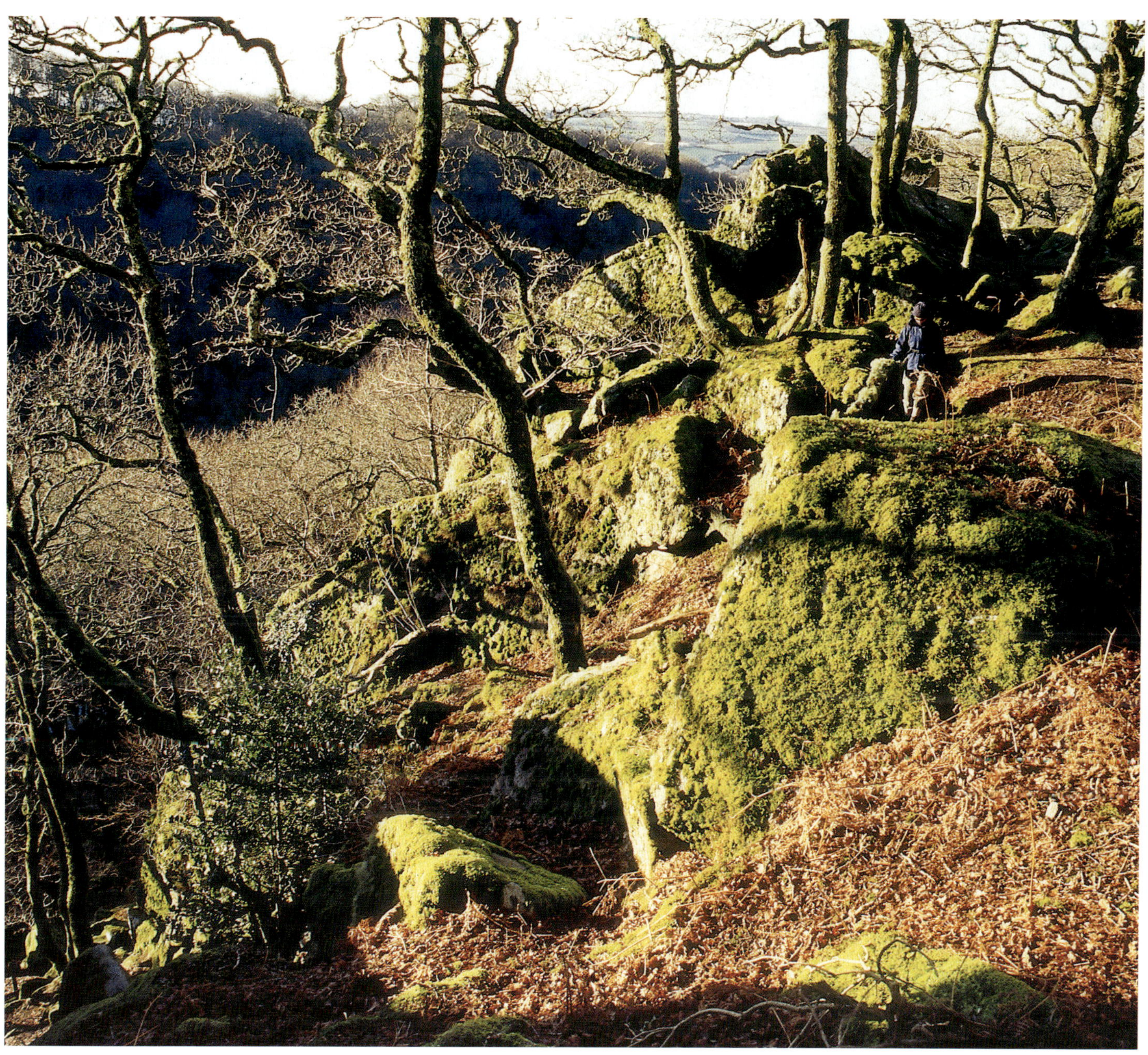

A beautiful morning in the woods by the Dewerstone

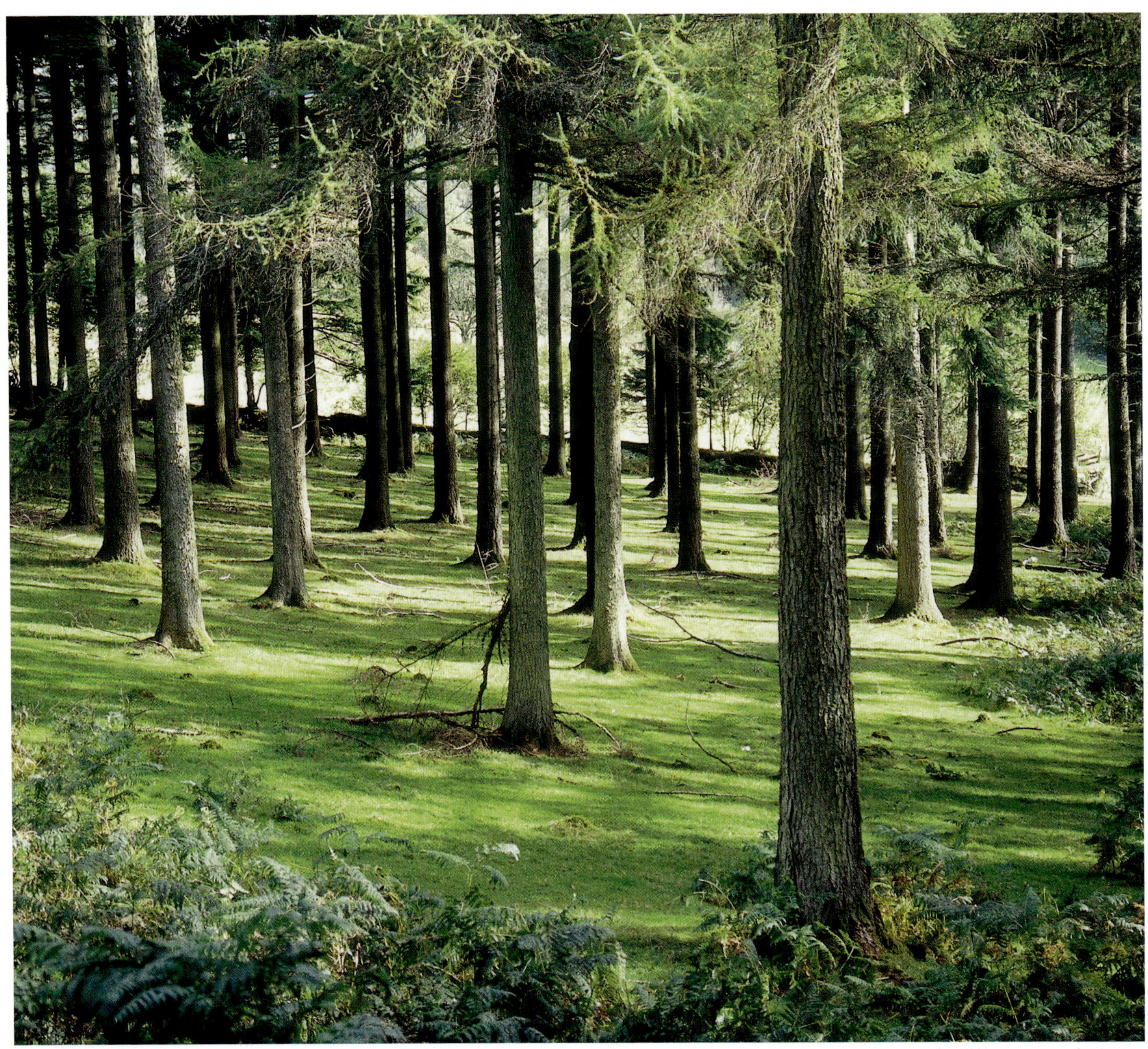

Mature, and rather stately, conifer plantations at Burrator Reservoir

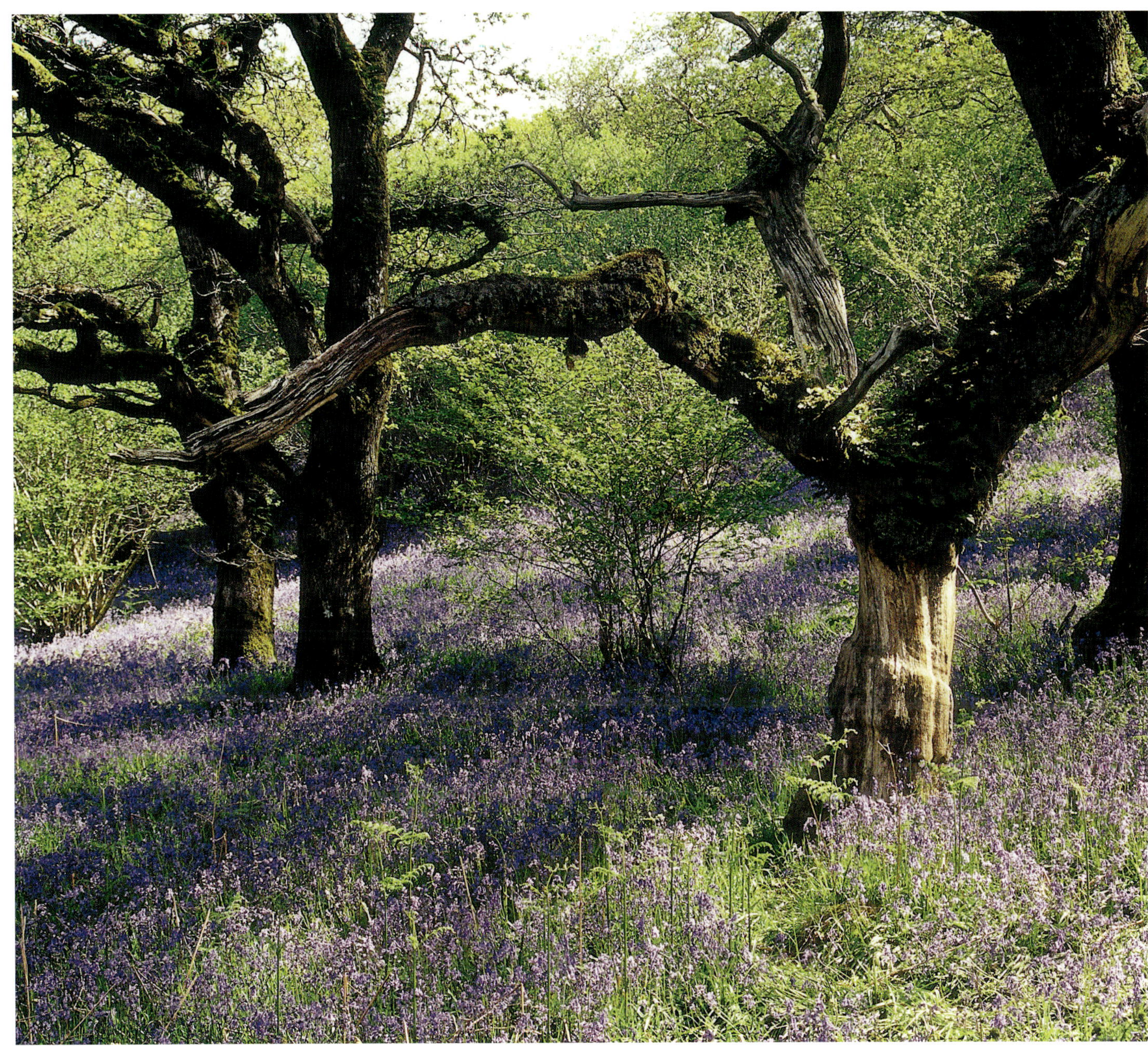

Meldon Wood, in the West Okement valley, known locally as Bluebell Wood

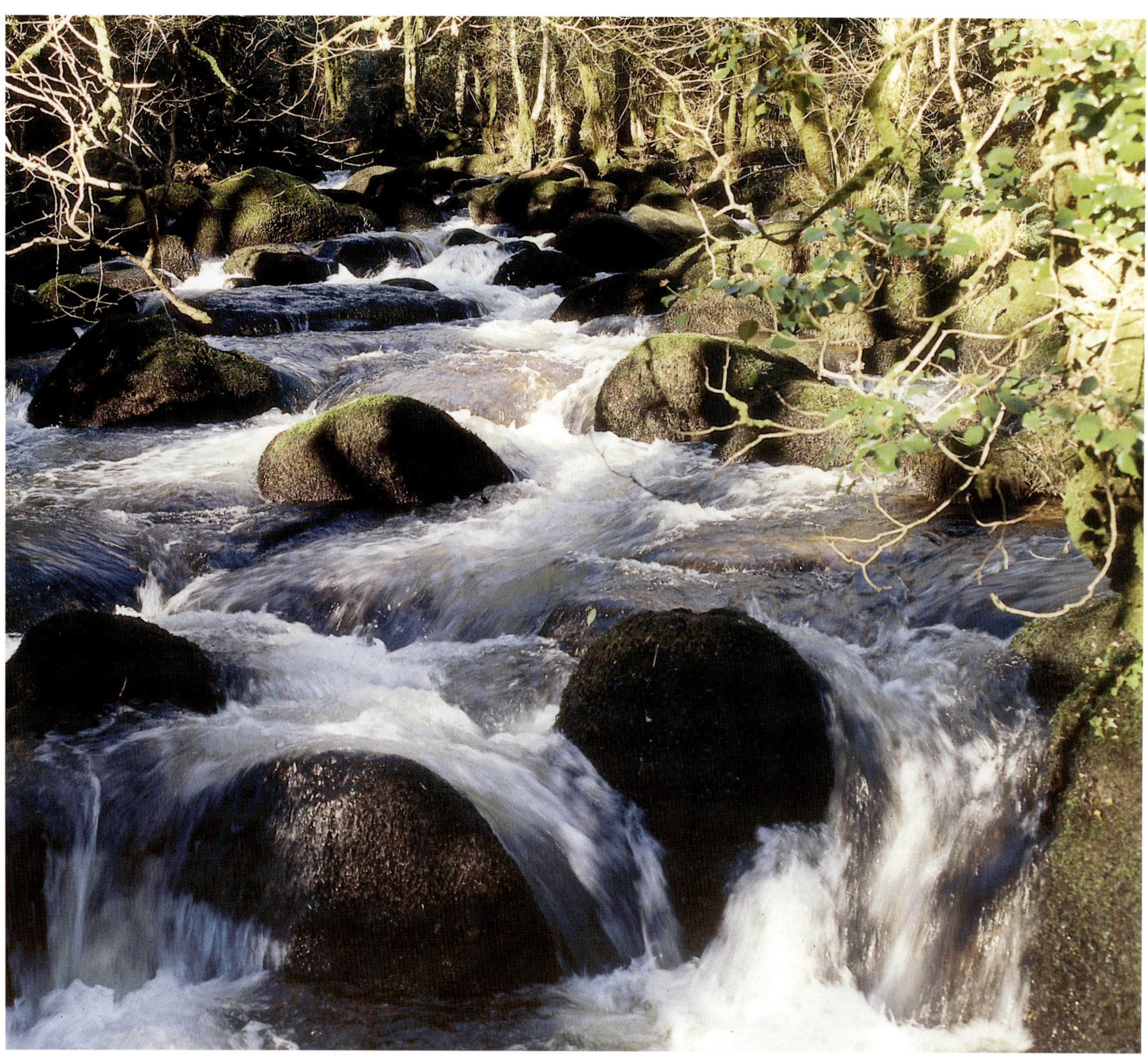

The River Bovey at Horsham Steps

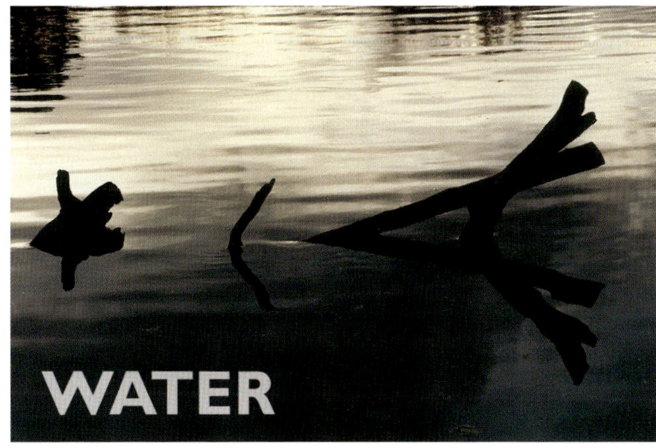

Ripples and reflections

Water adds life to a landscape – reflections and ripples or rapids and roaring torrents. It adds tranquillity and places for contemplation or at times excitement and even danger. It offers a refreshing swim in summer or some of the most challenging white-water canoeing in winter.

Many of Devon's rivers rise on Dartmoor. The blanket bog on the high ground acts like a great sponge, soaking up the winter rains and releasing them gradually in summer. Peat colours the water a beautiful golden brown, making it look almost like whisky as it tumbles over falls and swirls around boulders into pools which are deep and clear. Look down through the reflections – see the shafts of sunlight dappling the coarse sandy bottom and watch the brown trout keeping station in the flow. Sit by a waterfall and be hypnotised by the rushing water. Watch the armadas of big bubbles escaping from the white water and sailing away across the surface of the pool below. Be fascinated by the ever changing geometric patterns of ripples where the river squeezes through a gap between two stepping stones. But come back when the river is in flood – the stepping stones will be under feet of dark and heavy water, the bridge arches will be full to the top, the noise and the power will astonish you. You will begin to understand one of the elemental forces which has shaped this landscape.

Dartmoor is no Lake District. It has no large natural bodies of standing water, but it does have reservoirs, flooded quarries, and one or two artificial 'lakes'. Reservoir construction has in the past been a contentious issue on Dartmoor, and quarrying still is. Yes, landscapes have been destroyed, but new ones have been created. Visit Meldon Quarry Pool on a still morning when the huge rock overhang and the trees above are reflected in the water and you will not think that this is an intrusion into the landscape. If you carry on up the West Okement valley, and if water levels are high, you may find that Meldon Dam has been transformed from an ugly, blank, concrete wall into a beautiful cascade of feathery water and beyond it the reservoir winds its way into highest Dartmoor – not a natural landscape but different, dramatic and pleasing.

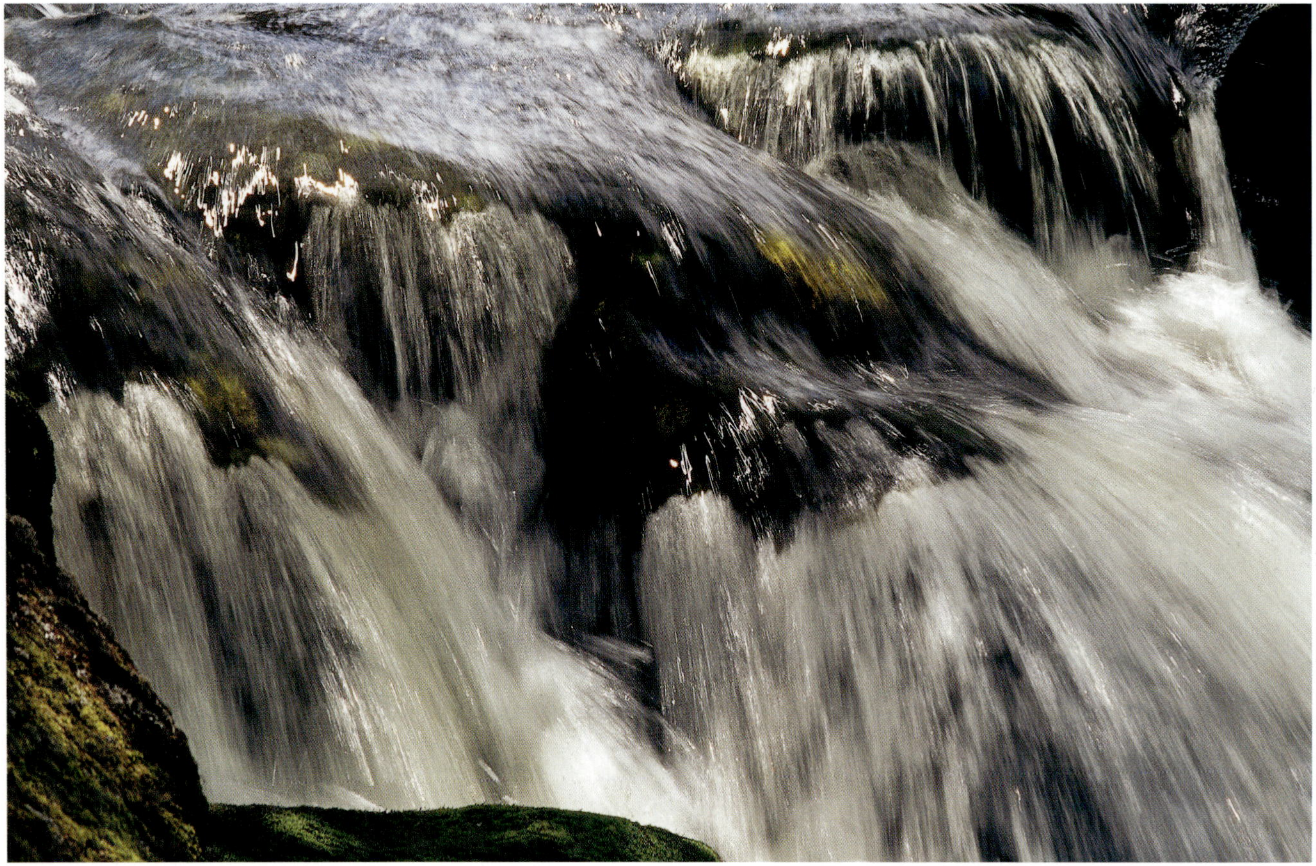

Falls on the West Okement above Vellake Corner

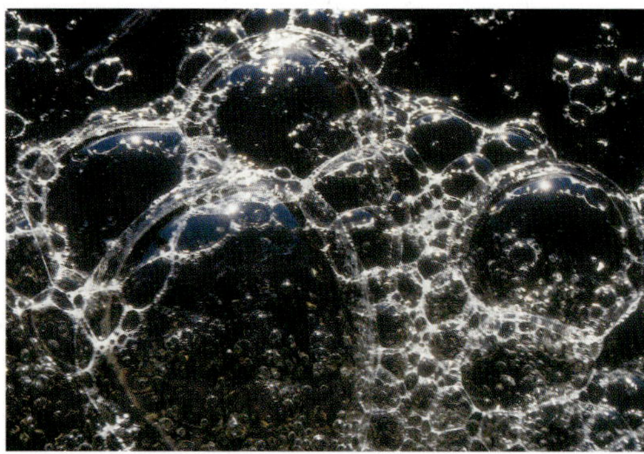

Armadas of bubbles

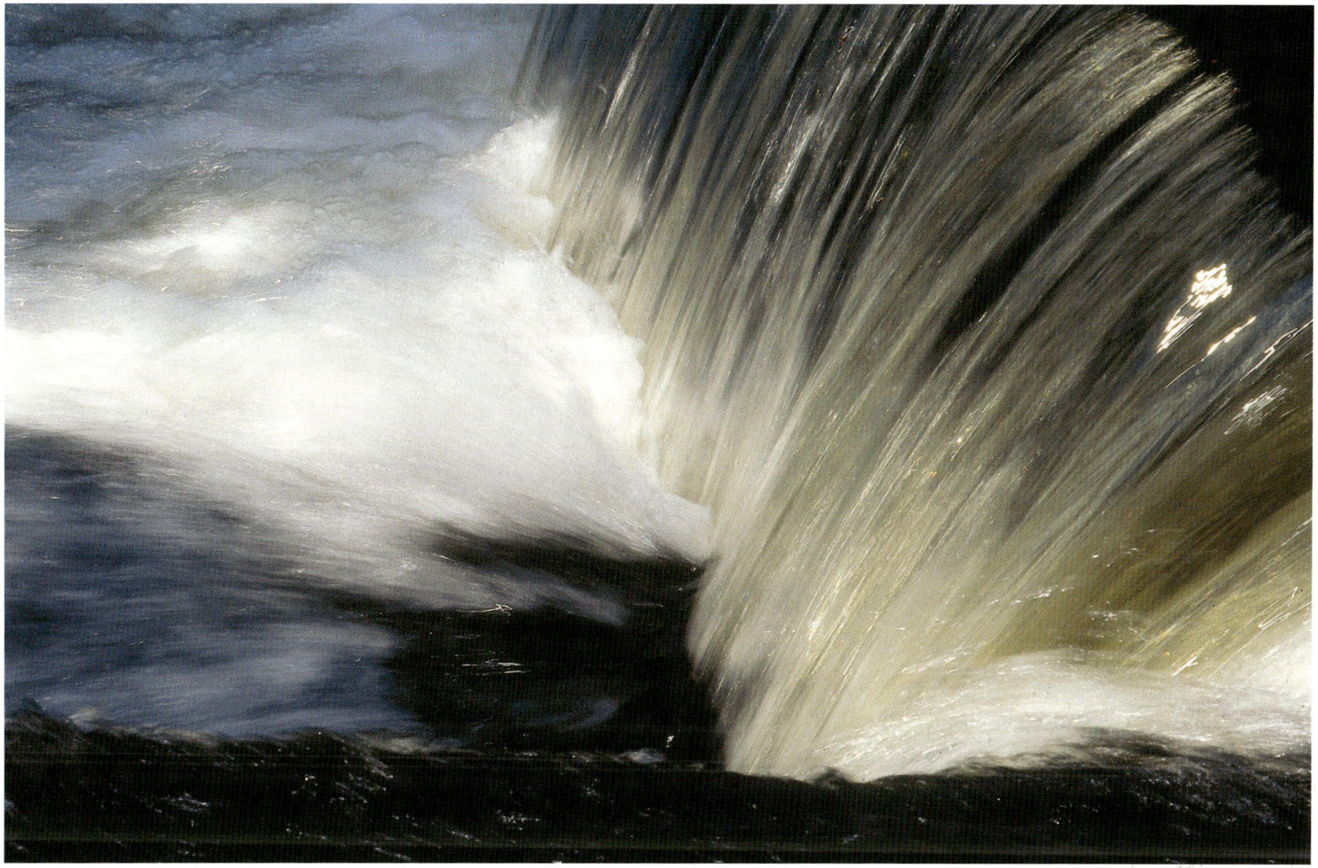

A fall on the Dart below Dartmeet

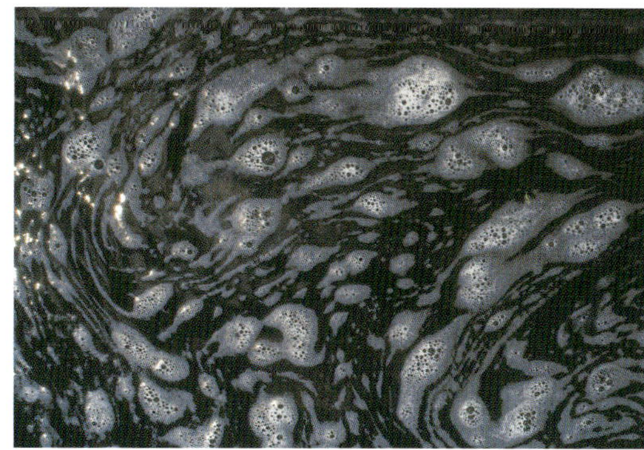

Swirling patterns

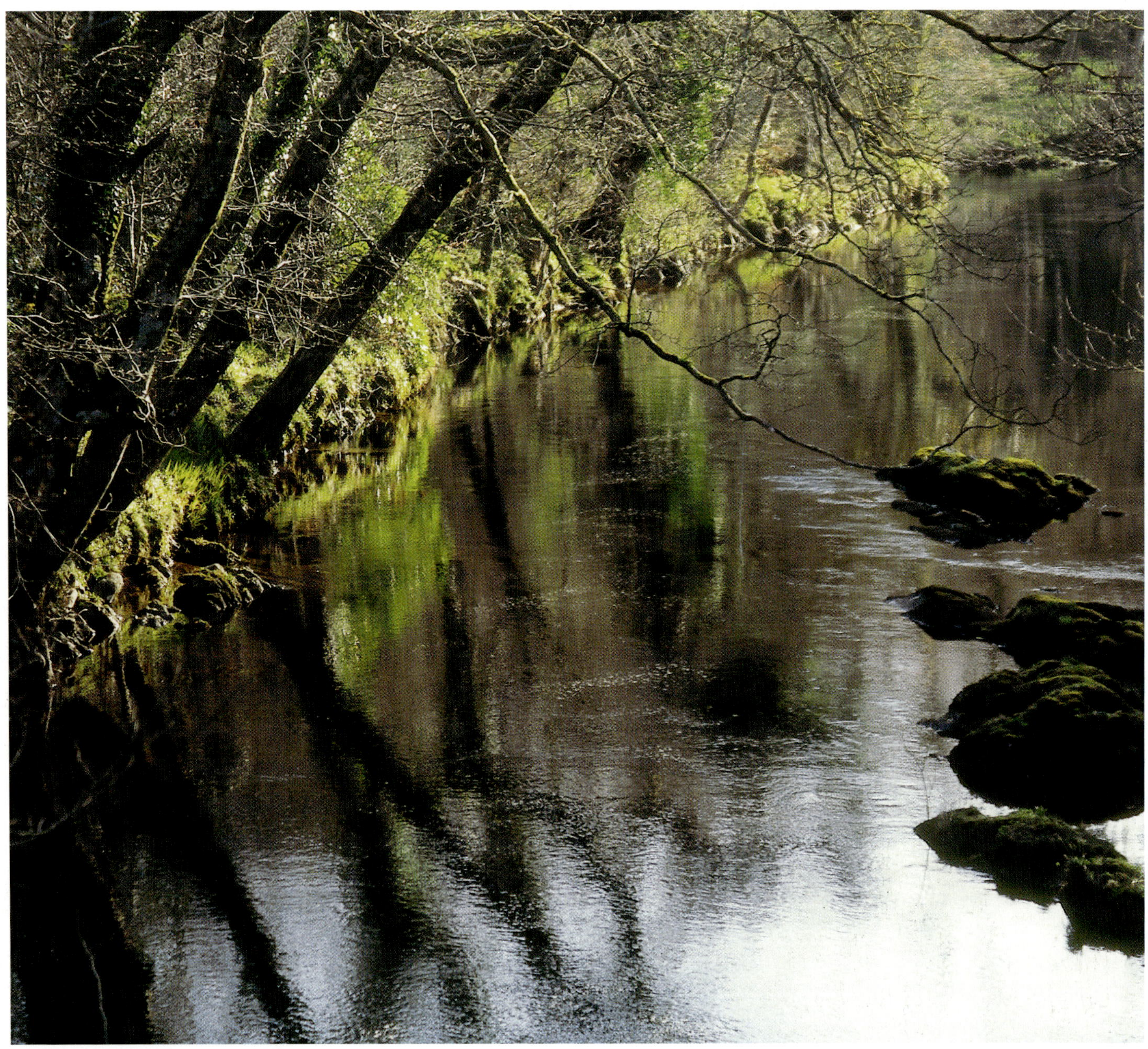

The Dart, looking downstream from Holne Bridge

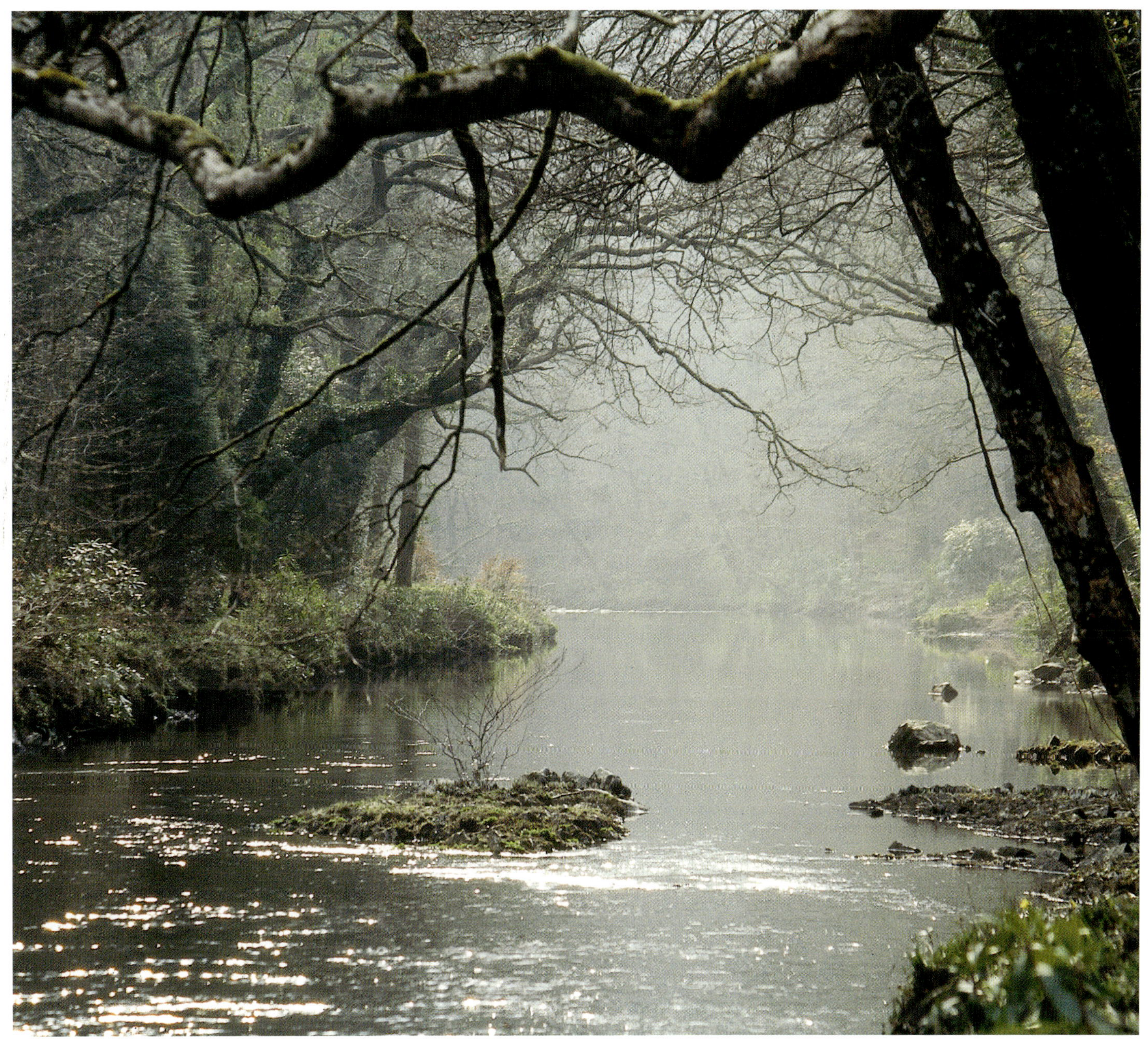

The Dart at Hembury Woods – a big river by this stage

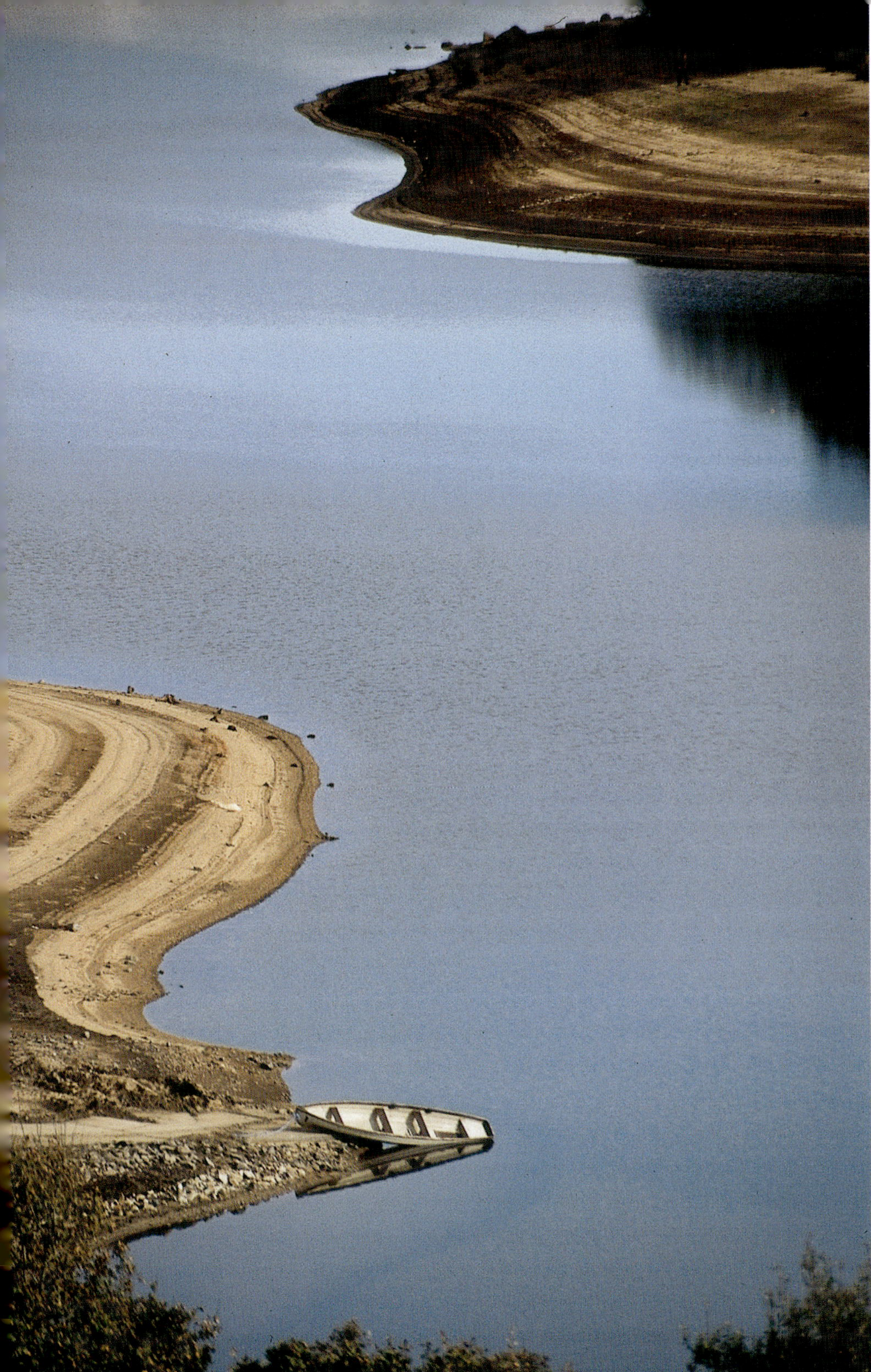

Low water levels at Burrator Reservoir

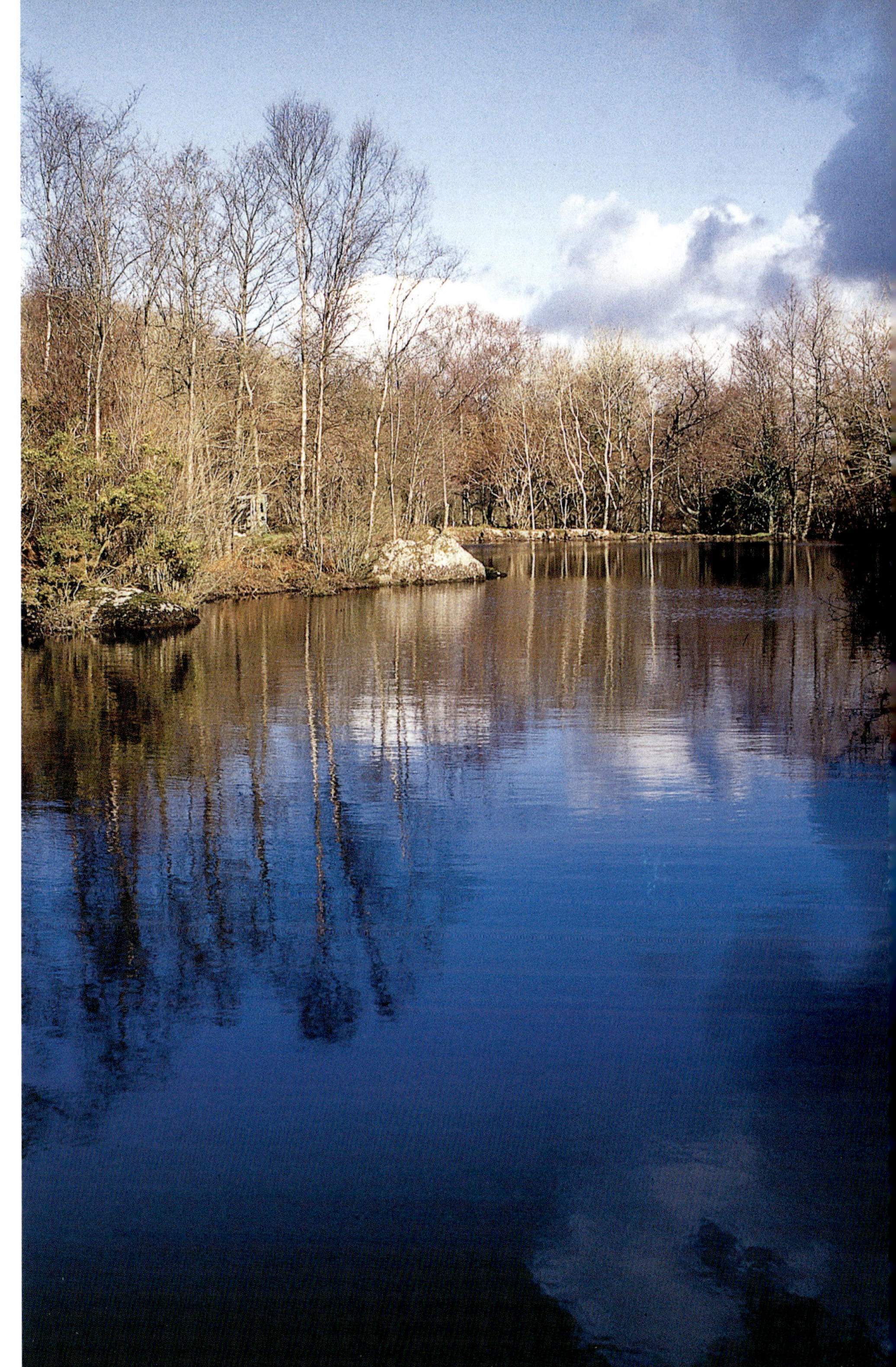

Reflections in the lakes on the Becka Brook below Hound Tor

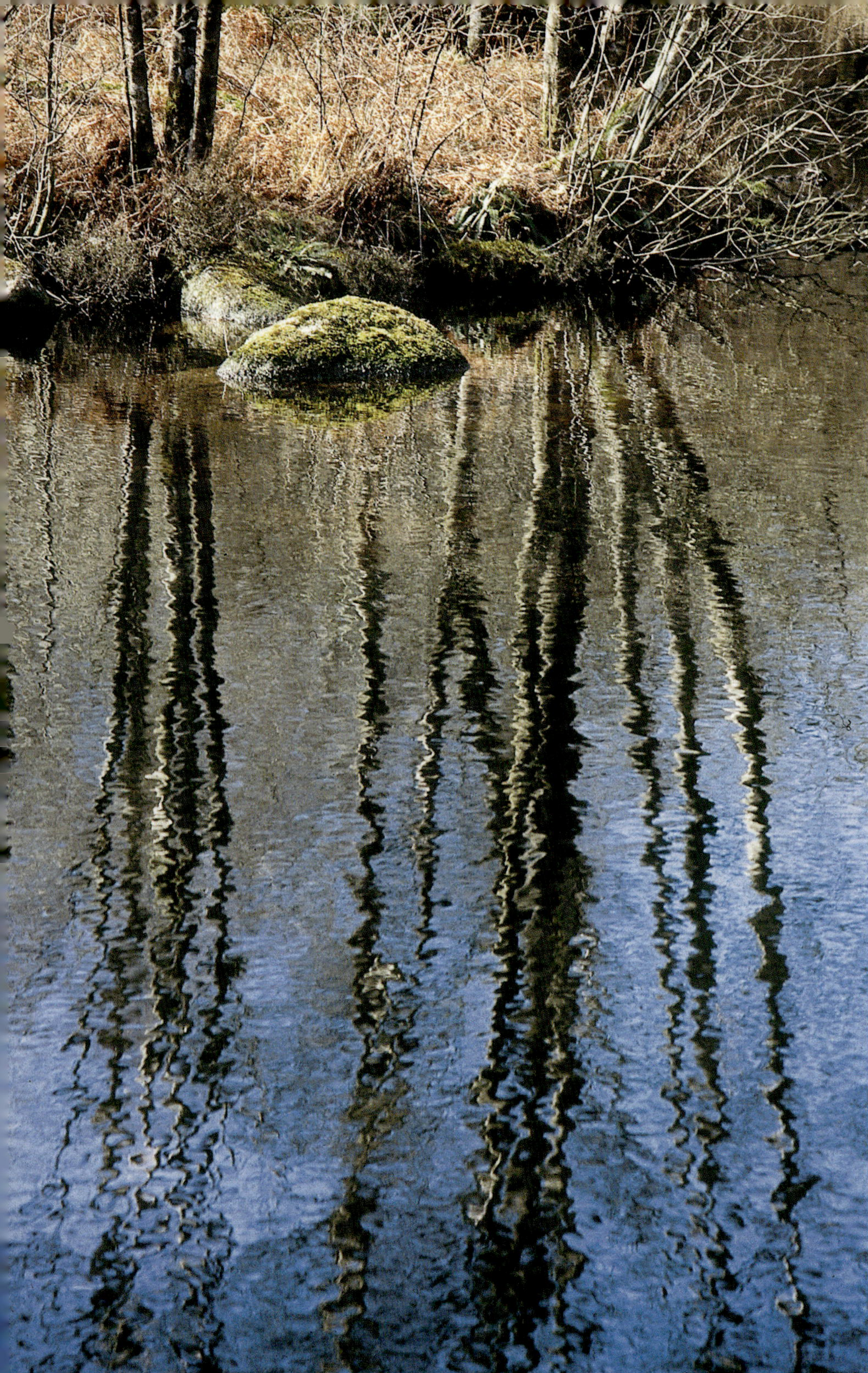

Reflections in blue

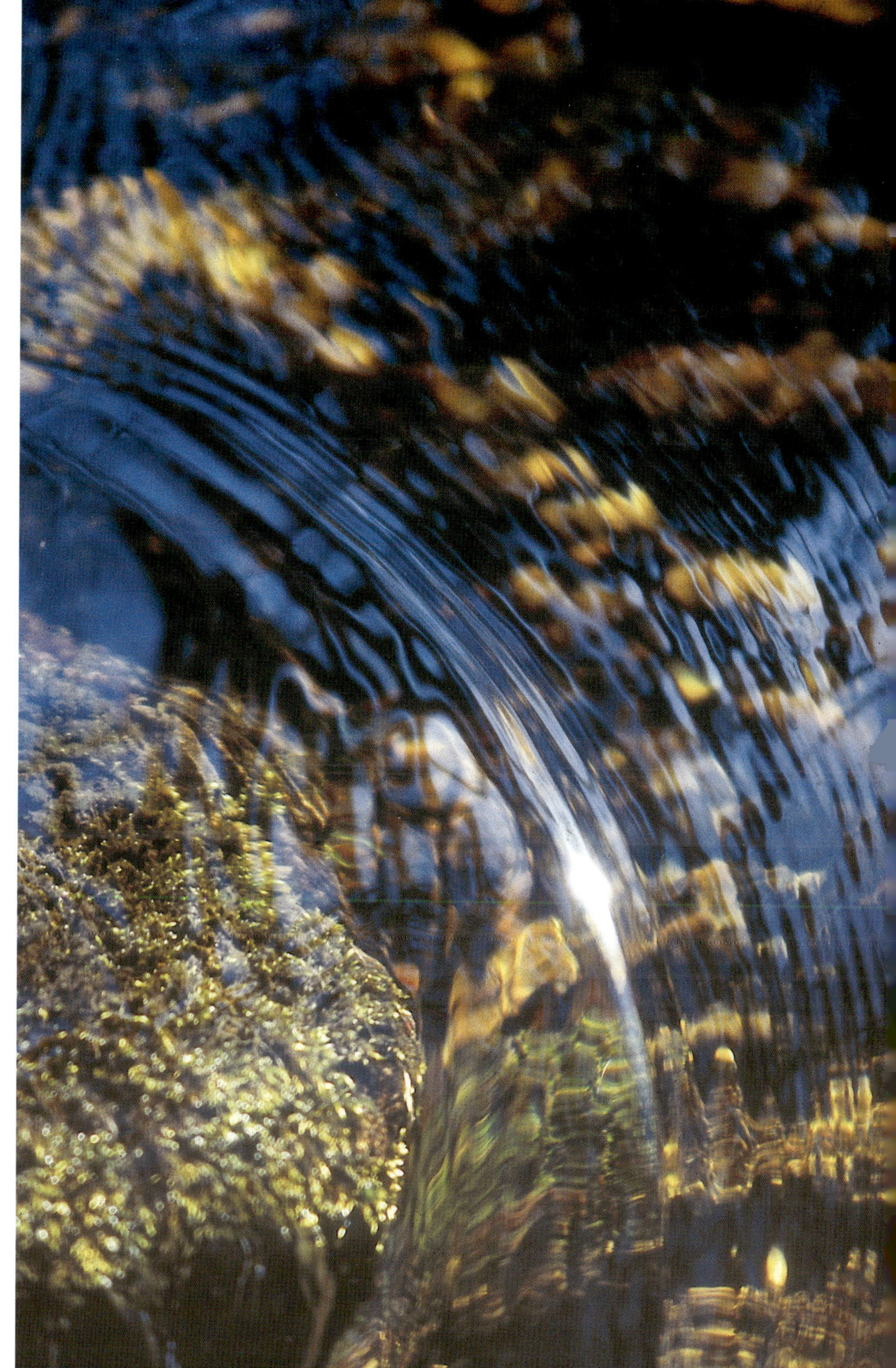

Rainbow ripples in the Becka Brook

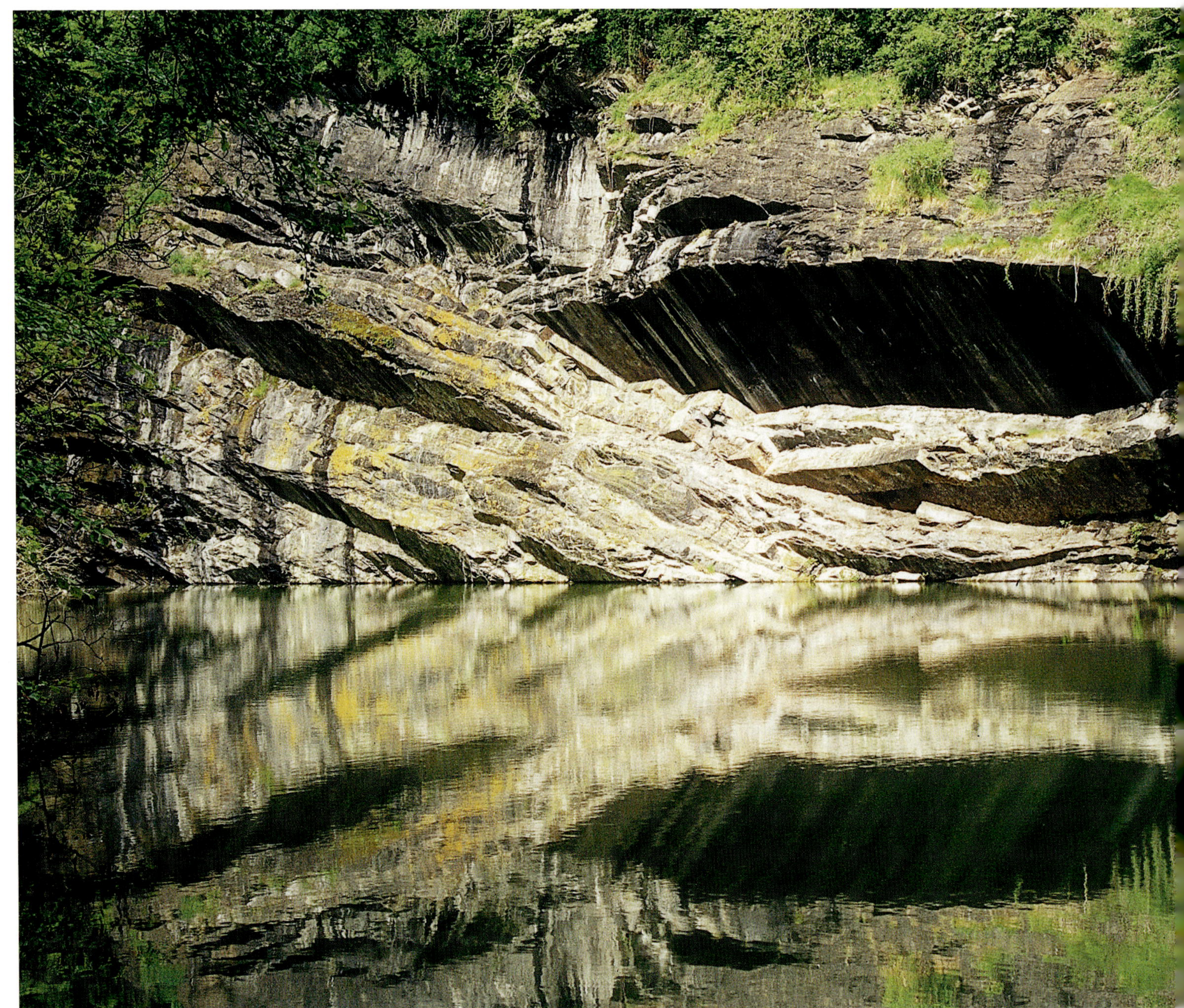

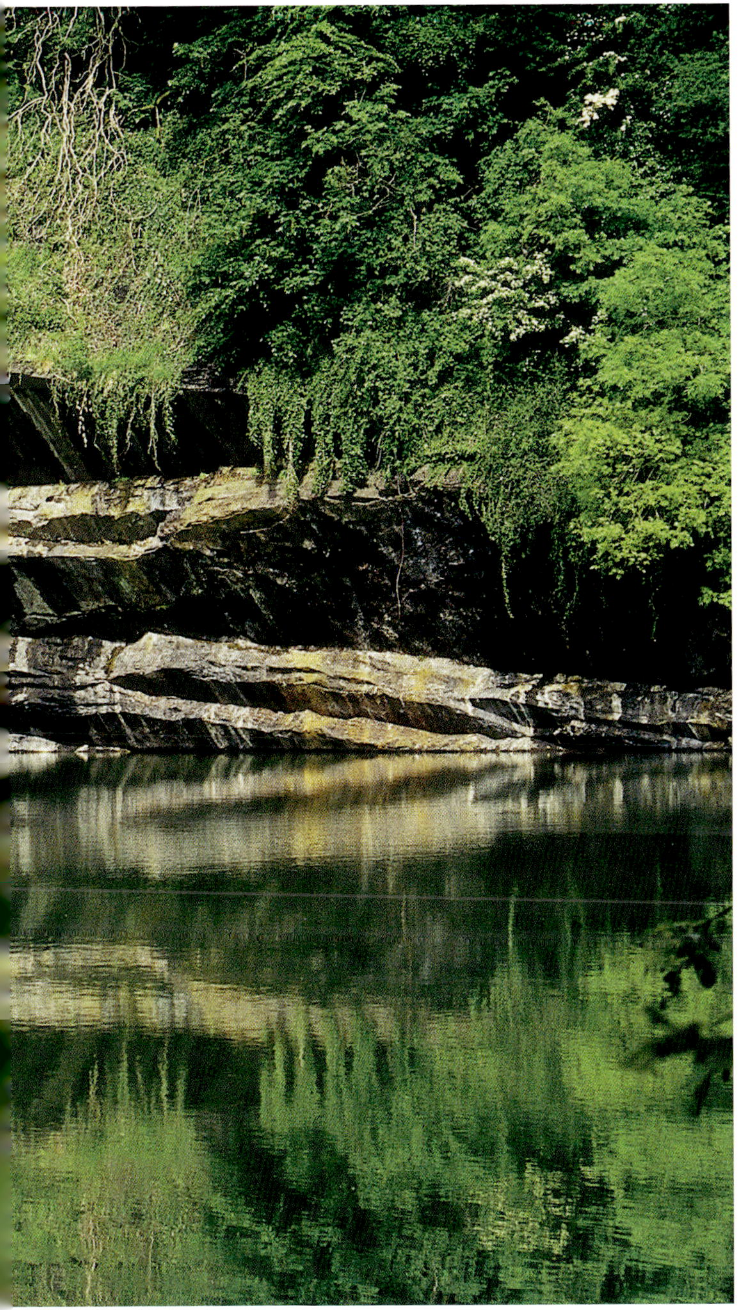

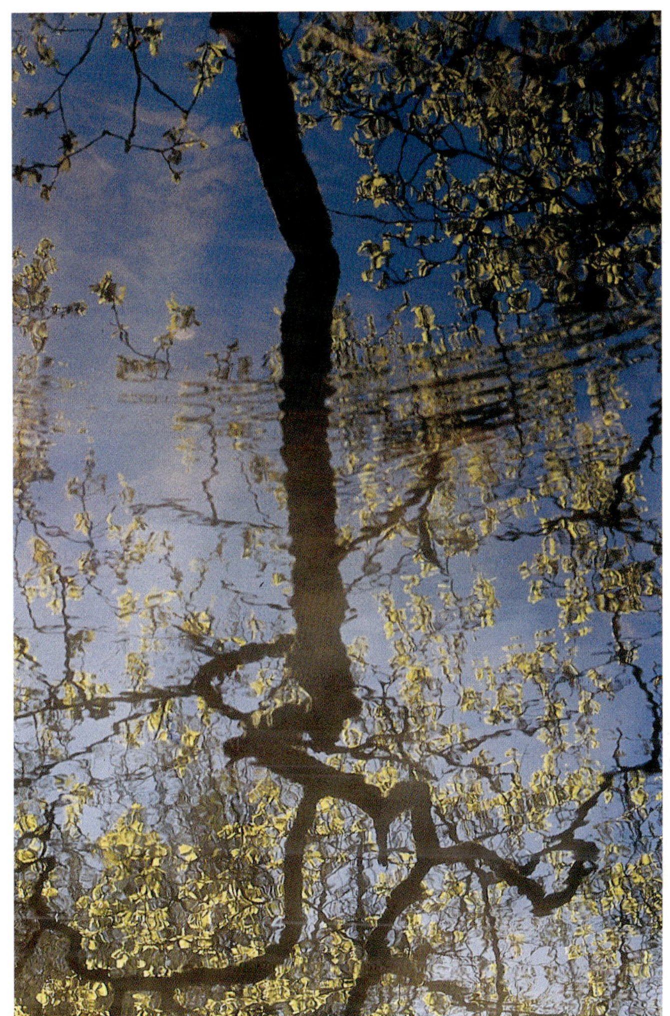

Spring leaves reflected

The great rock overhang reflected in Meldon Quarry pool

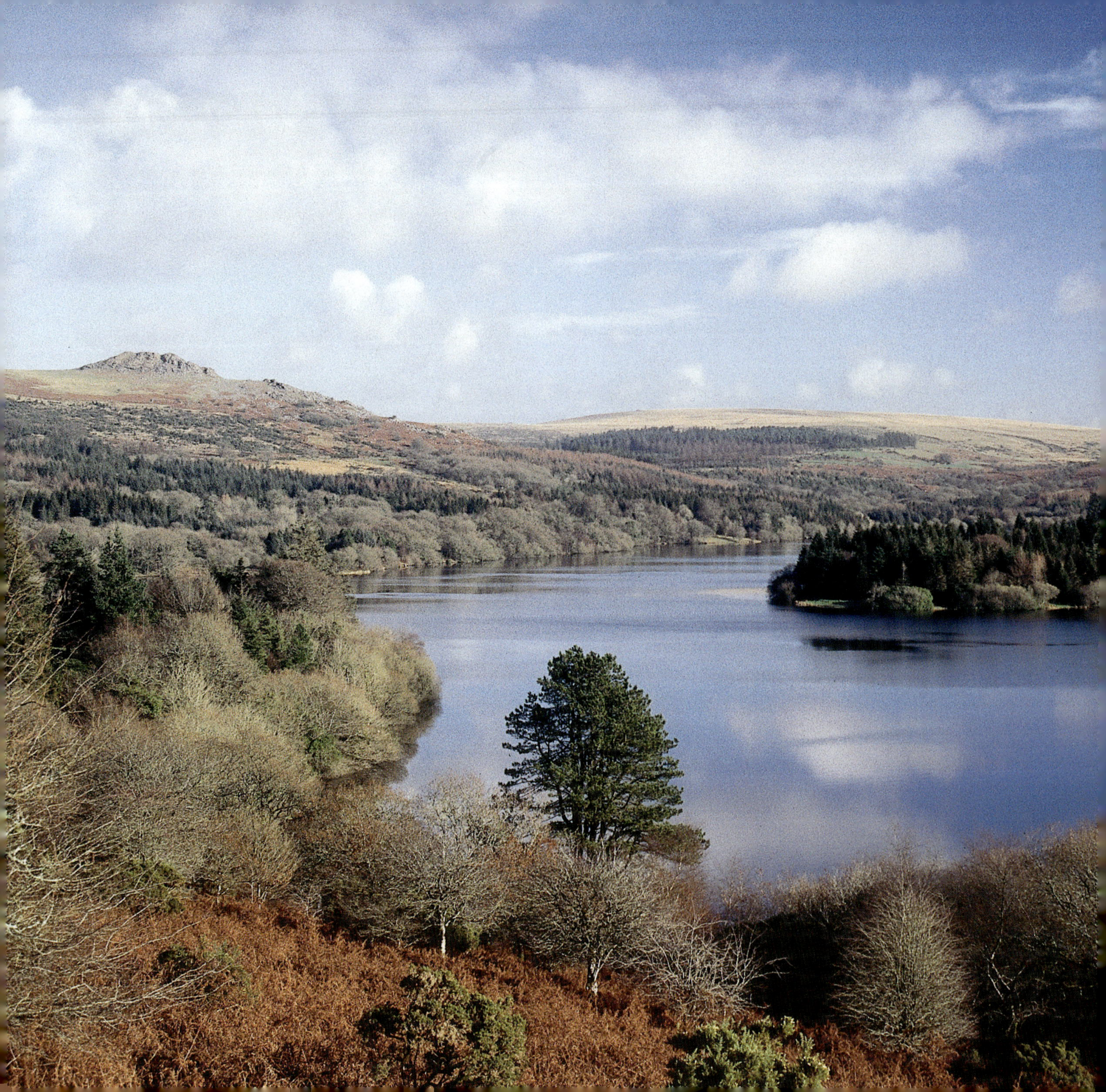

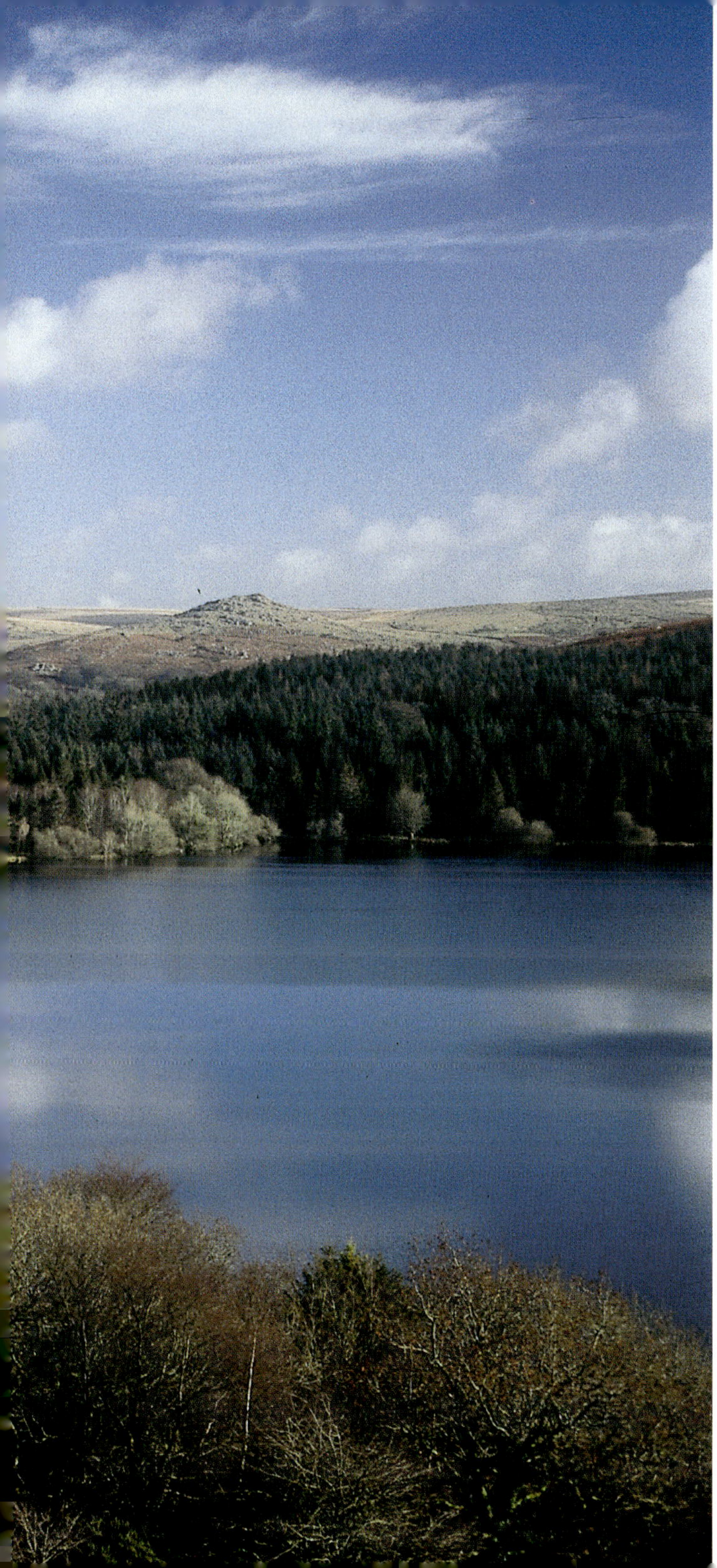

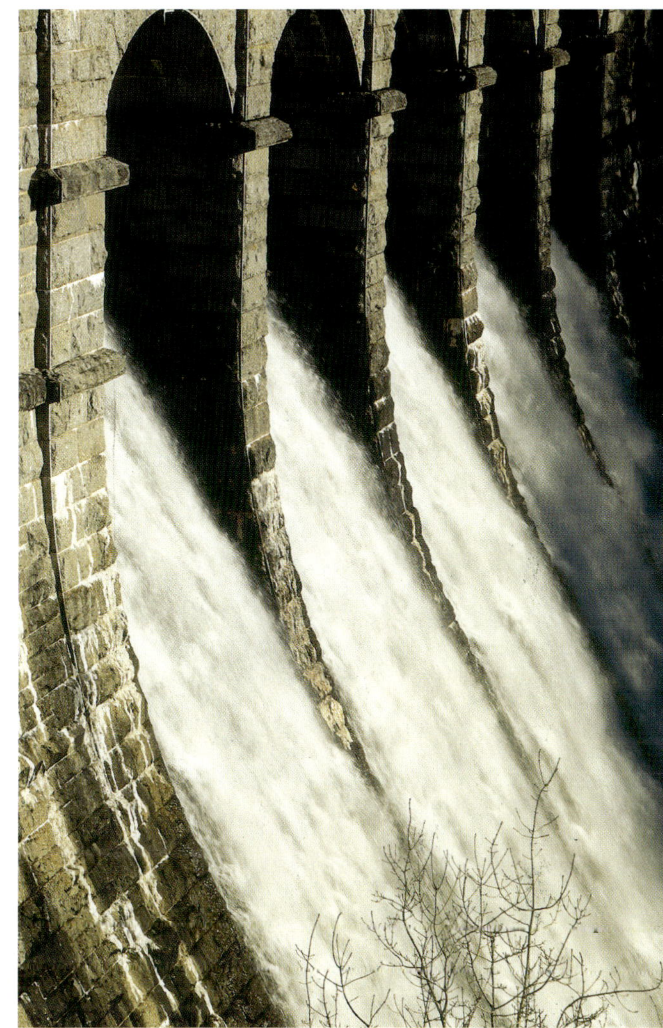

Burrator Dam – one of the older granite dams, and cascading beautifully

Burrator Reservoir from the old railway line on Yennadon Down

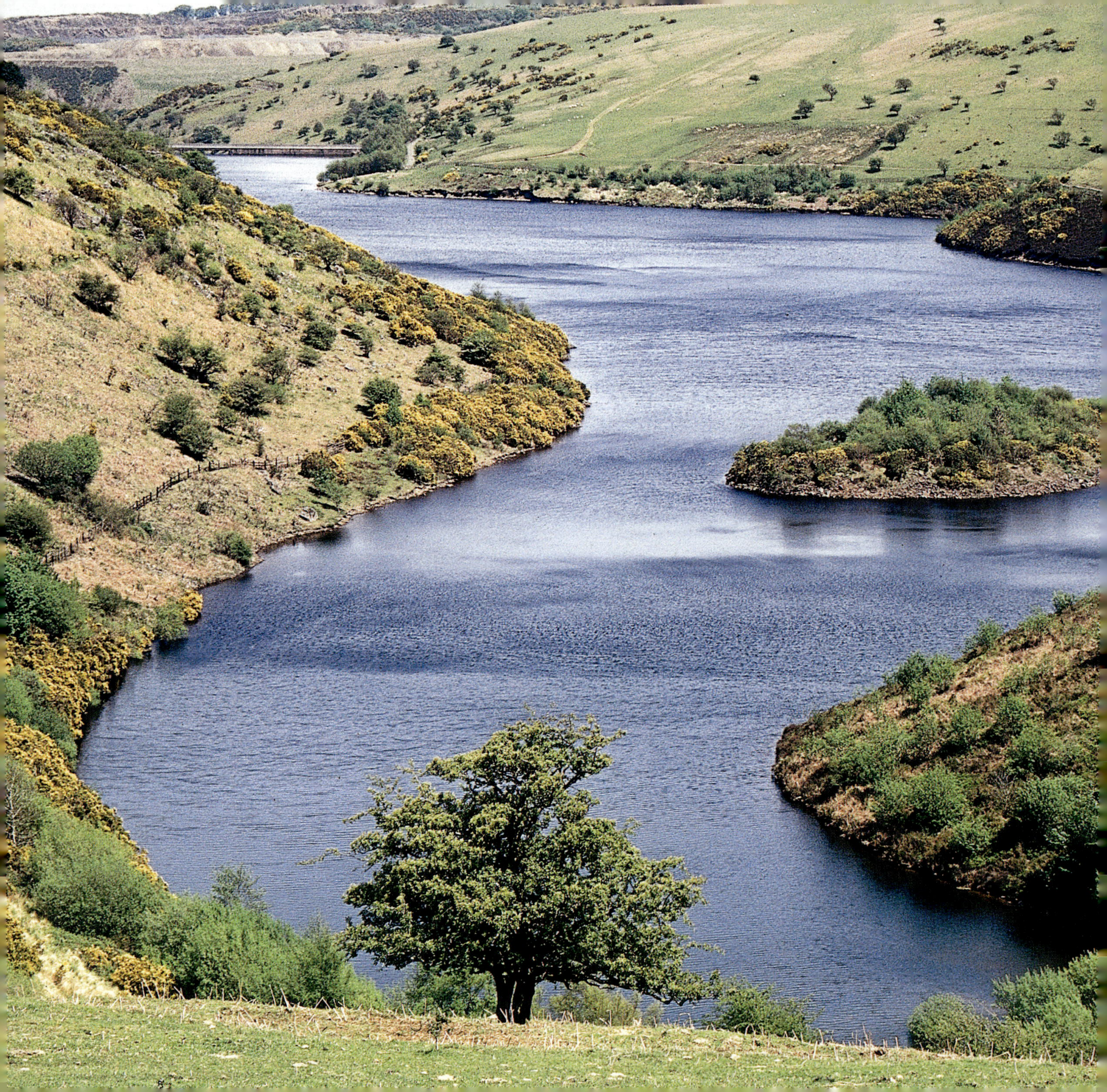

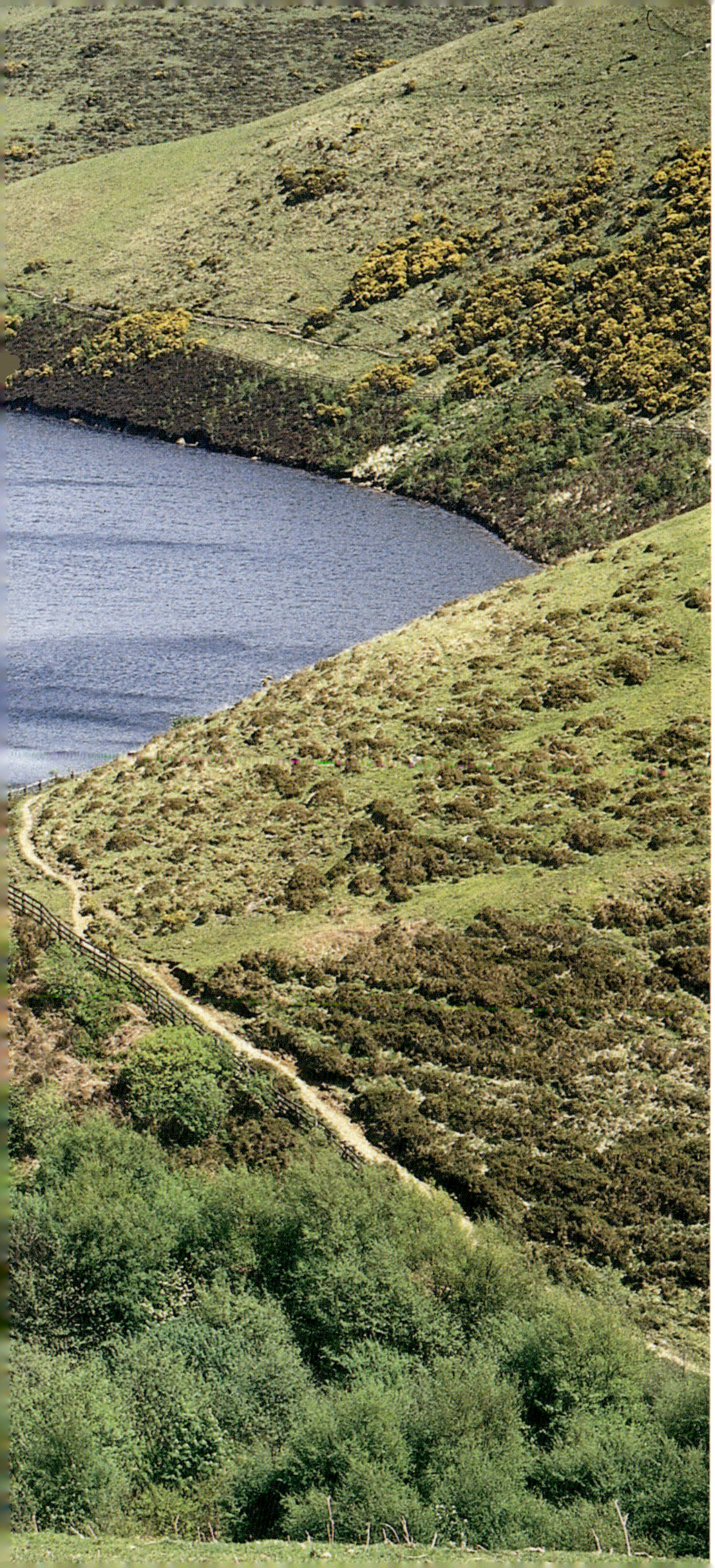

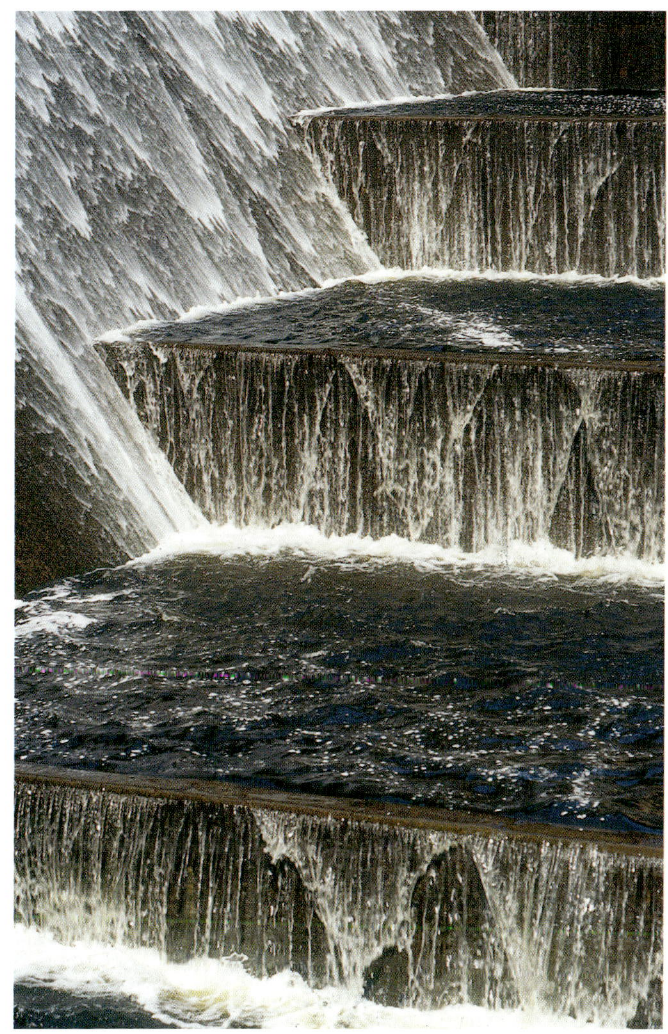

The spillways at Meldon Dam – an almost abstract geometric pattern

Overleaf: *Fernworthy Reservoir at low-water level*

The sinuous shape of Meldon Reservoir, which penetrates Dartmoor's highest country

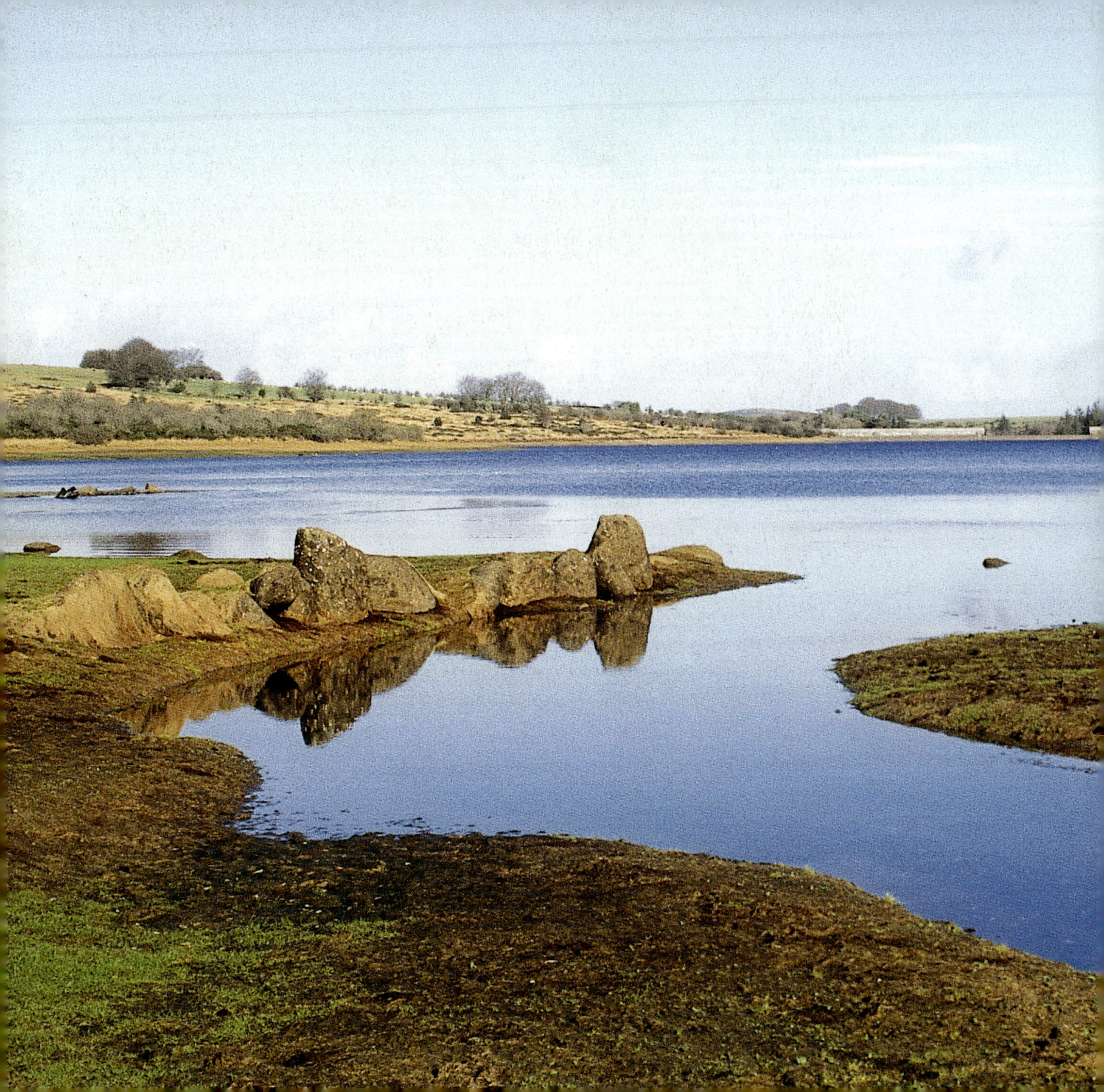

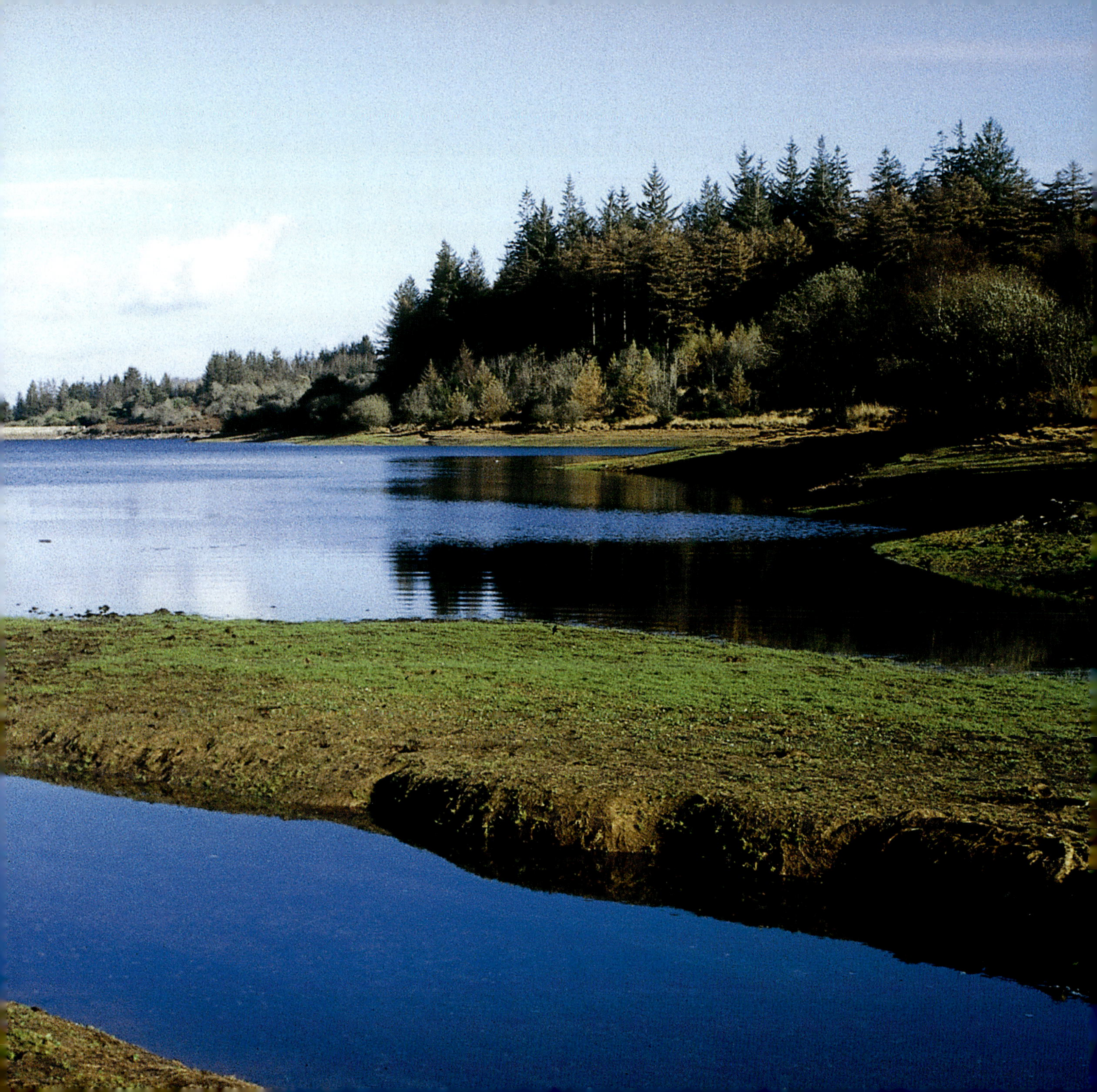

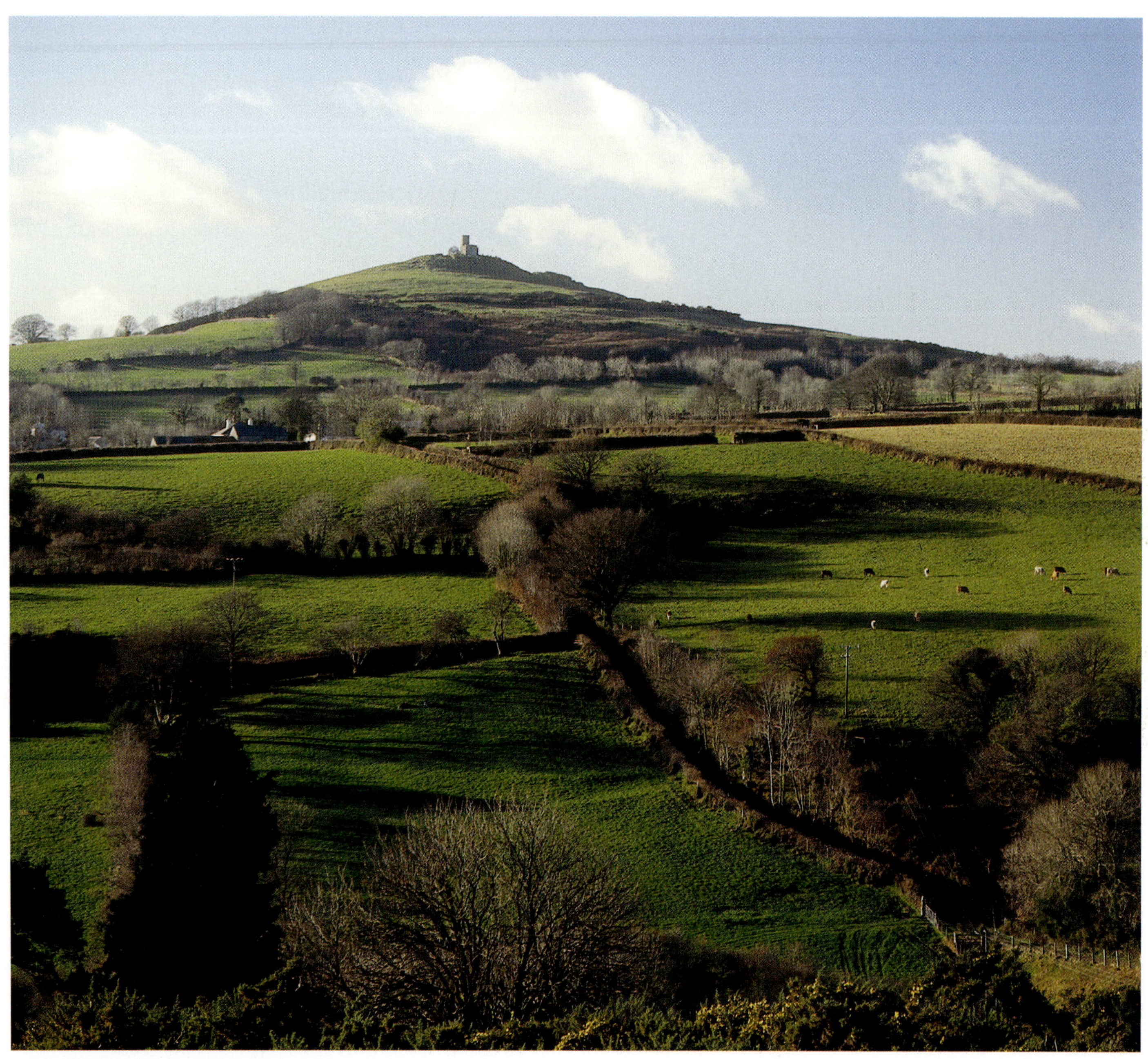

Brent Tor and its tiny church – a landmark on the western side of the moor

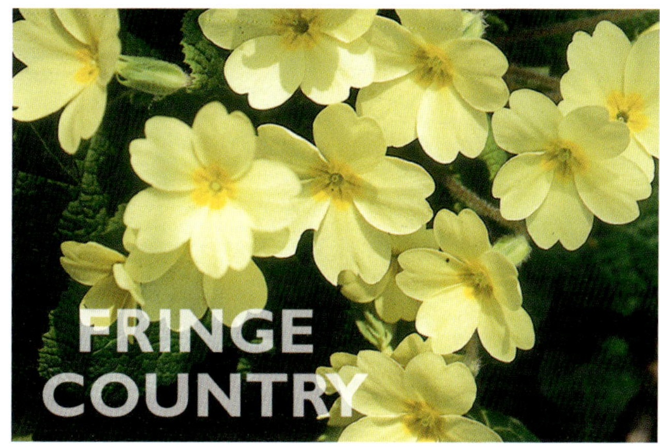

The human landscape

Around the moorland core, and extending up the major valleys, is the fringe country of fields, farms and villages. In many ways it is similar to farmed landscapes outside Dartmoor, but there are significant differences. Many traditional buildings are granite, and there are more walls and stone-faced banks than elsewhere. The juxtaposition of farmland and moorland creates a pleasing contrast and highlights the centuries of effort that have gone into enclosure and improvement of the 'in-bye' land. The simple fact that you can stand up high on the moorland and look down on the field patterns gives them greater impact and further emphasises the contrast between the cosy detail of the country below and the untamed wide open spaces above.

Field patterns can be stunning. When the sun is low in the sky giving that wonderful warm glow, and casting long shadows which pick out every feature and every gentle fold in the ground, this random patchwork looks as if it has been designed just for our pleasure. Many of the farmsteads dotted over this landscape are ancient and beautiful. Most still have some of their traditional outbuildings – barns, linhays, ash houses and the like, many still in use. Others are derelict but still attractive, and an important part of the history of the moor.

Many of Dartmoor's villages are well known and loved: Lustleigh with its beautifully thatched buildings and sylvan setting; tiny Sheepstor huddled around its church; Belstone perched on top of its cleave; Chagford with its hustle and bustle. Widecombe-in-the-Moor is of course known the world over for that song, its annual fair and for its great church – the cathedral of the moor! Princetown is an oddity, with 90 inches of rain a year, endless days of mist and low cloud, grey buildings, and the infamous prison. But visitors love it and so do the stalwart residents. Ashburton and Buckfastleigh are the only settlements in the National Park which can really be called towns. You can walk from them directly into the paths and lanes of the fringe country, which provides a beautiful setting for the wilder parts of the Park and which no lover of Dartmoor should neglect to explore.

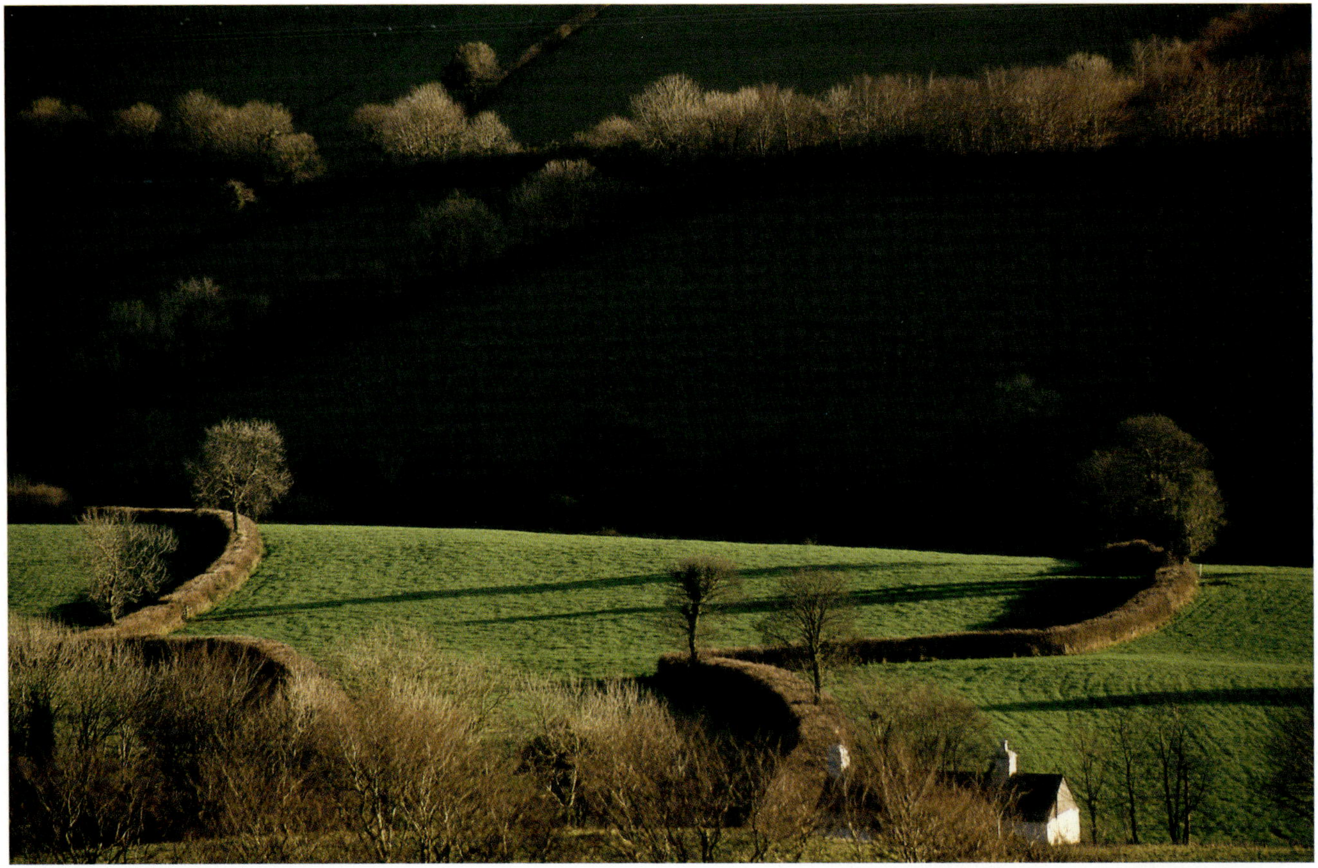

Patterns in the landscape. Looking south from Brent Tor

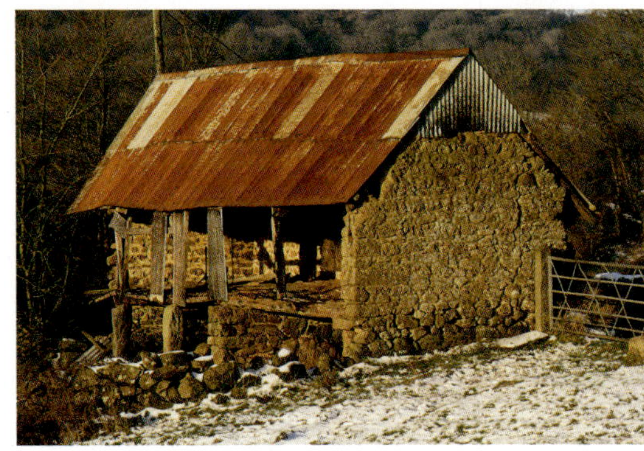

An old linhay near Lustleigh

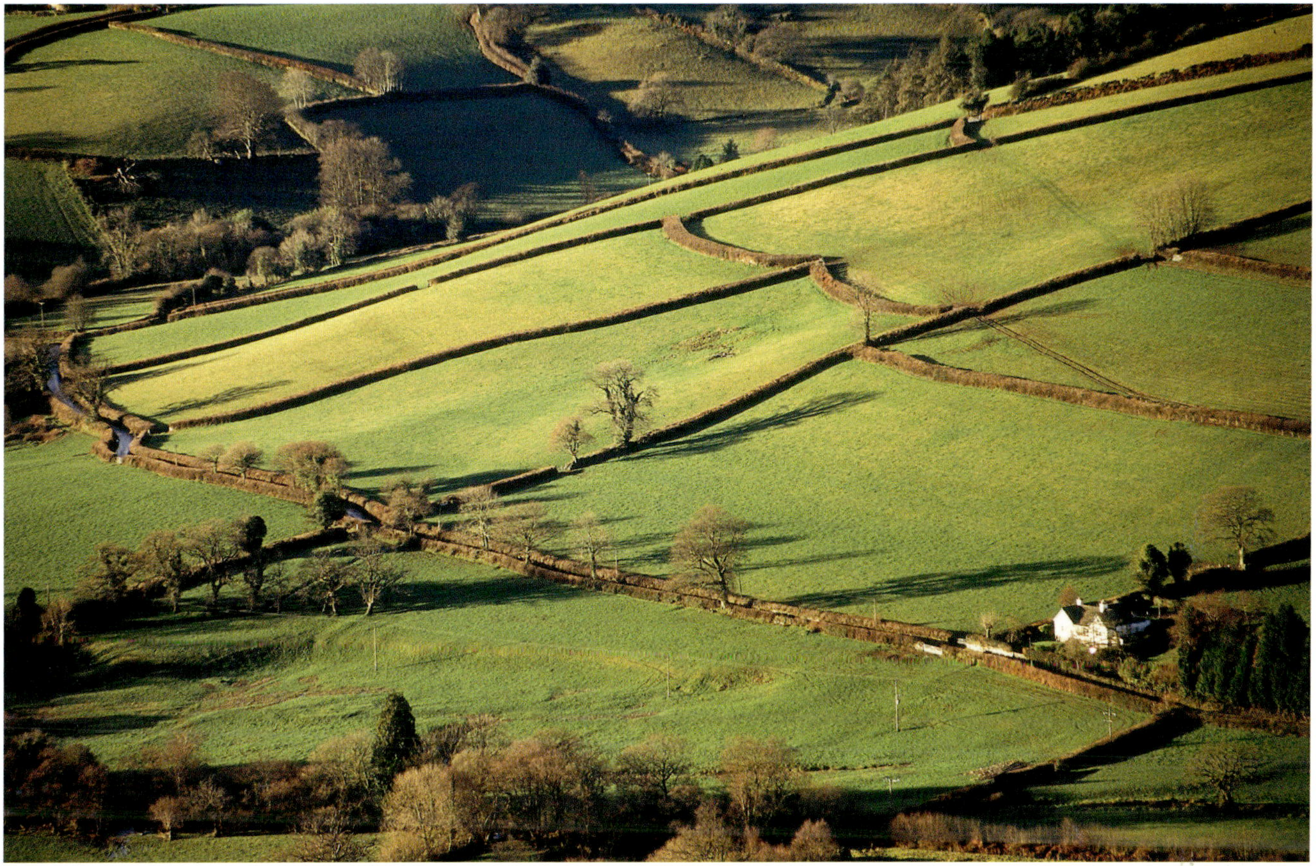

Early-morning light in the Widecombe valley, seen from Bell Tor

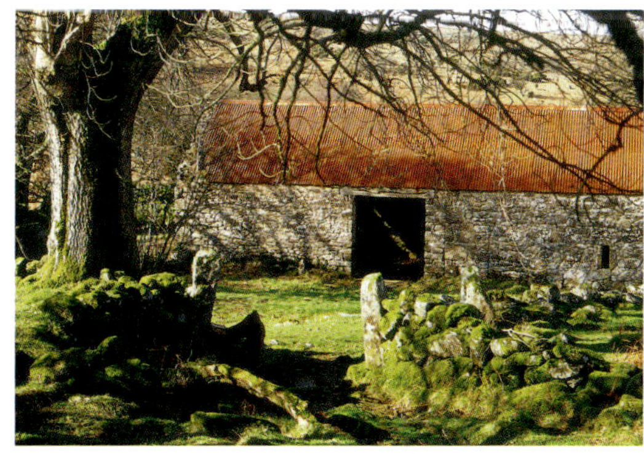

The old barn at Emsworthy, near Widecombe-in-the-Moor

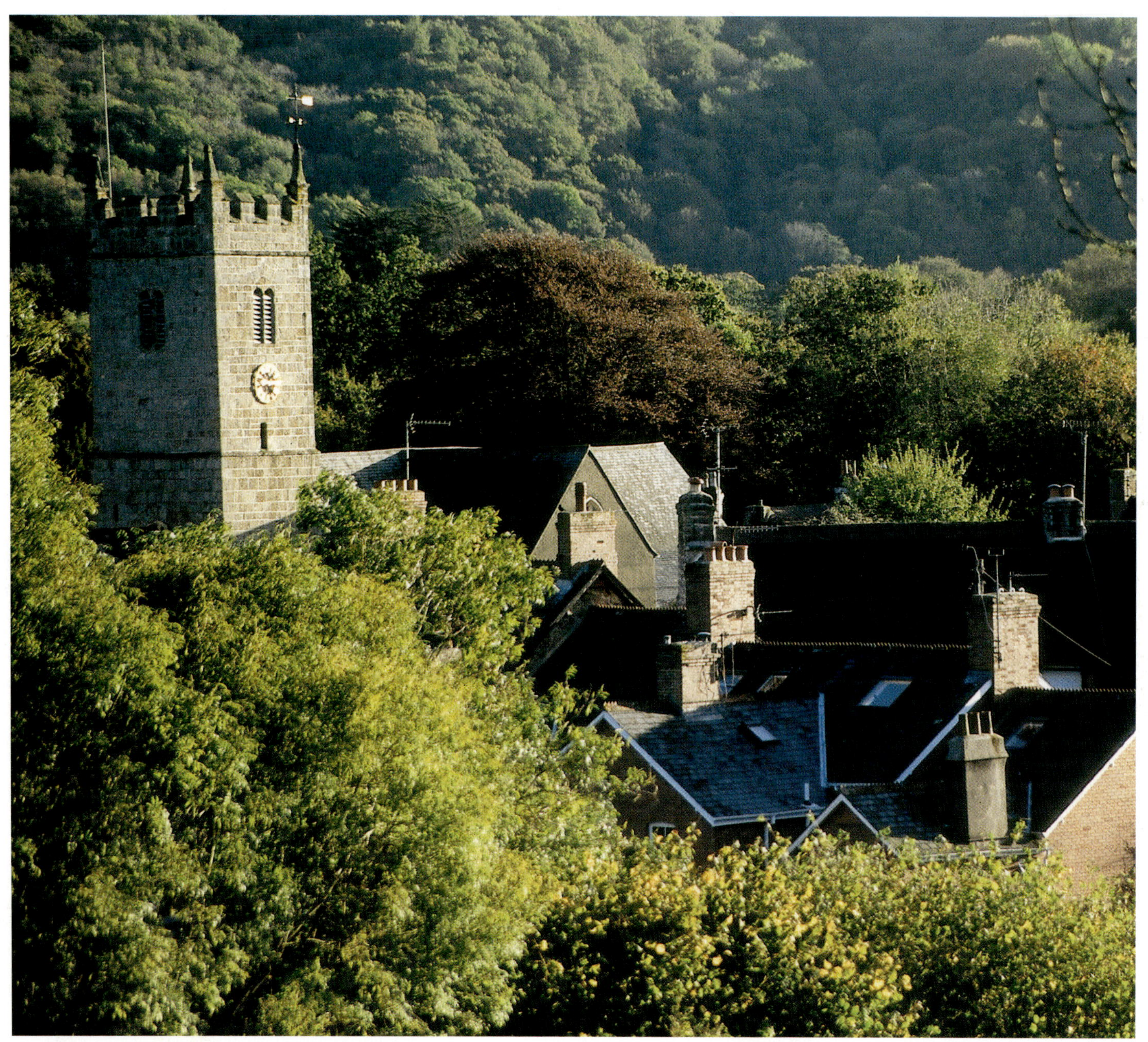

Lustleigh – a sylvan setting in the Wray valley

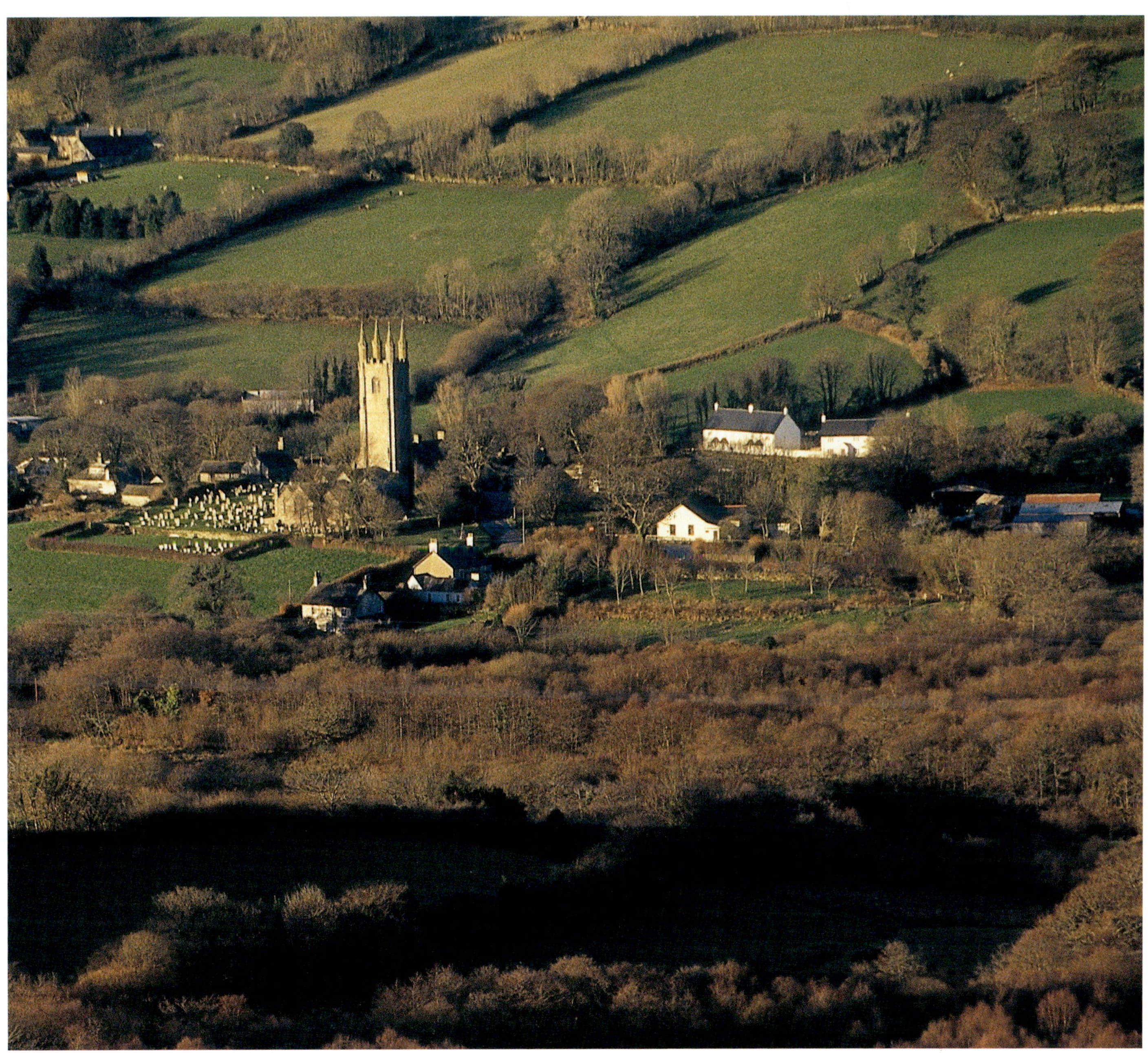

Widecombe-in-the-Moor from Bell Tor

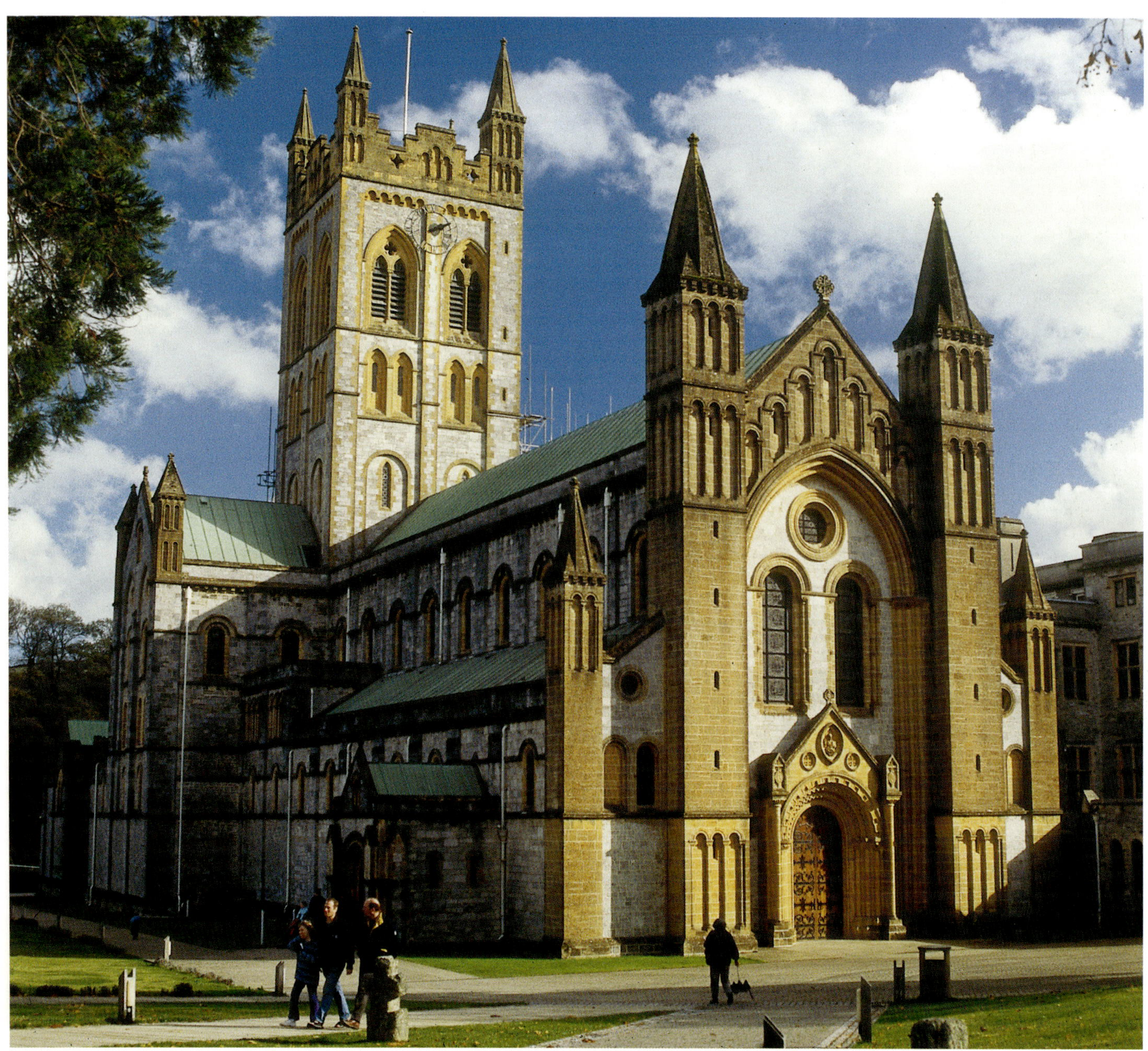

Buckfast Abbey – Dartmoor's most popular visitor attraction

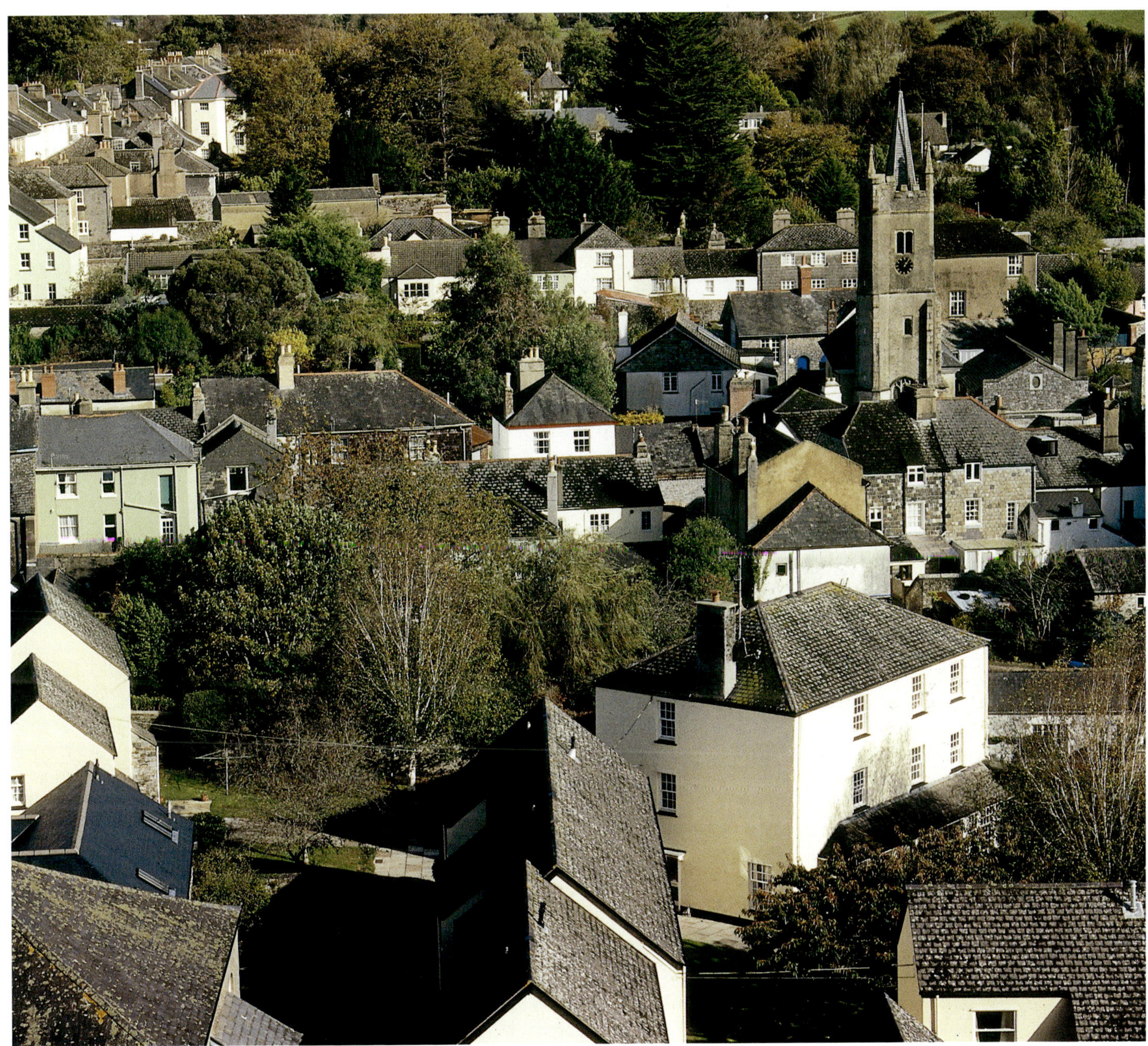

Ashburton, an ancient stannary town, seen from the church tower

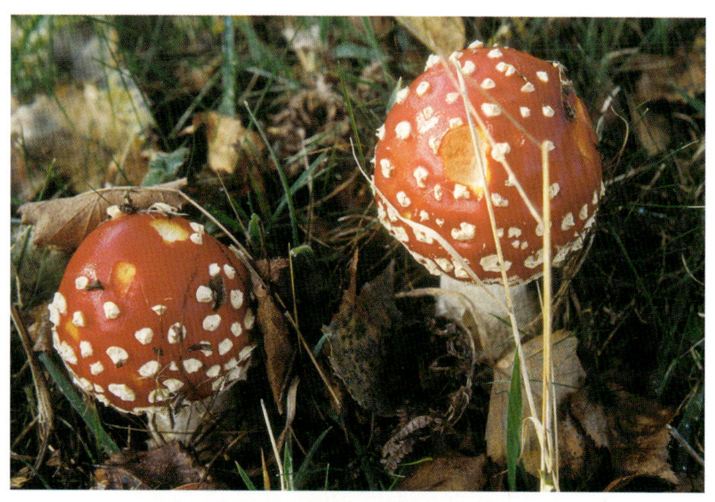

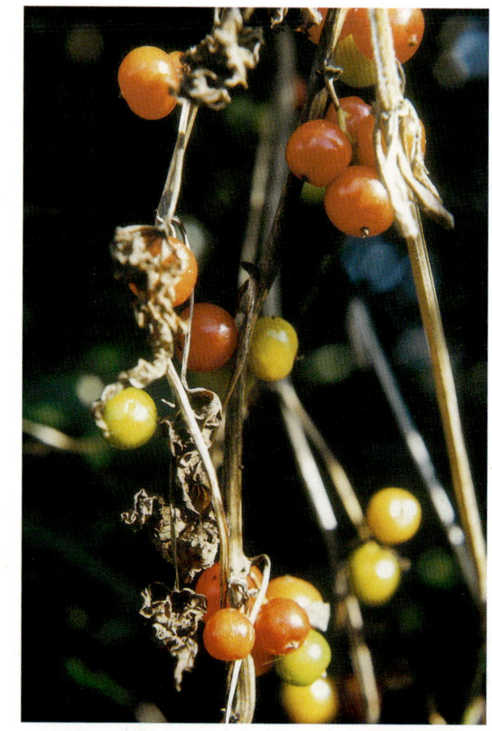

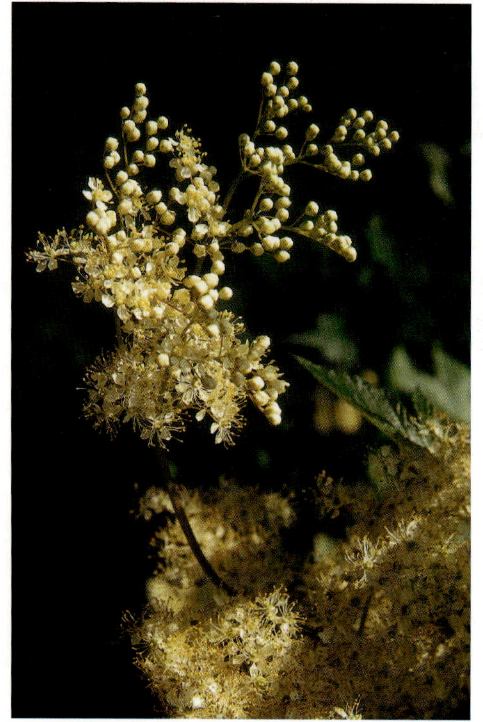

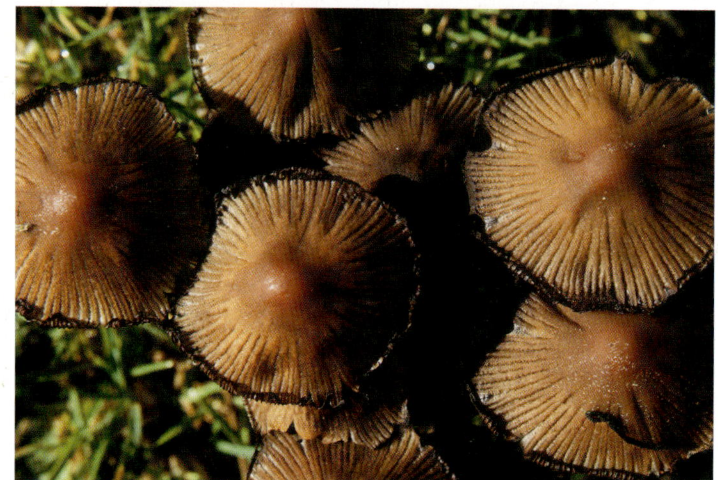

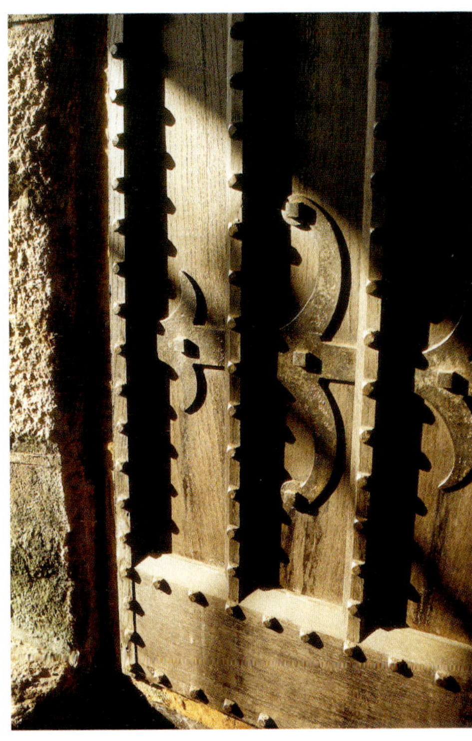

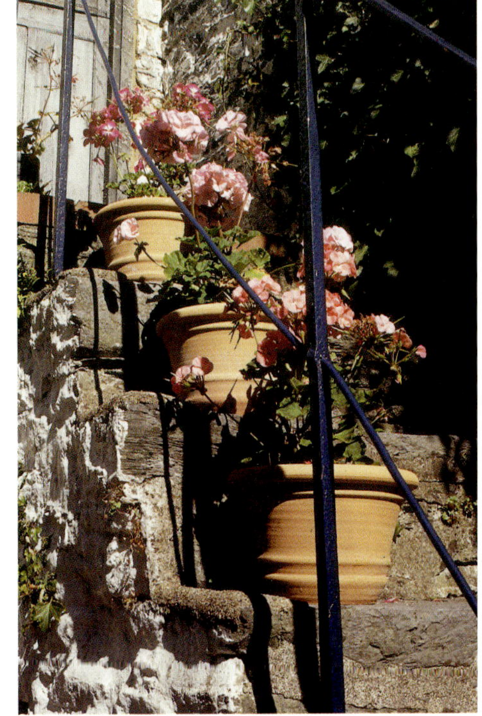

It is often the detail which makes the fringe country so interesting. Here we have (left) flowering meadowsweet; bryony berries and fascinating fungi, and (right) the 'My dear mother' clock on the church tower at Buckland in the Moor, the church door at Hennock, and a quiet corner in Buckfastleigh

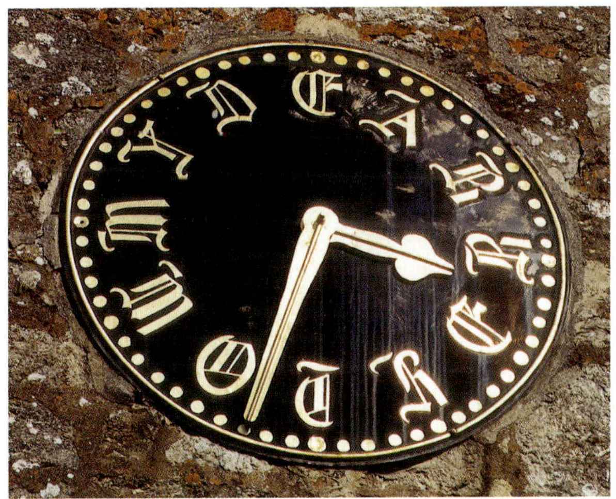

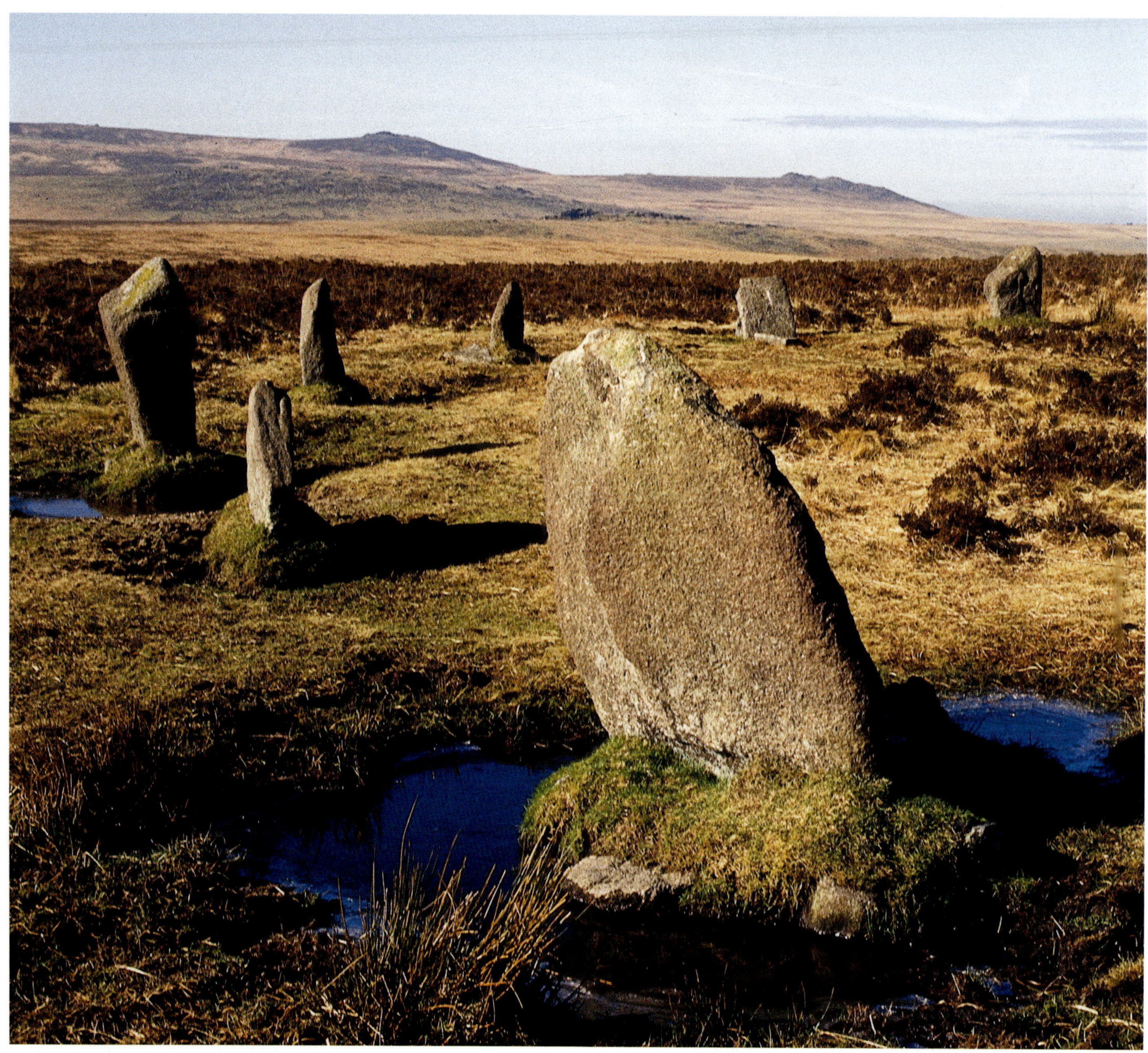

A prehistoric stone circle near Little Hound Tor

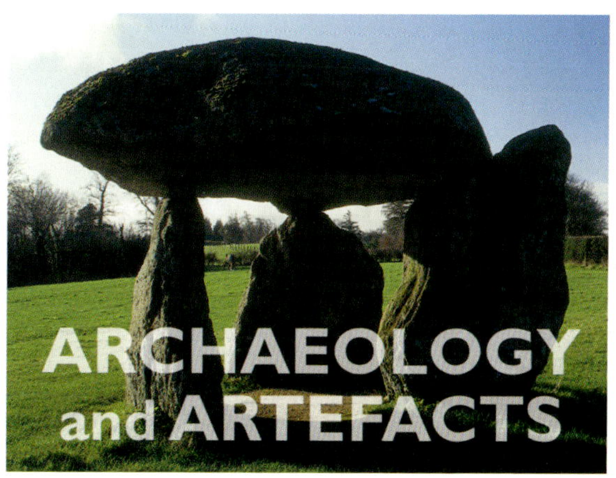

History and prehistory

As we have seen already, almost all of the Dartmoor landscape is influenced by man's activities. In the fringe country the man-made additions – walls, banks, hedges and buildings, in fact, make up the landscape and provide its essential character. But all over the moor there are thousands of prehistoric and historic artefacts which add enormously to the interest of Dartmoor. If you read a guidebook before you go, or study the OS map carefully, or just keep your eyes open, you will find them on almost any walk you might do. Some will hit you in the eye, like Meldon Viaduct or the Wheal Betsy engine house. Others are more subtle – the arrangement of boulders that looks slightly artificial and which is in fact a Bronze Age hut circle; or the indistinct but straight line across a hillside which can only have been a leat serving a long-gone mining operation. Many are full of atmosphere, and evocative of our own past. Stand at the end of one of the big stone rows in the Plym valley or on Stall Moor and think about the society which erected these monuments. Some have tales attached to them, like Childe's Tomb overlooking the lonely bowl of Foxtor Mires. Some might be considered as eyesores were it not for their historic interest. Not many people would argue that the remains of the old crane in Haytor Quarry should be removed, but how old does something have to be to acquire a heritage value?

'Today's eyesores are tomorrow's archaeology' is a well-worn phrase, but does raise difficult dilemmas for those who have to make the decision on whether to remove some structure or building that no longer has a function, or whether to repair and consolidate it as part of Dartmoor's cultural heritage. Most old quarries pose similar dilemmas – should they be 'landscaped' back into the scenery, or should they remain untouched as dramatic monuments to past industry, to be gradually reclaimed by nature?

Interest and beauty do not always go hand in hand in a landscape, and who is to say which gives us more pleasure? The balancing act is not easy.

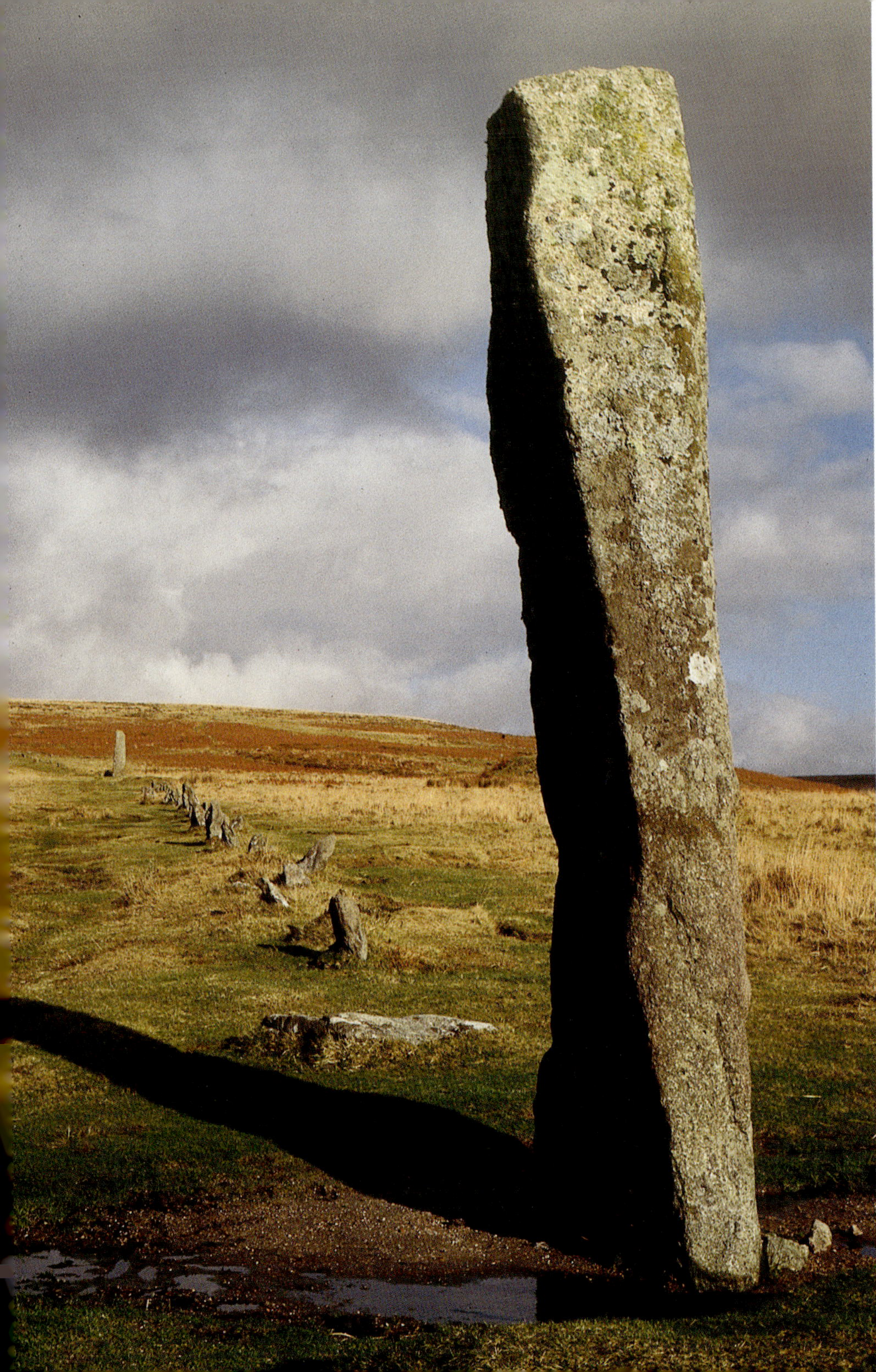

A prehistoric stone row in the upper Plym valley

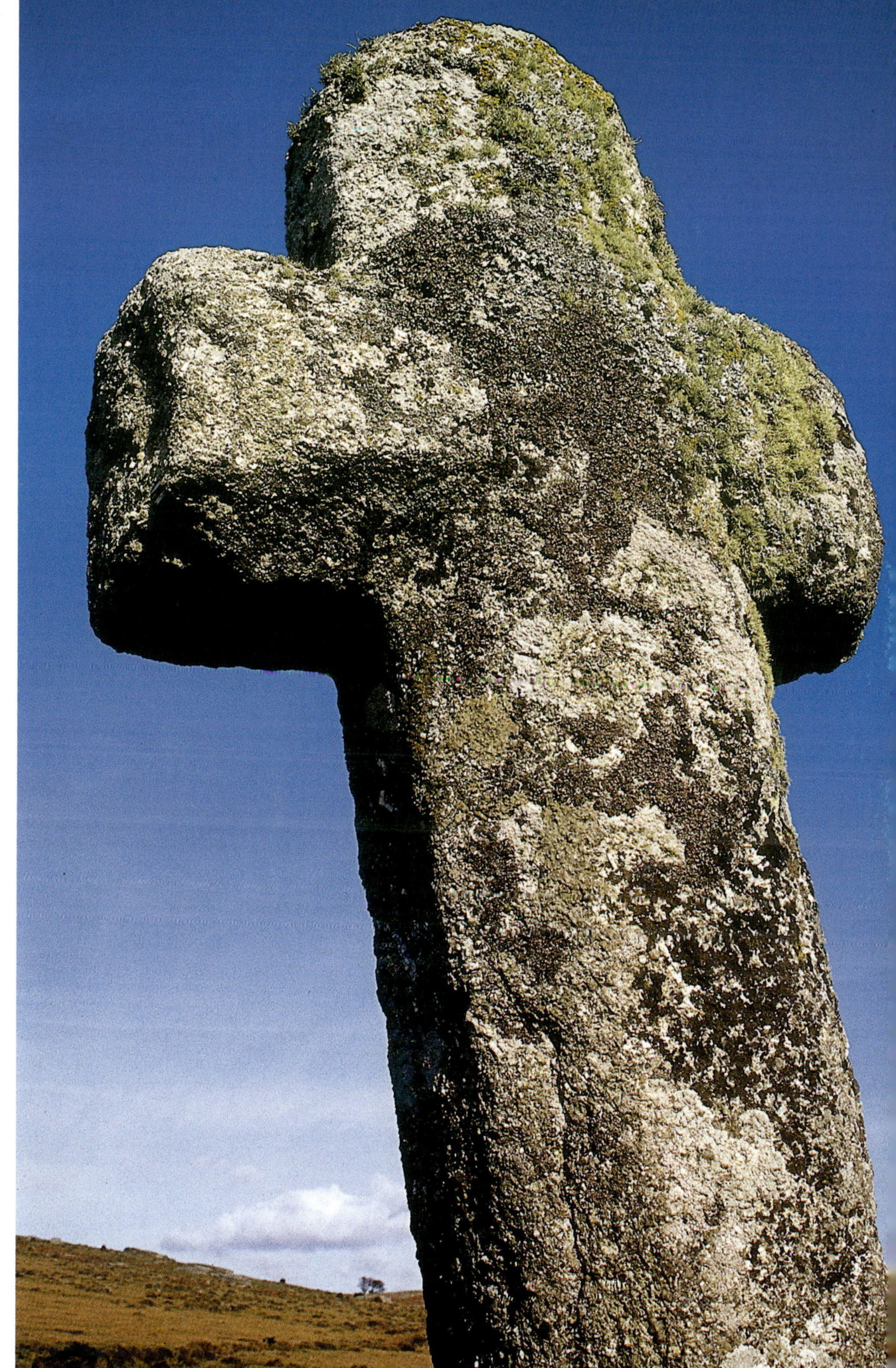

*Windy Post on Whitchurch Common, marking an
ancient trackway across the moor*

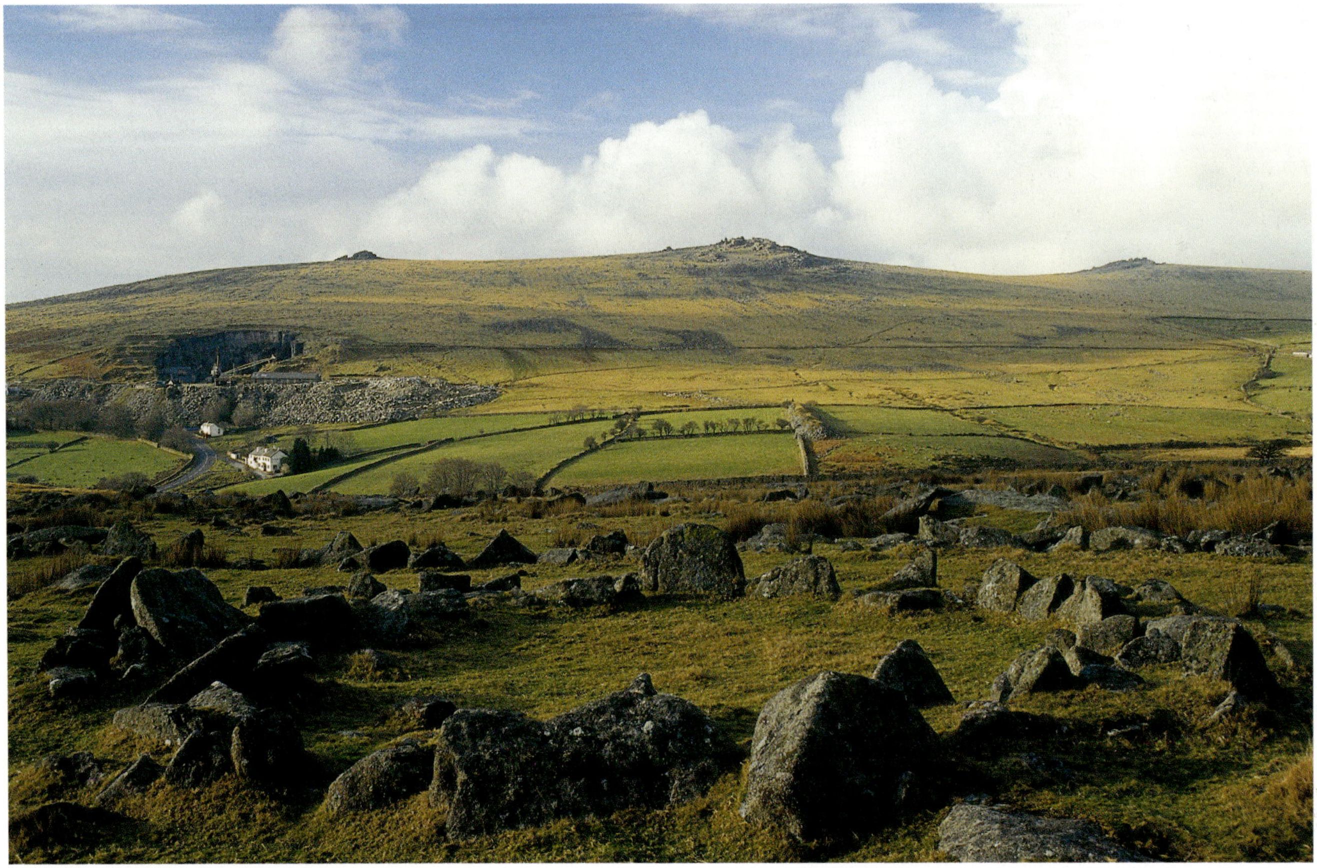

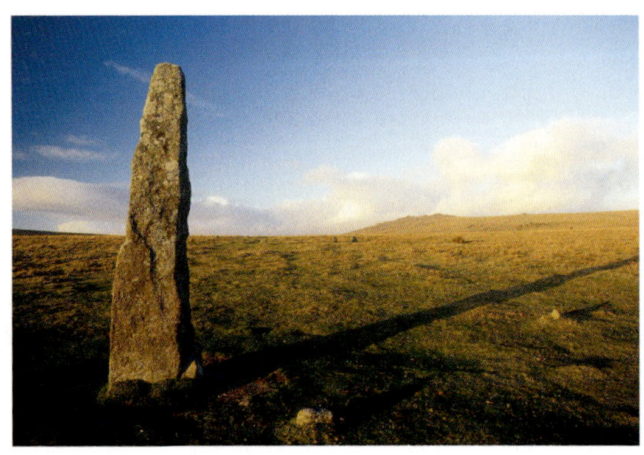

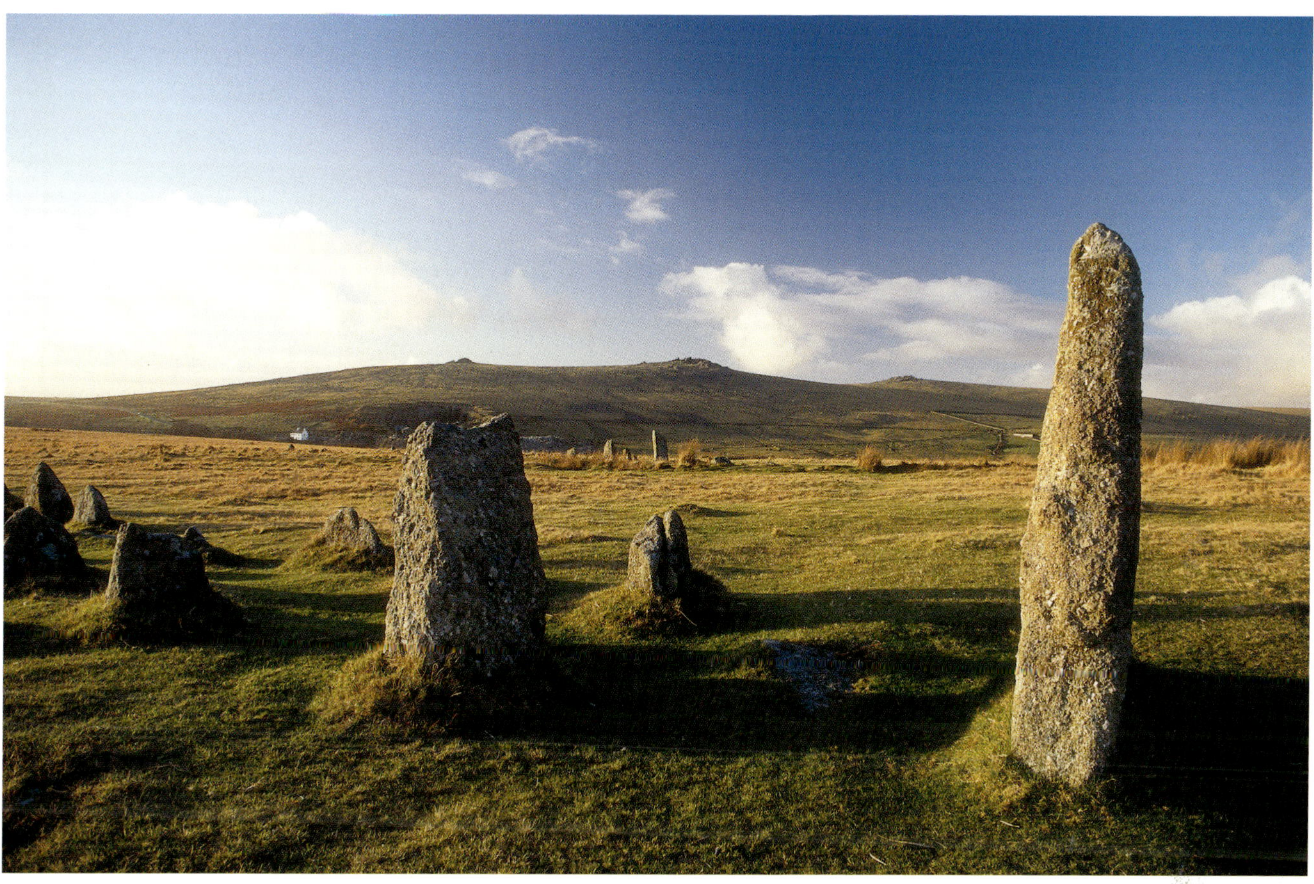

Left and above: *Merrivale. A wonderful collection of Bronze Age hut circles, stone rows and standing stones, all right next to the Princetown–Tavistock road*

Overleaf: *The stone circle at Scorhill, near Gidleigh*

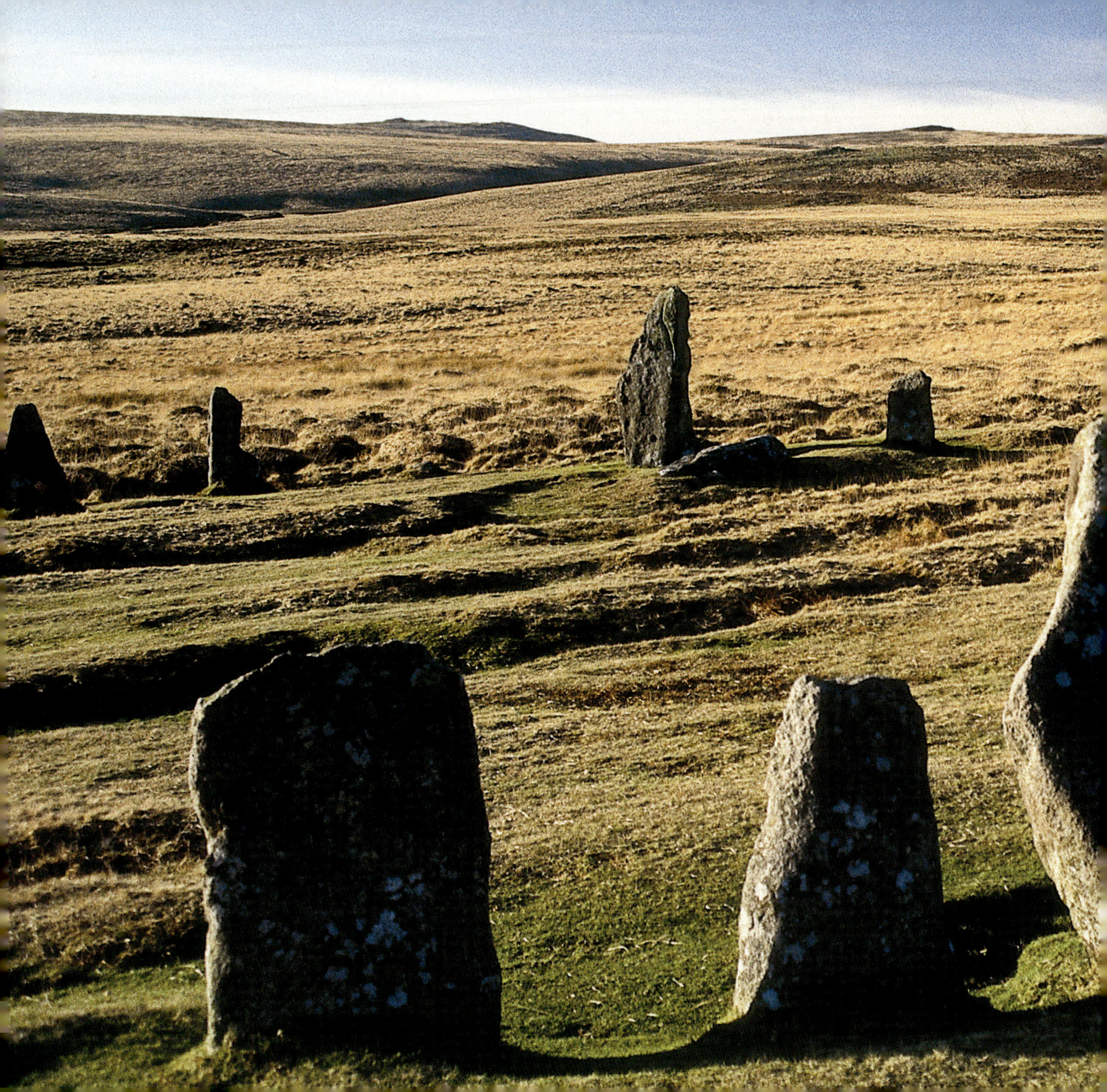

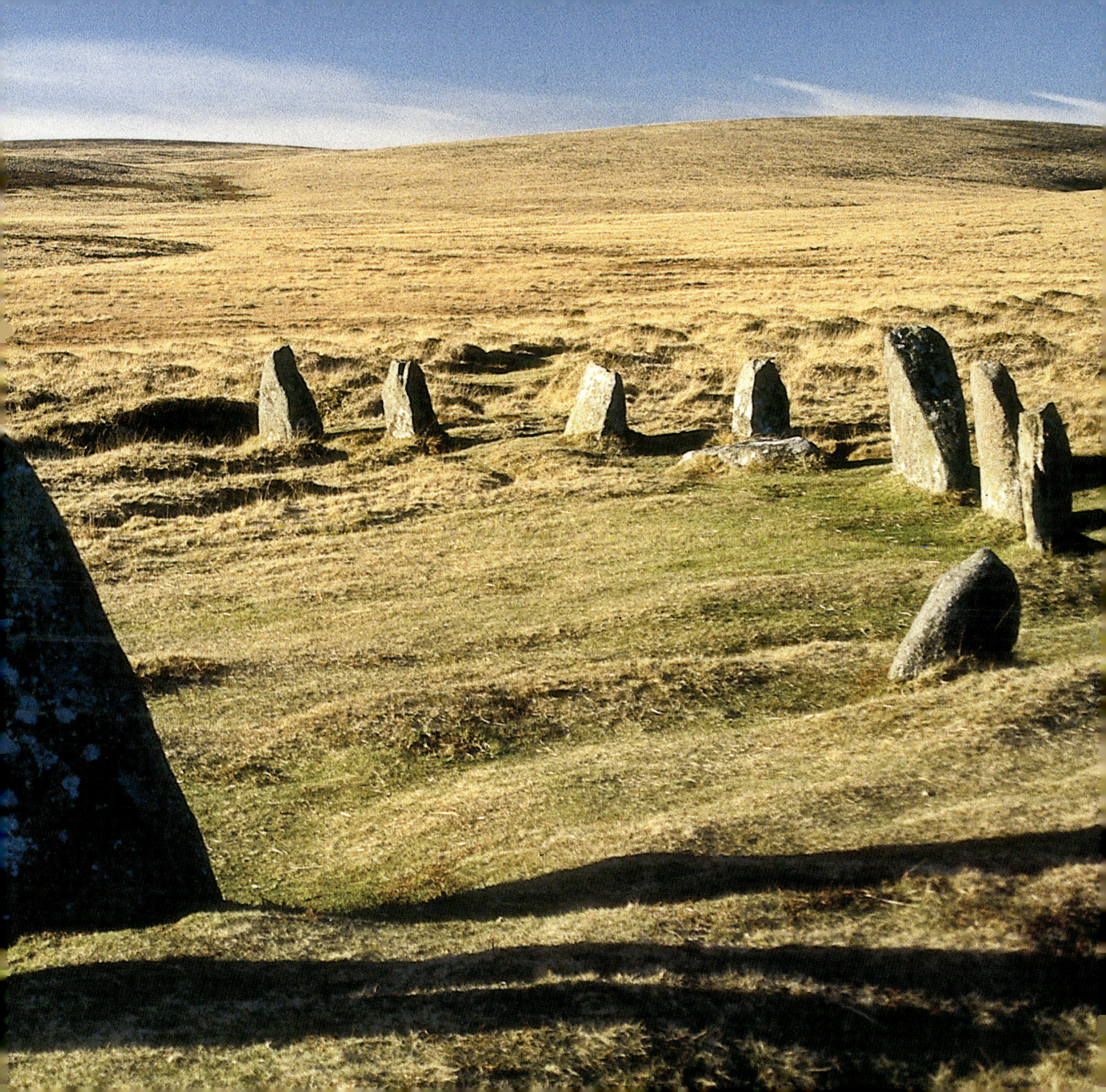

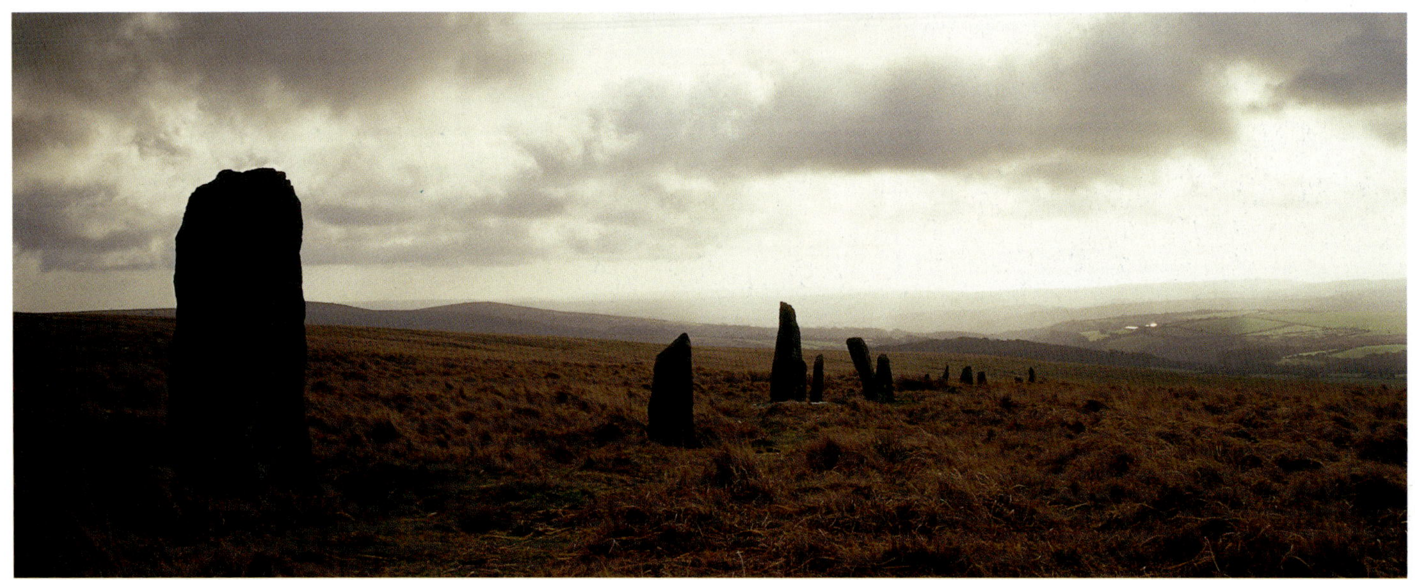

A stone row on Stall Moor

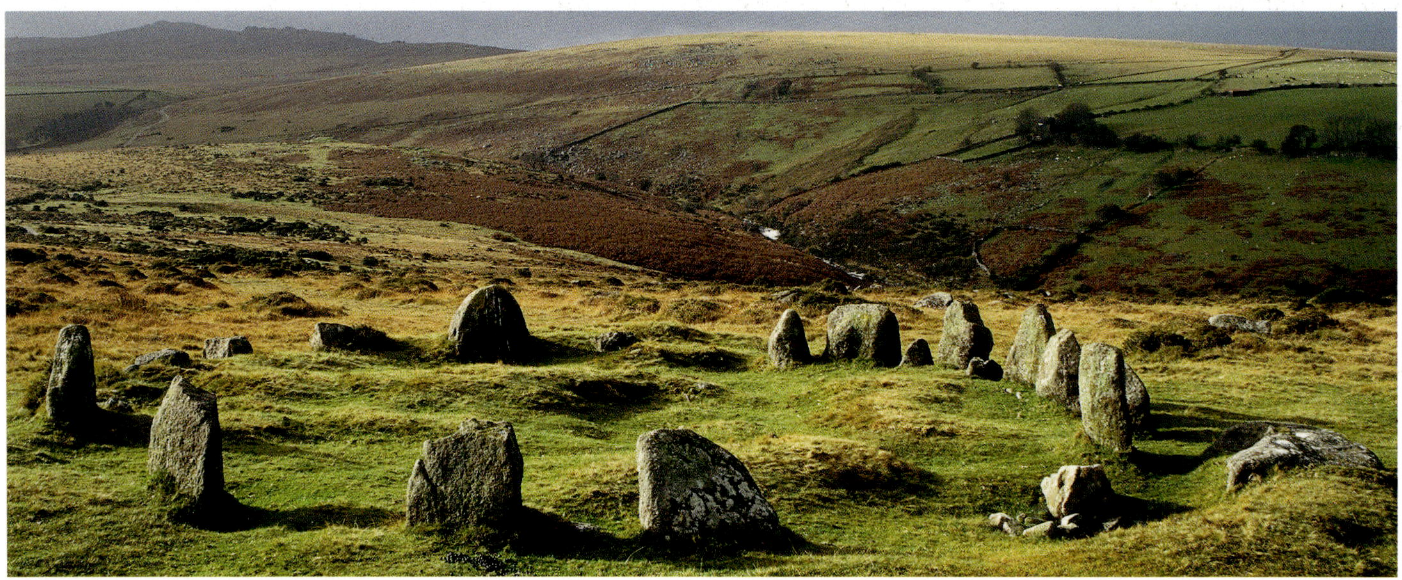

Nine Stones, a stone circle near Belstone

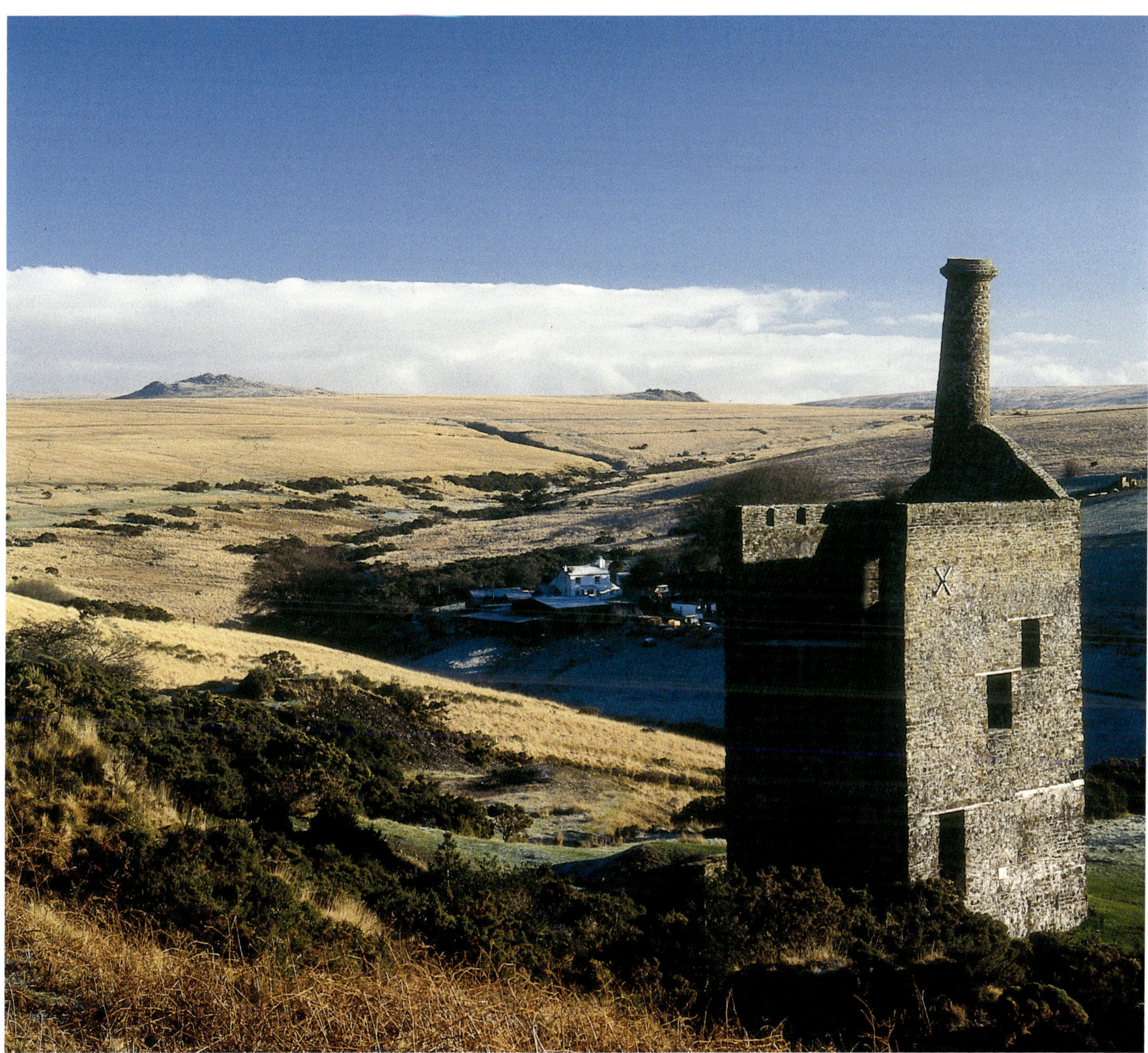

The engine house at Wheal Betsy mine near Mary Tavy, worked in the nineteenth century for lead, copper, silver and arsenic

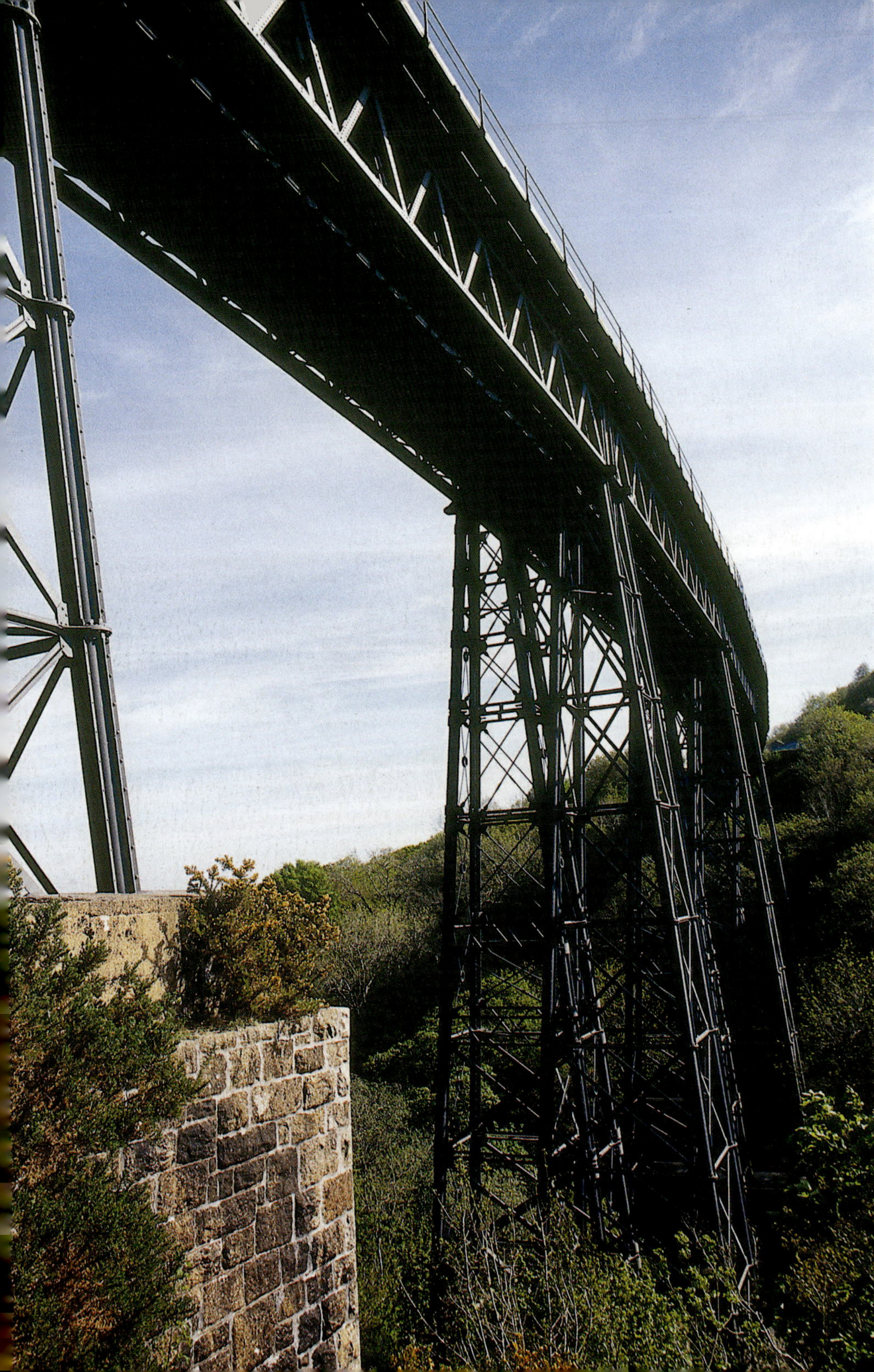

Meldon Viaduct once carried the Southern Railway line over the West Okement valley, and now carries part of the National Cycle Network

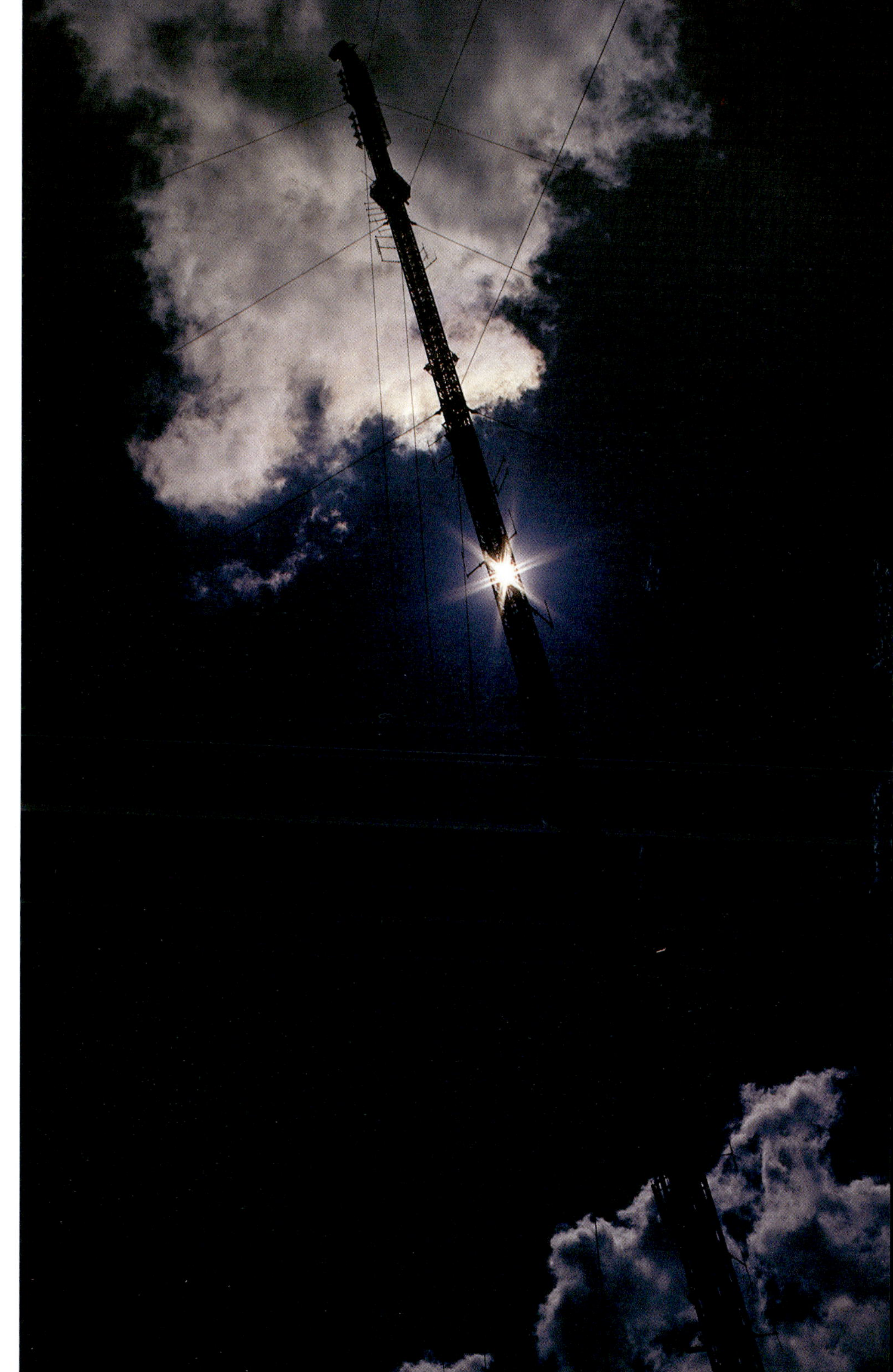

The radio mast on North Hessary Tor. Even modern
'intrusions' can be dramatic

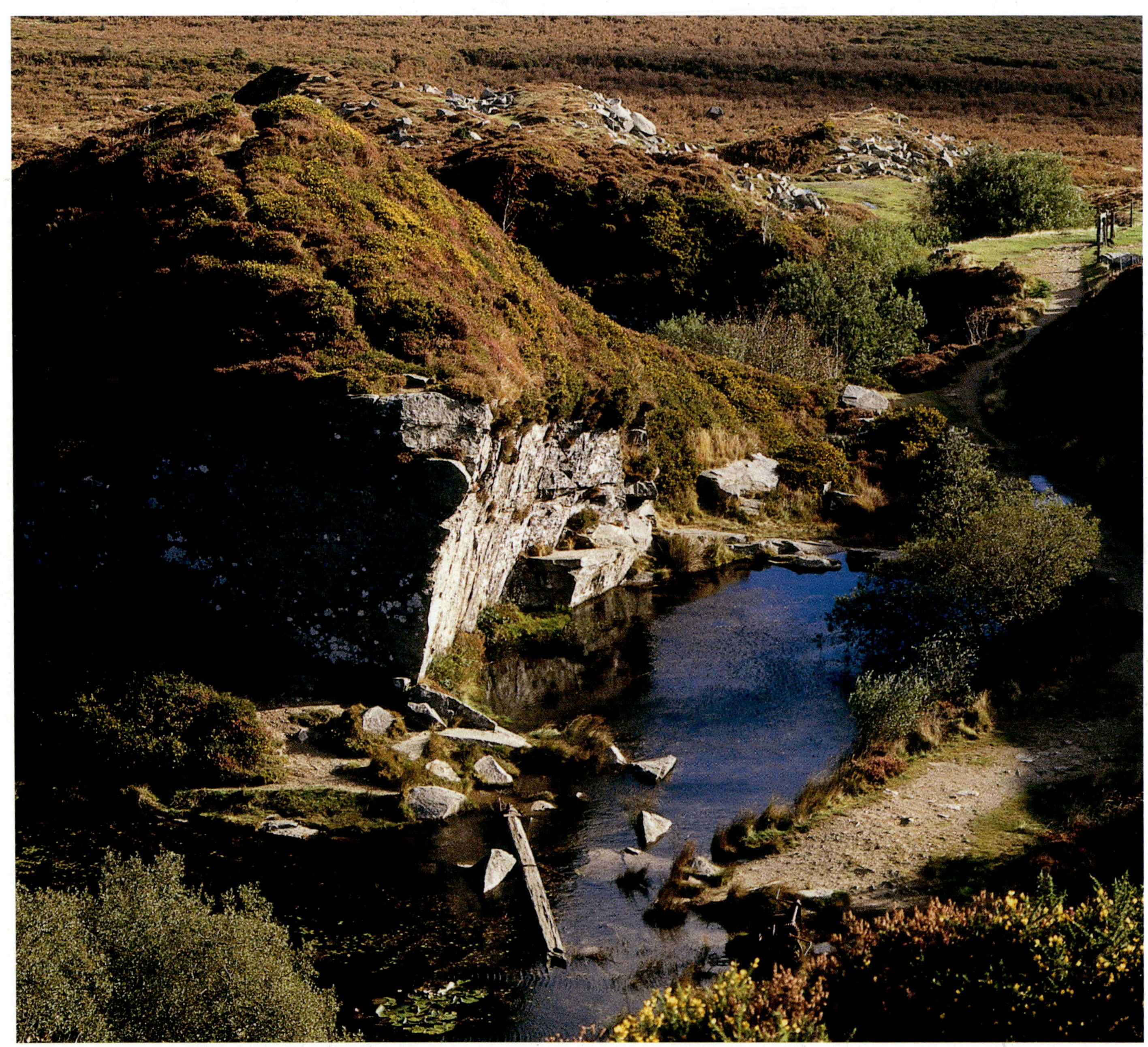

Haytor Quarry, source of granite for the old London Bridge

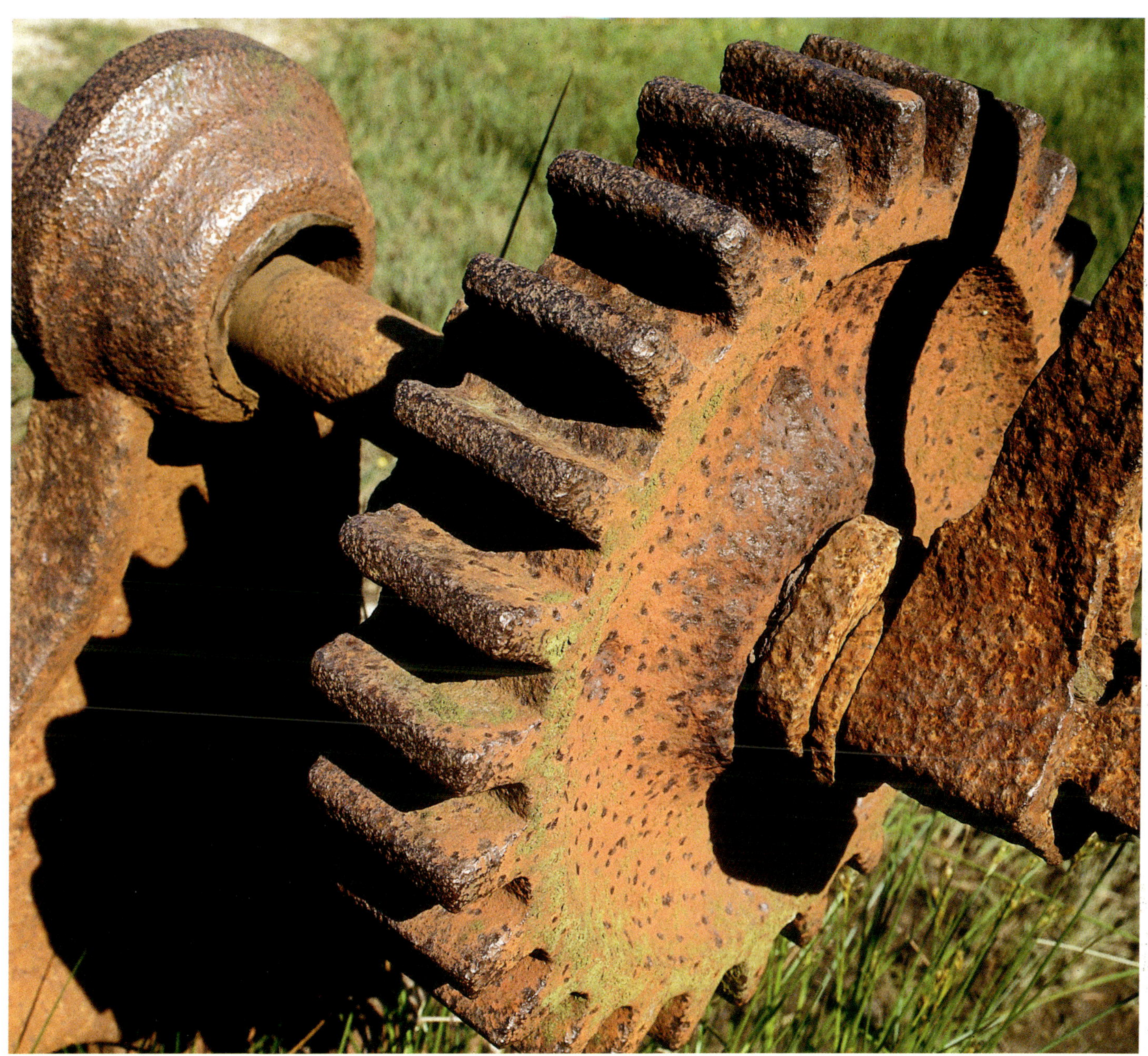

Part of the old crane in Haytor Quarry

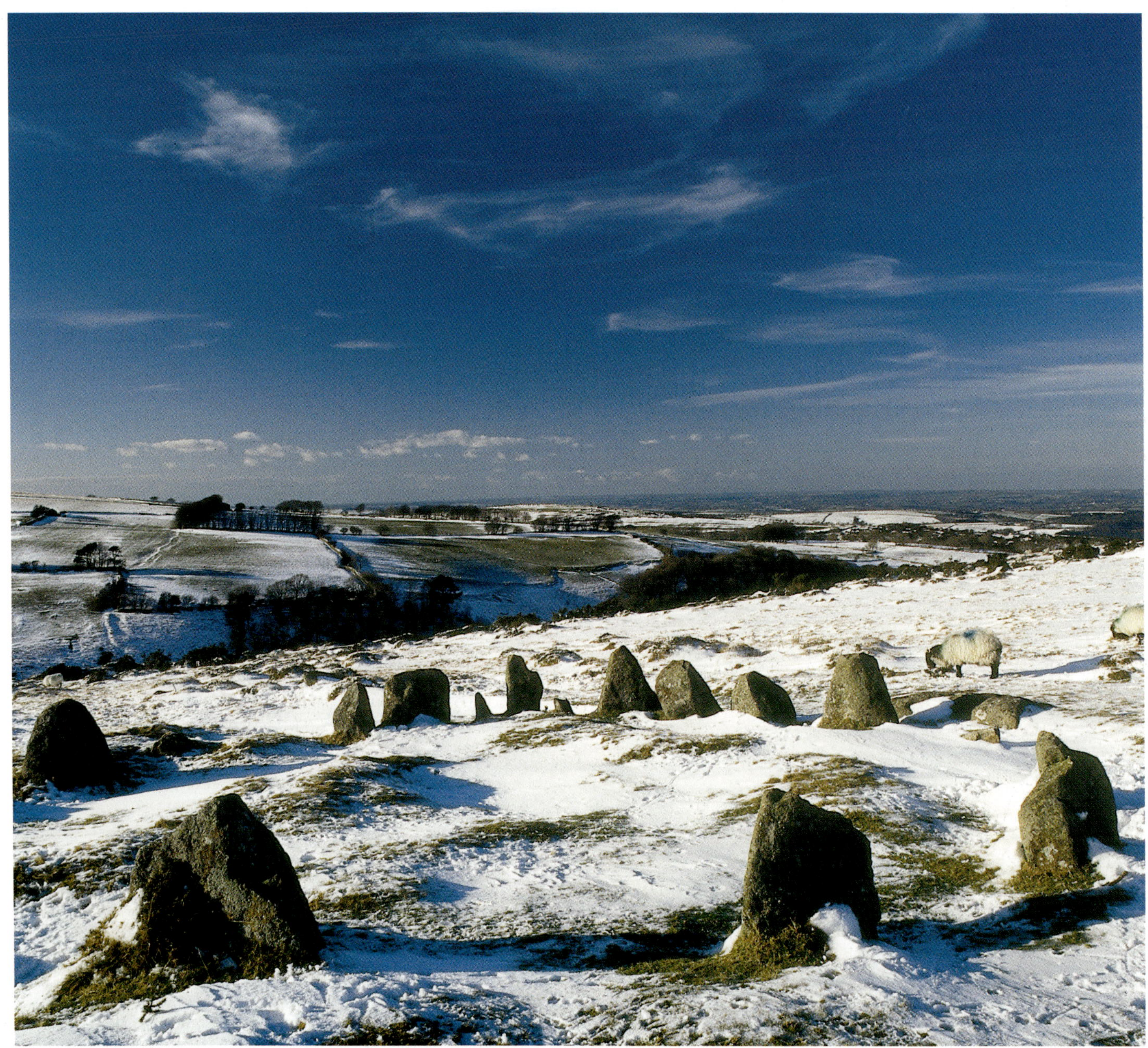

Nine Stones at Belstone

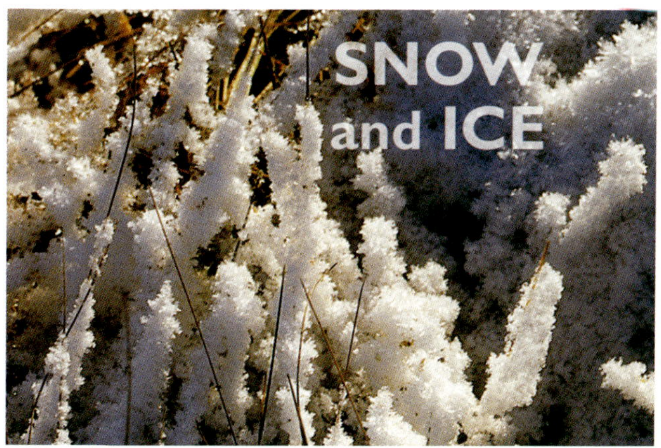

Magic in the landscape

Ice and snow work magic on the Dartmoor landscape. They don't come that often, but when they do the commonplace is transformed into the weird and wonderful; the mundane object that normally doesn't get a second look becomes a thing of beauty, and the vastness and remoteness of the high hills are accentuated. The moor becomes a far greater challenge for the serious walker, but it also becomes a winter wonderland for every small child (and a few larger ones!) with a toboggan and a yearning to throw a few snowballs.

When it is really deep you may struggle to get anywhere unless you have cross-country skis or snowshoes, and in the past Dartmoor villages have been cut off for weeks at a time. That hasn't happened for many years, but even a modest fall is dramatic. If the sky is heavy and grey over the moorland there is that sense of enormous desolation and foreboding. The landscape becomes threatening – you start to think of the consequences of a twisted ankle or a navigational error. Properly equipped and prepared, you can revel in challenging conditions. If the sun shines and skies are blue, everything sparkles and it feels good to be alive. Marvel at the wind-fluted shapes of snowdrifts; realise from all the little paw prints how much unseen wildlife there is about you.

Hard frosts add another dimension. Look under the overhangs on the tors for ice formations that put Kent's Cavern to shame. Walk up any tumbling stream to find those places where the spray from a fall has frozen onto everything around it, coating it in clear ice – boulders with a silvery sheen and skirts of icicles; grasses and rushes transformed into works of art. If there's a hoar frost, everything becomes beautiful. Trees turn into icing-sugar sculptures, and fallen leaves become intricate works of art. If there is moisture in the air fantastic crystals grow into the wind from rocks and plants. Frozen pools and puddles develop incredible patterns in the ice as water levels change, and if it rains on frozen surfaces they can become coated in a thick layer of black ice – known on Dartmoor as 'ammil.' In severe conditions power lines can be brought down by the weight, and tree branches break. The frozen moor is a wonderful place, but it can also be a dangerous one. Enjoy it, but respect it.

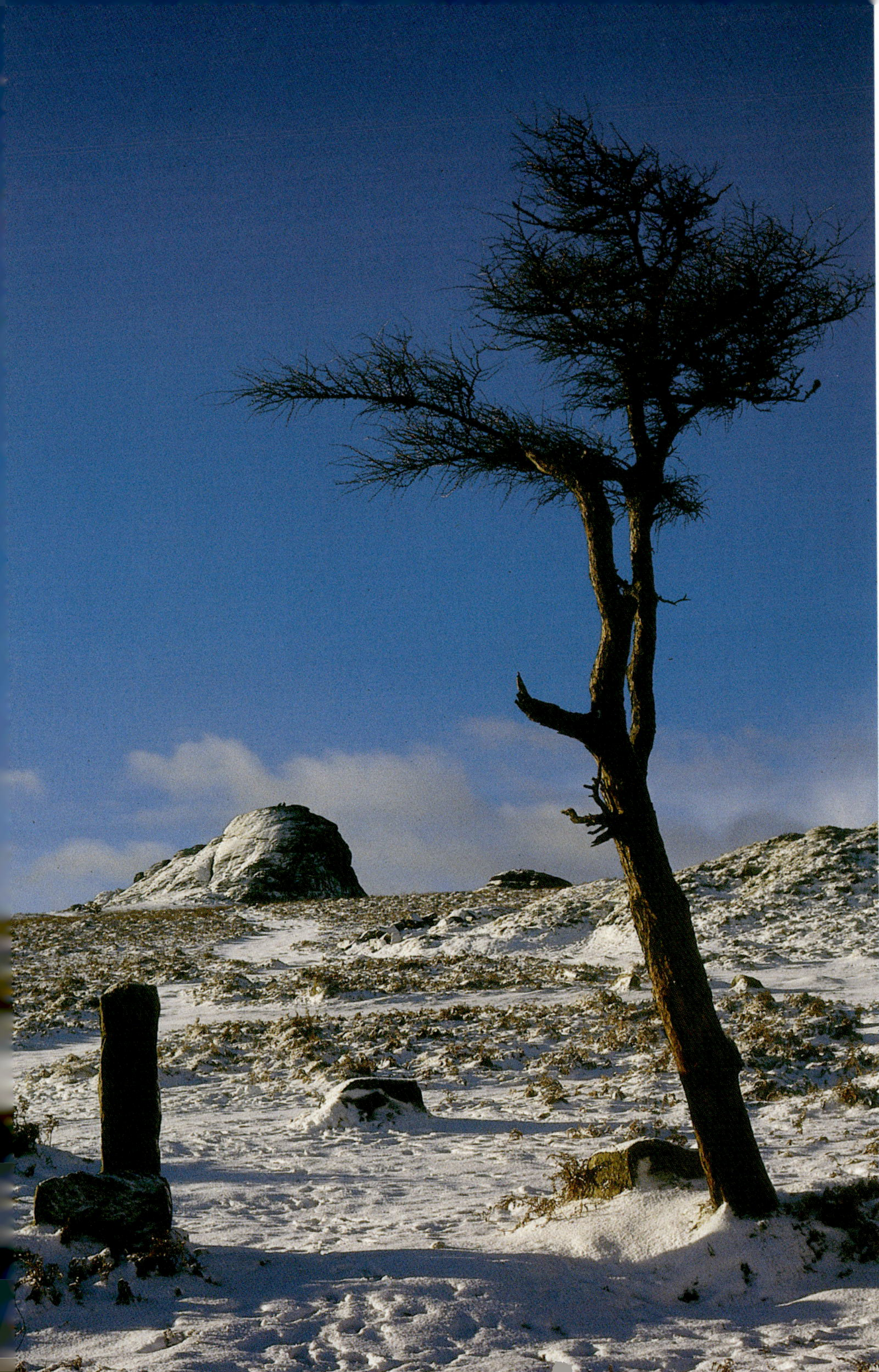

Haytor from near the old quarry

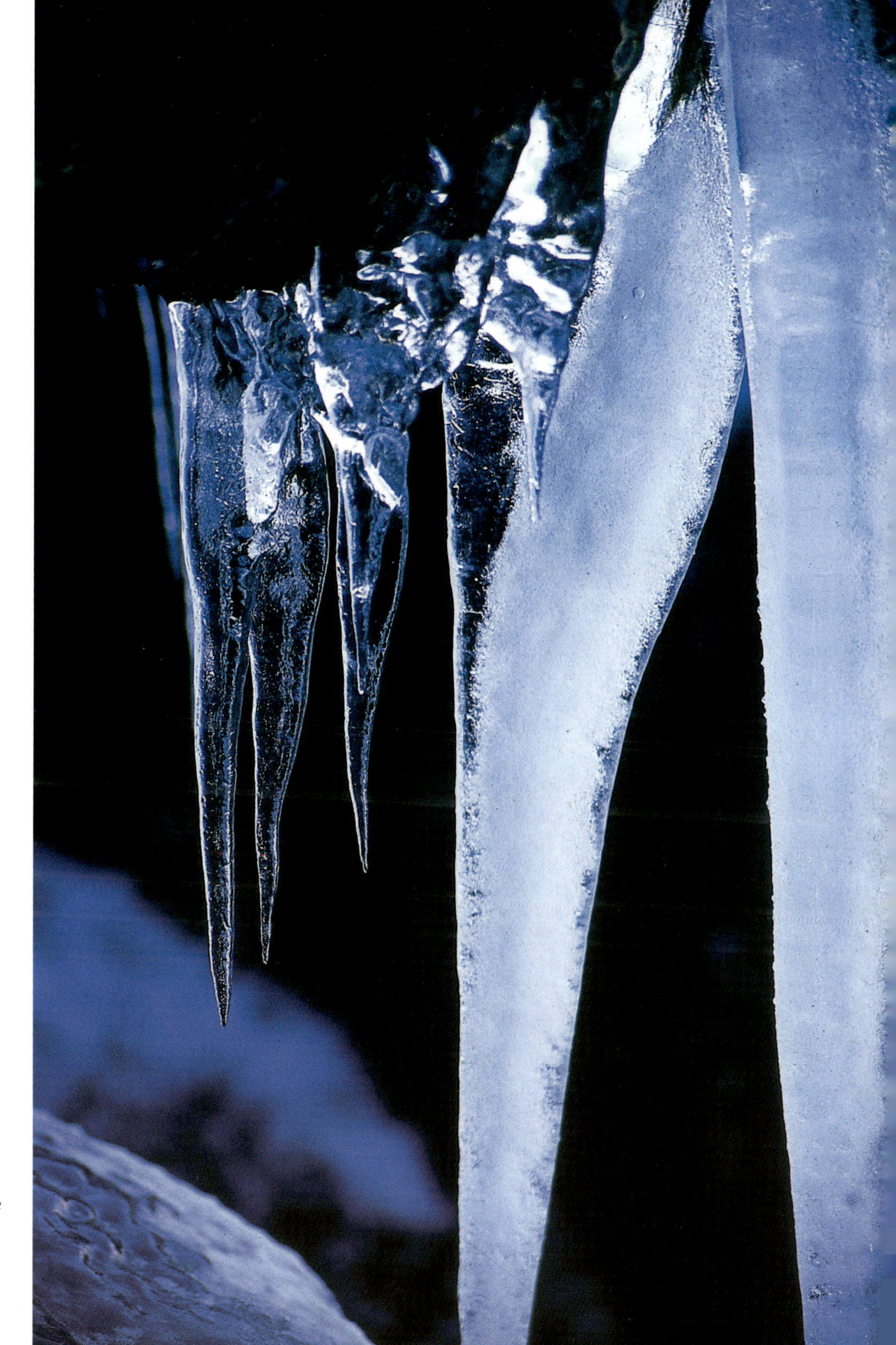

Look under the overhangs for an icy Aladdin's cave

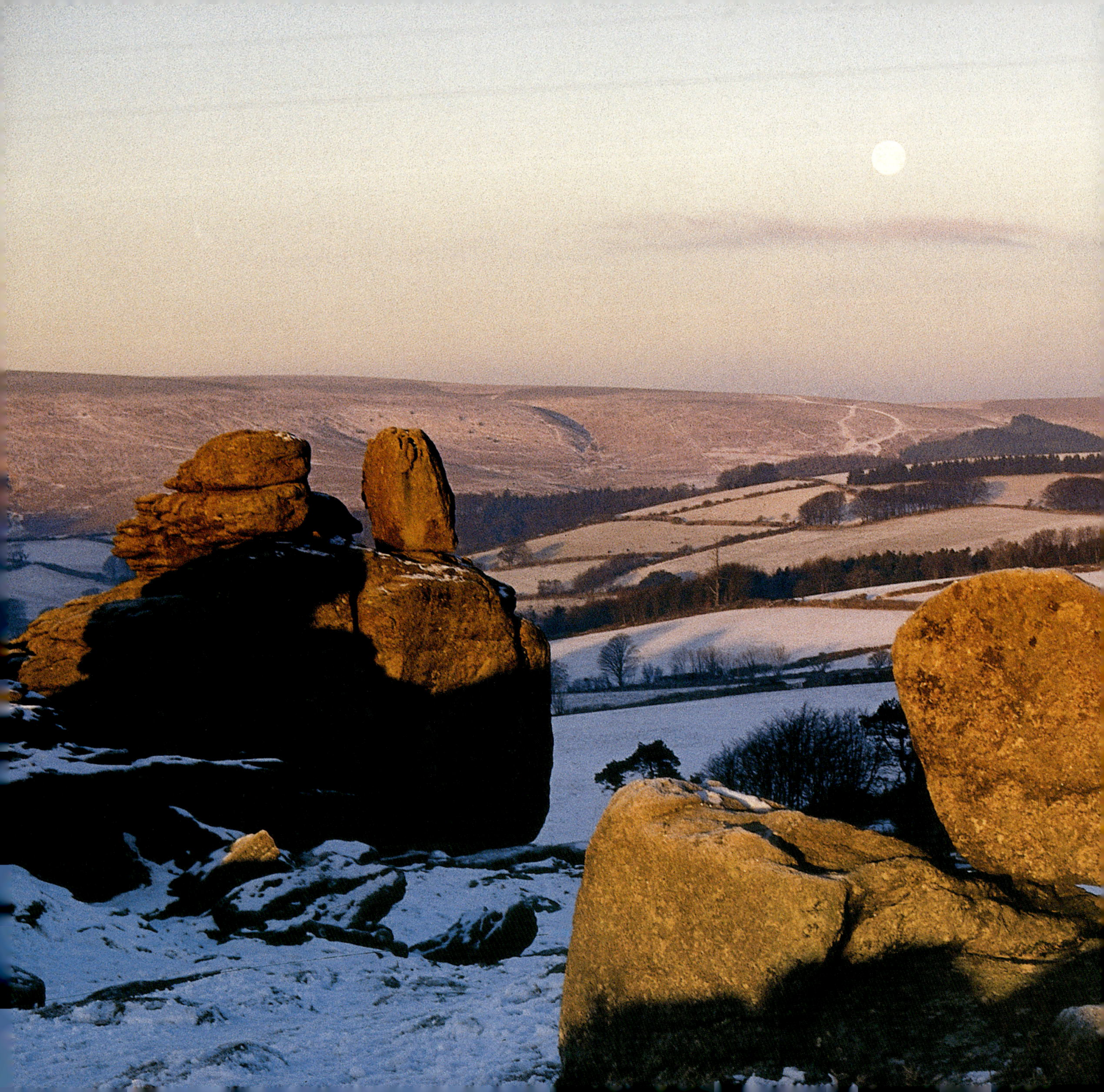

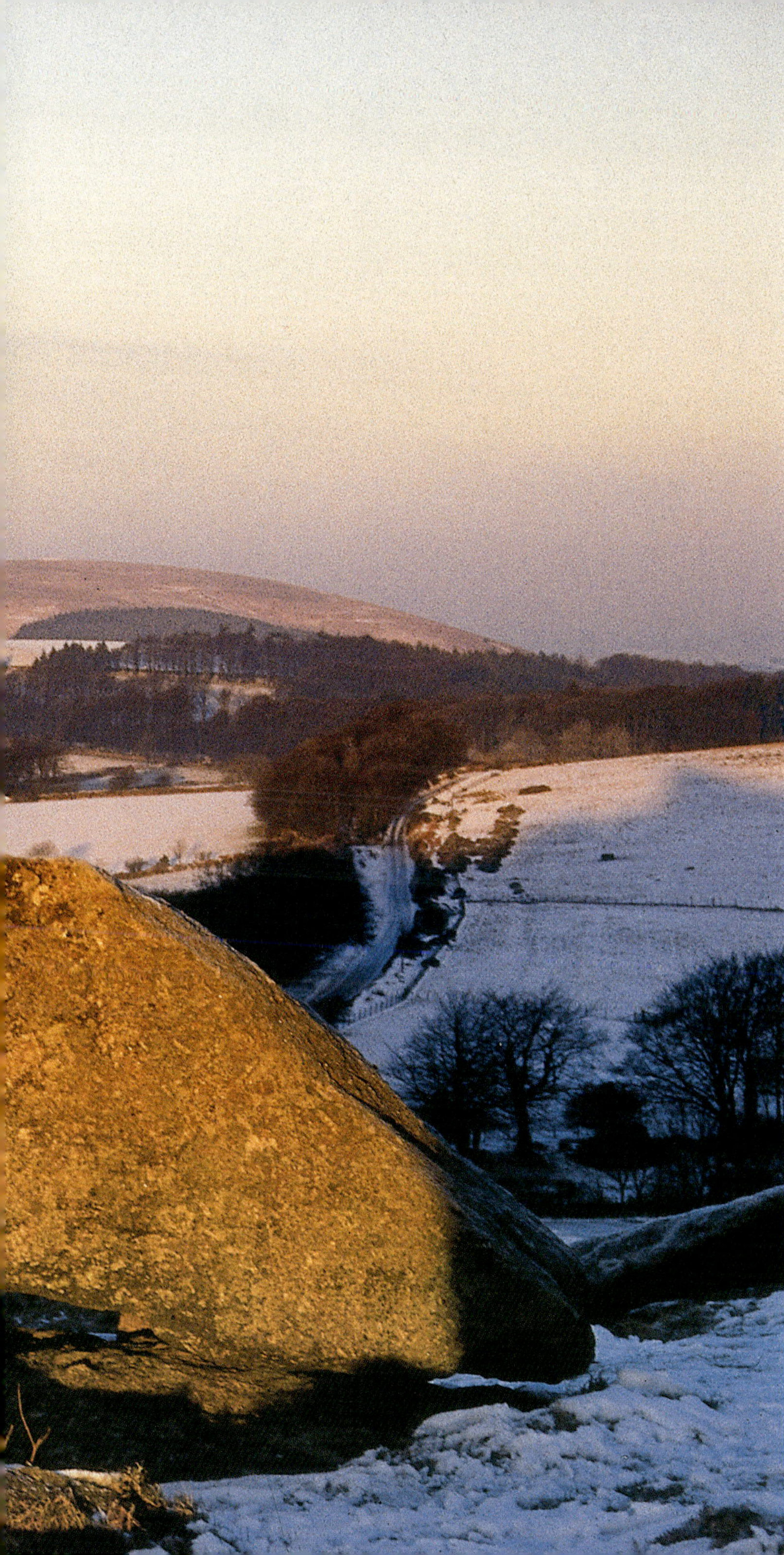

Sunrise and moonset at Hound Tor

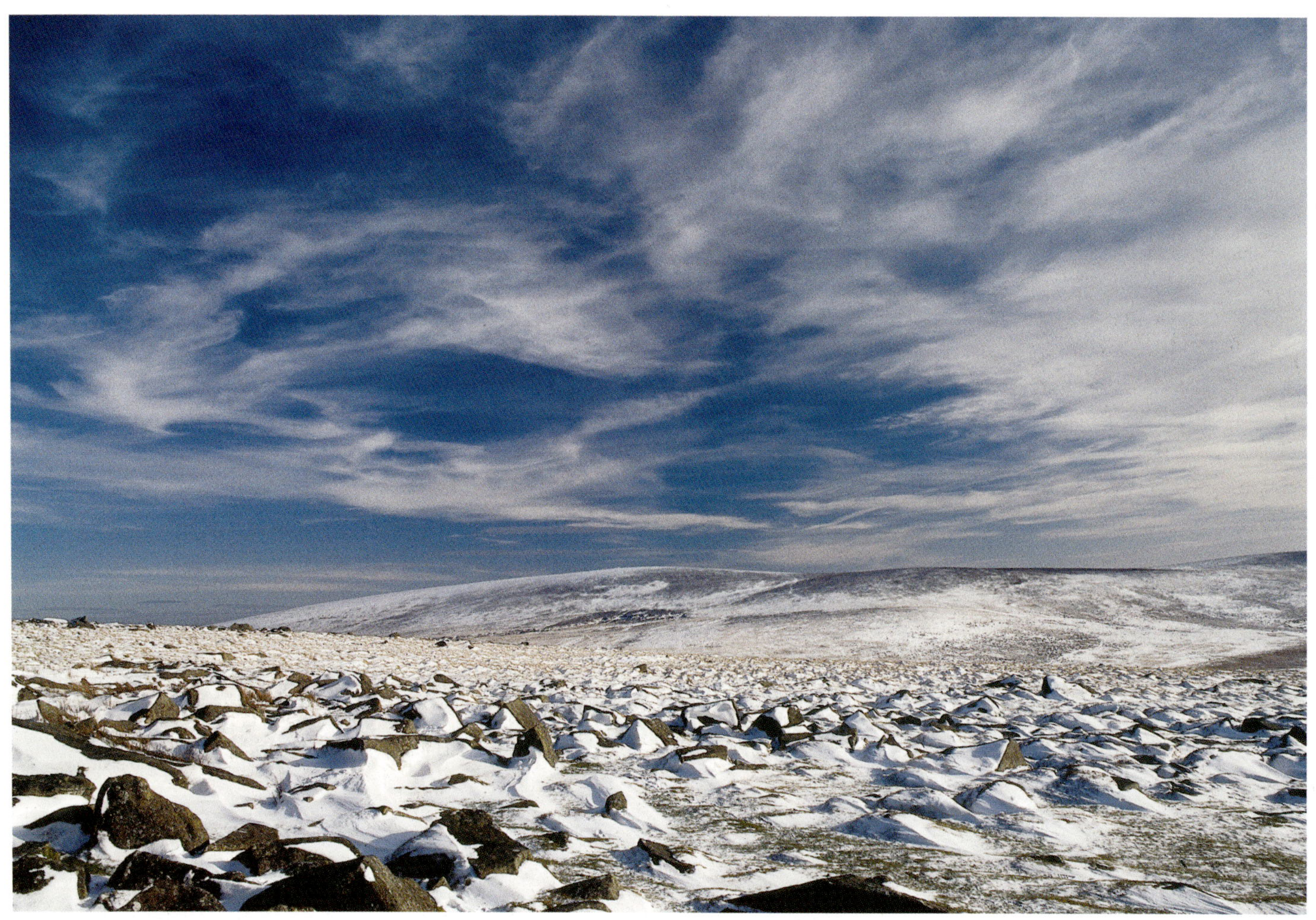

A wonderful sky over Cosdon Beacon

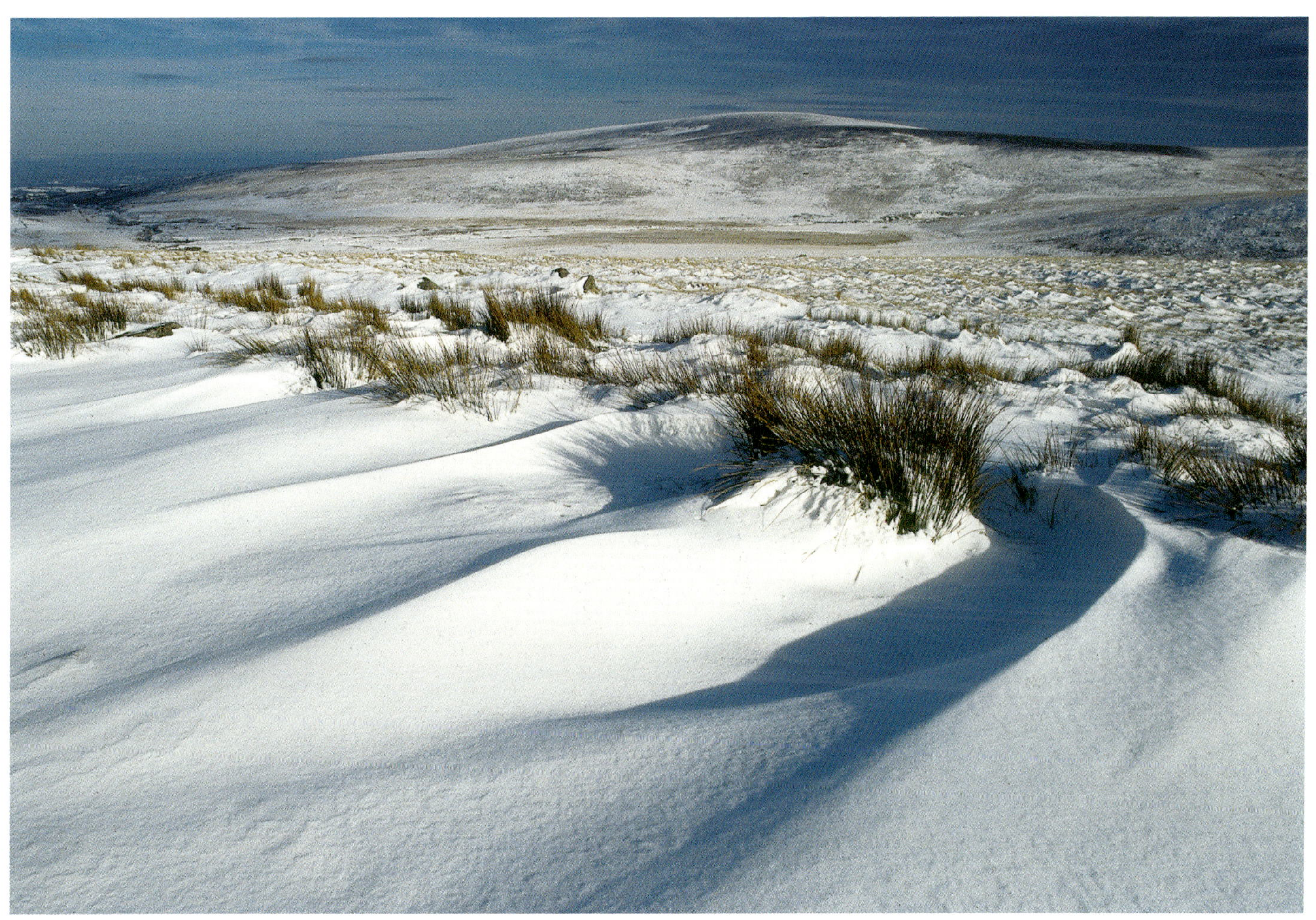

On the Belstone Tor ridge

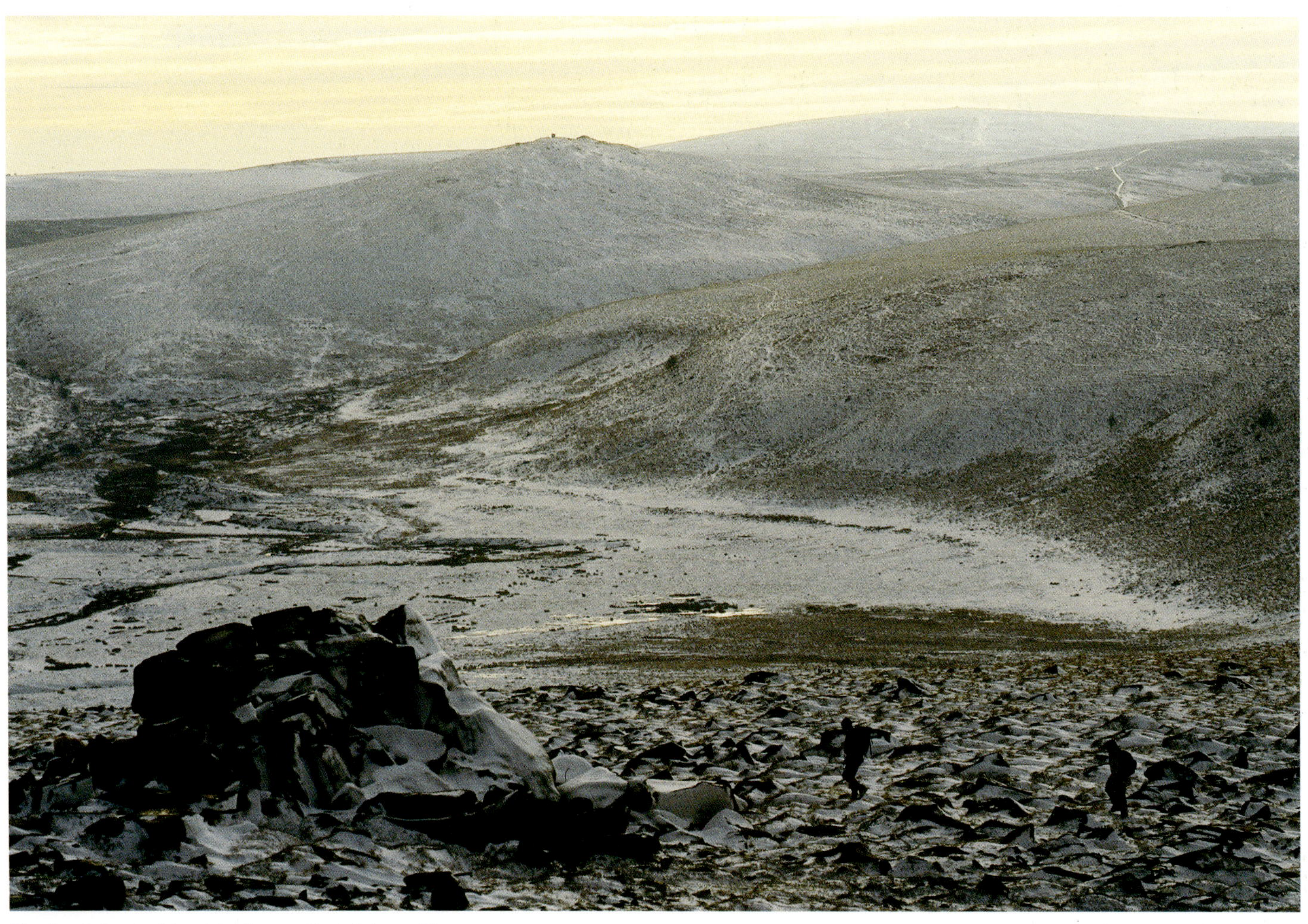

The lonely bowl of Taw Marsh, seen from Belstone Tor

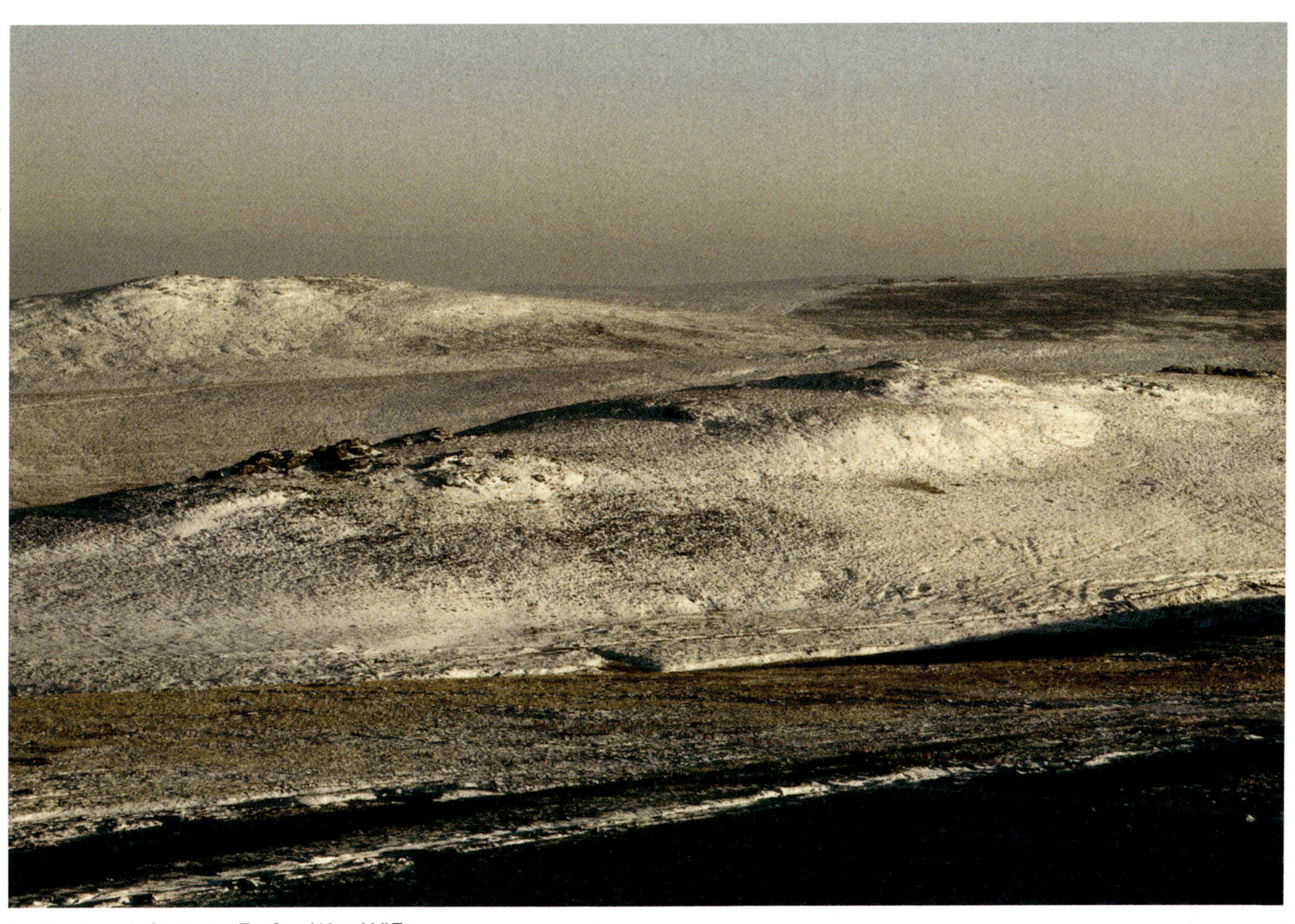

Looking towards Steeperton Tor from West Mill Tor

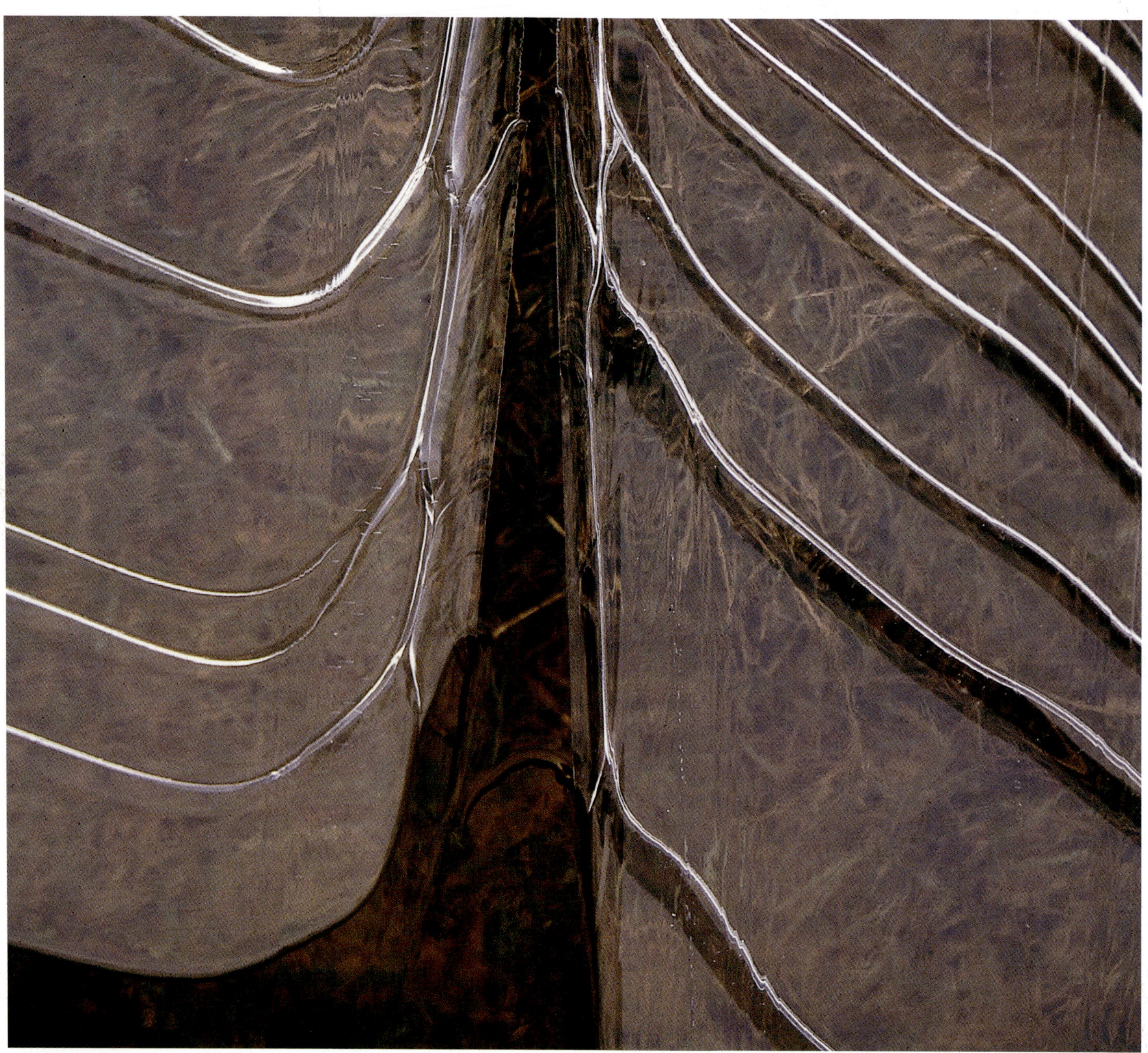

Patterns in the ice may be simple…

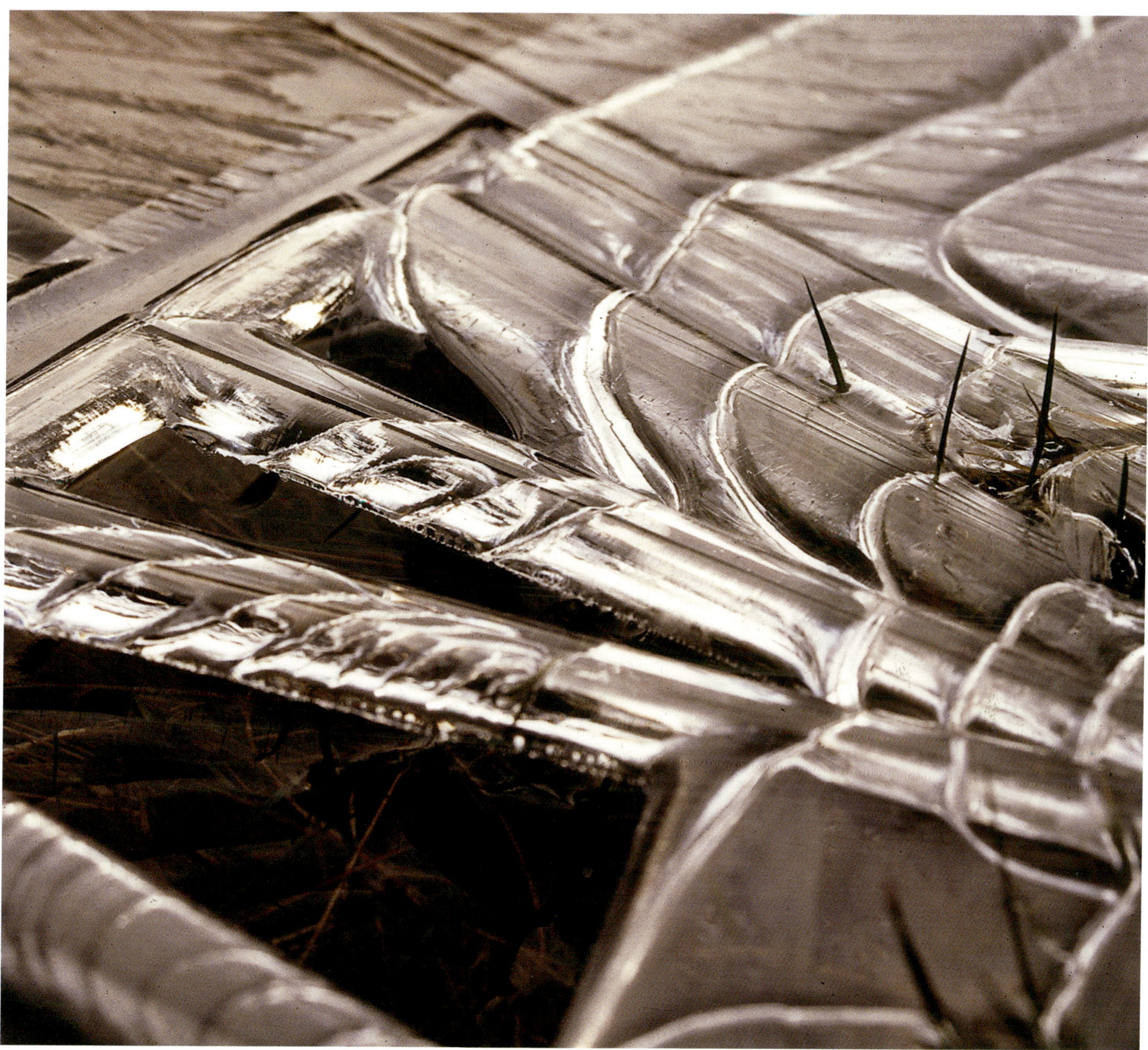

...or complex

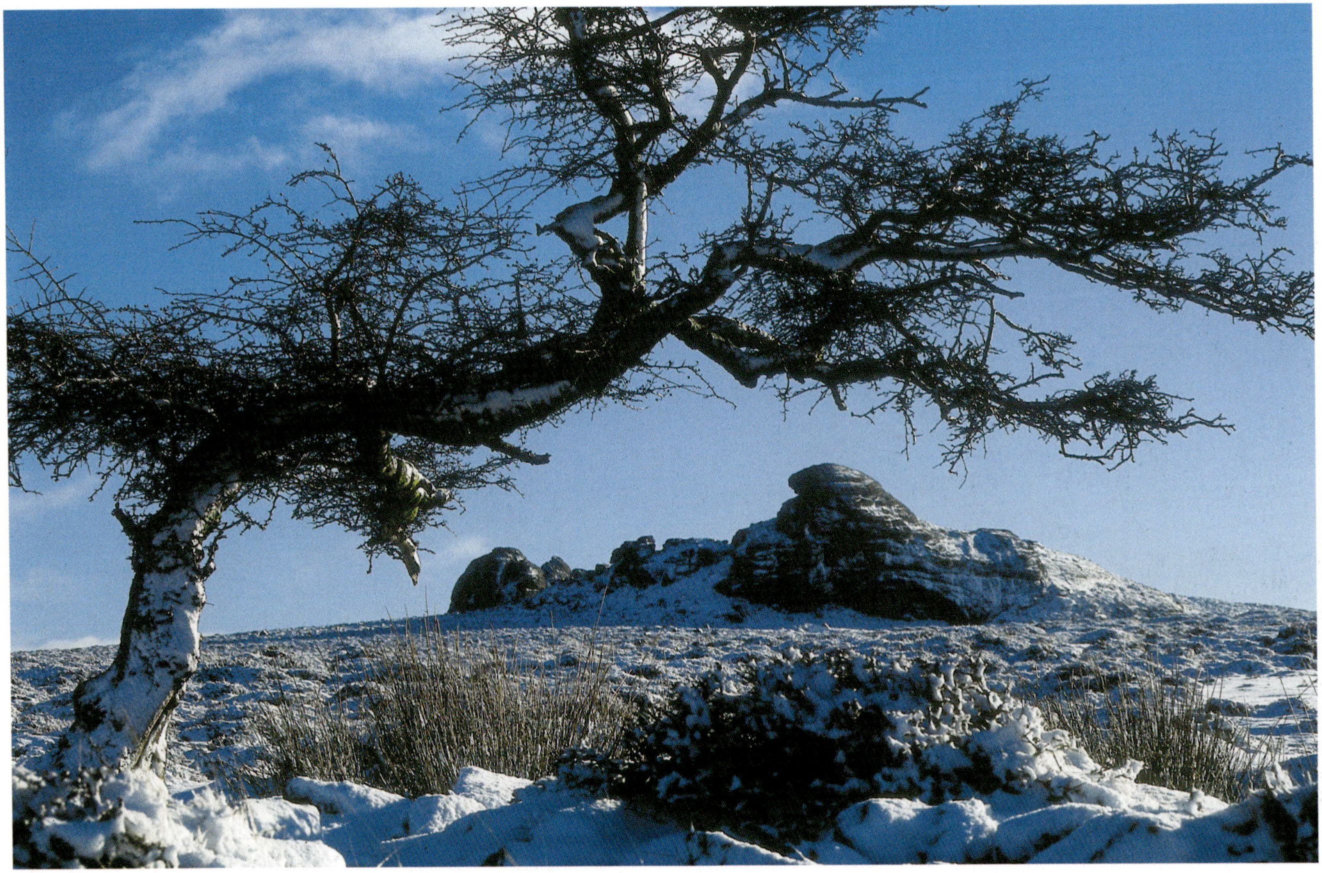

Haytor, dramatically framed

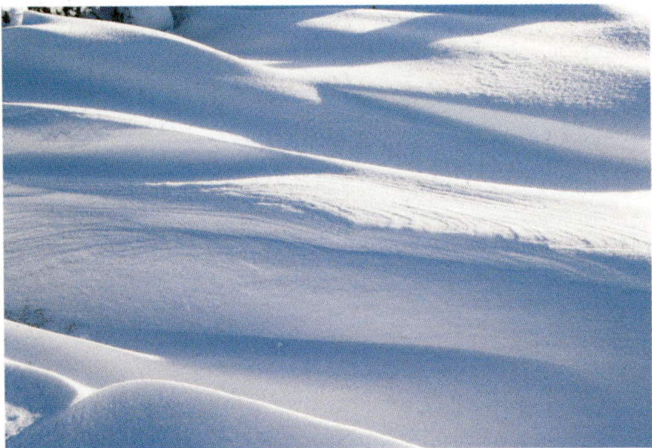

Wind-fluted snow

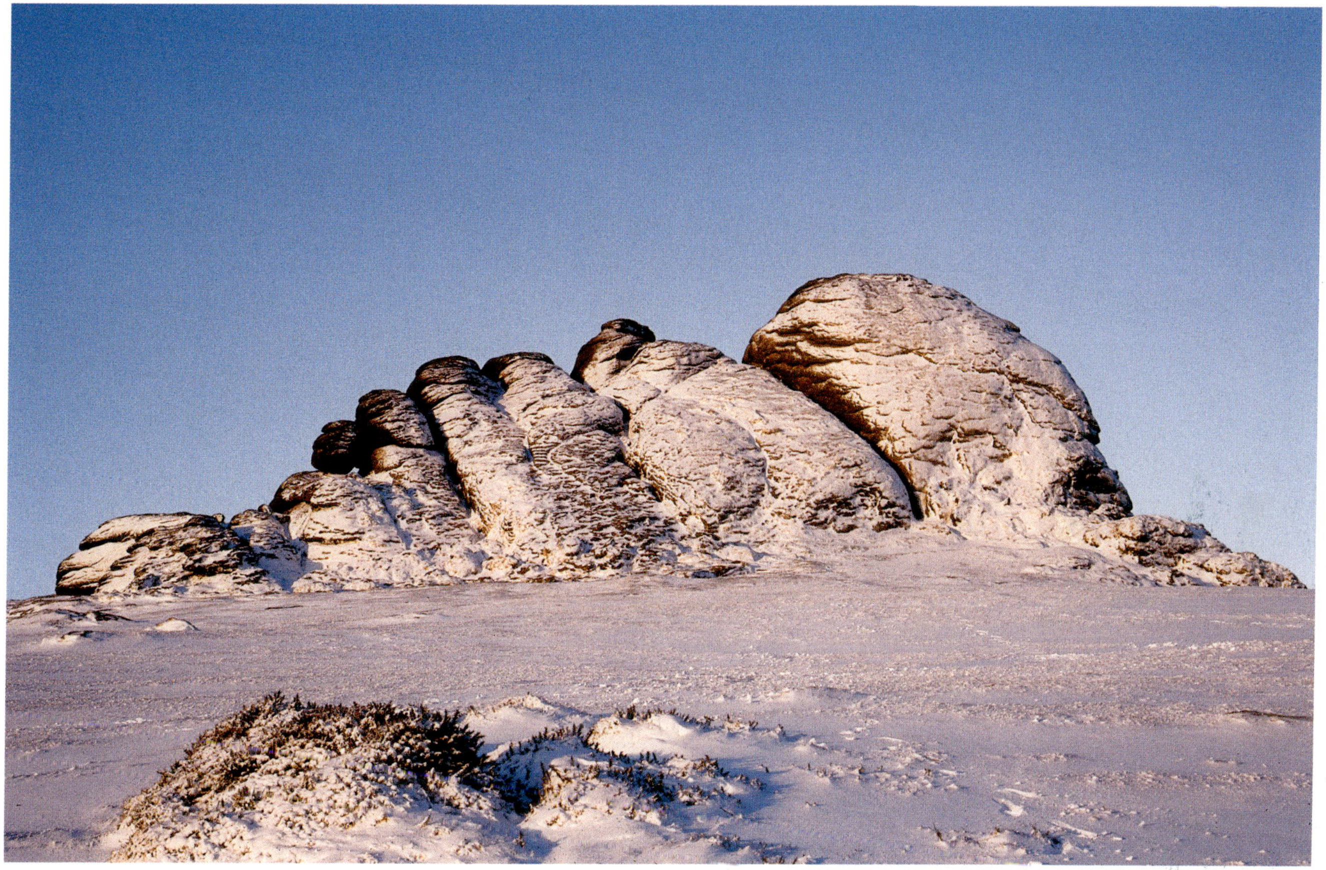

Haytor, plastered in snow, at dawn

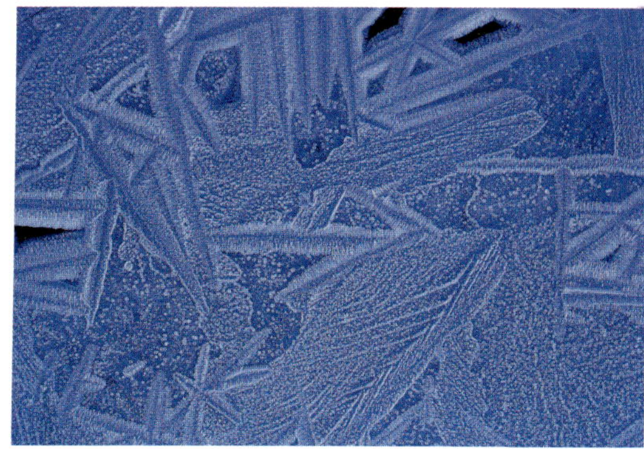

Frost patterns on an iced puddle

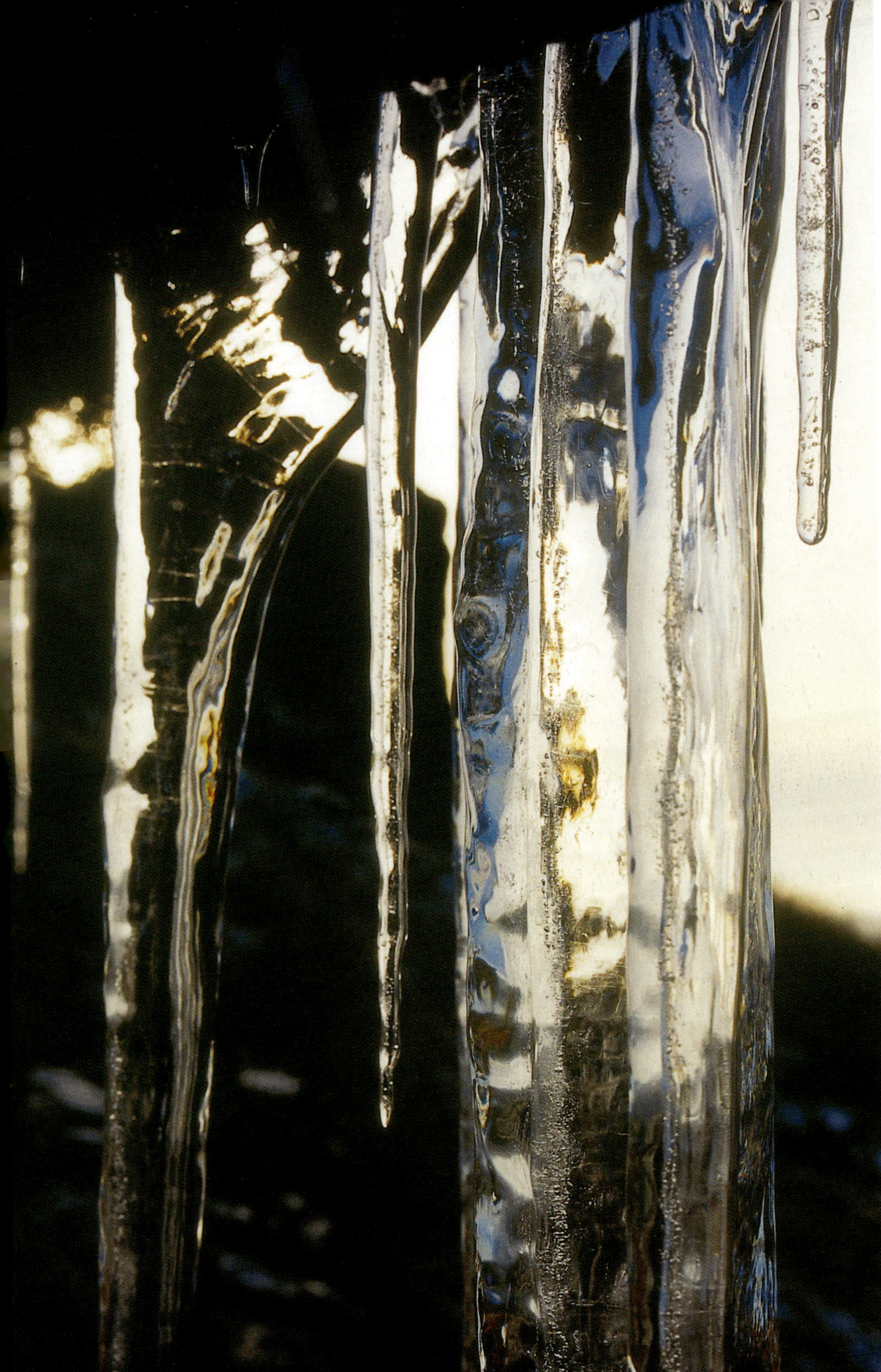

Evening light on icicles…

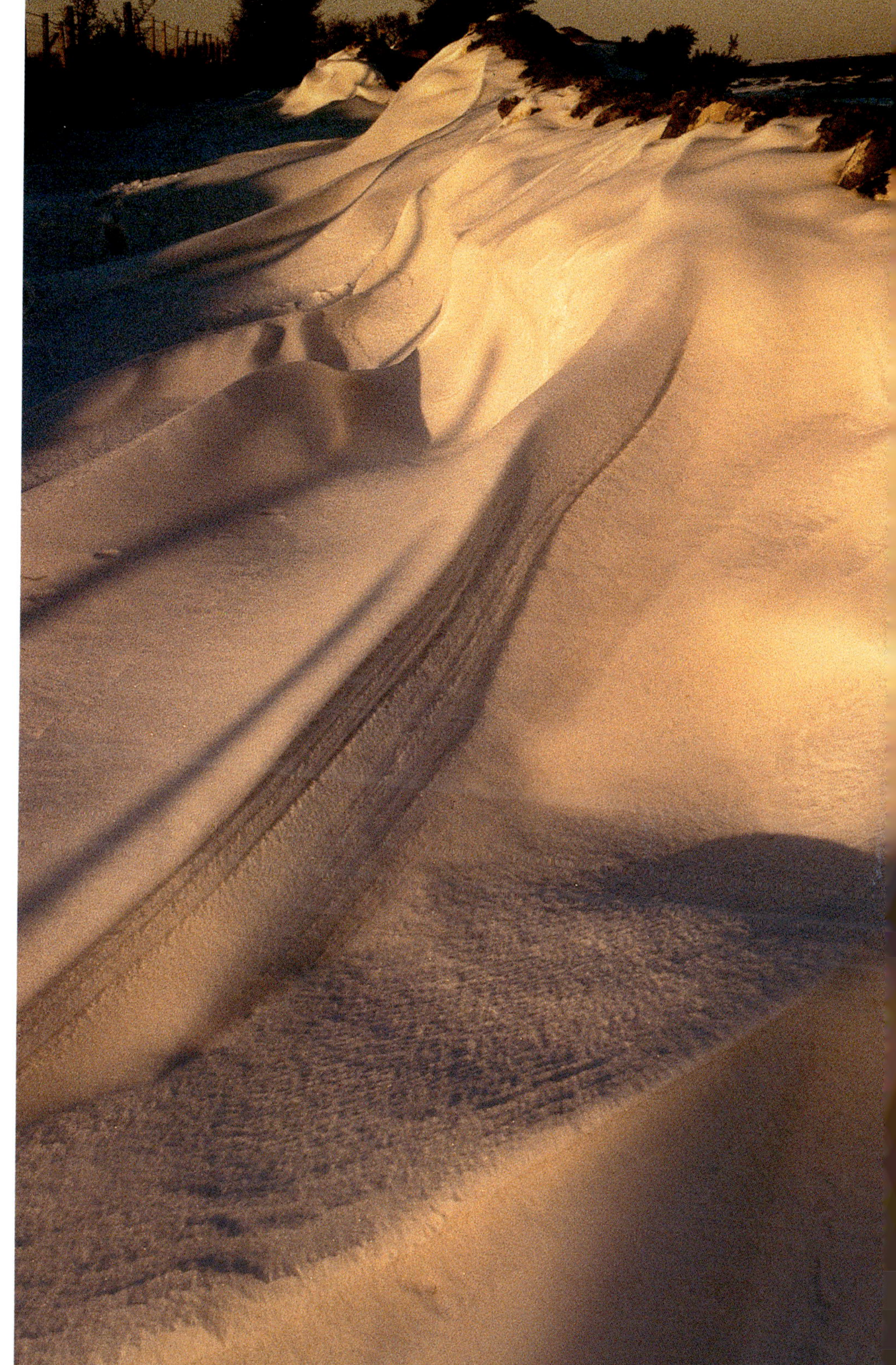

...and on snowdrifts in a lane above Prewley

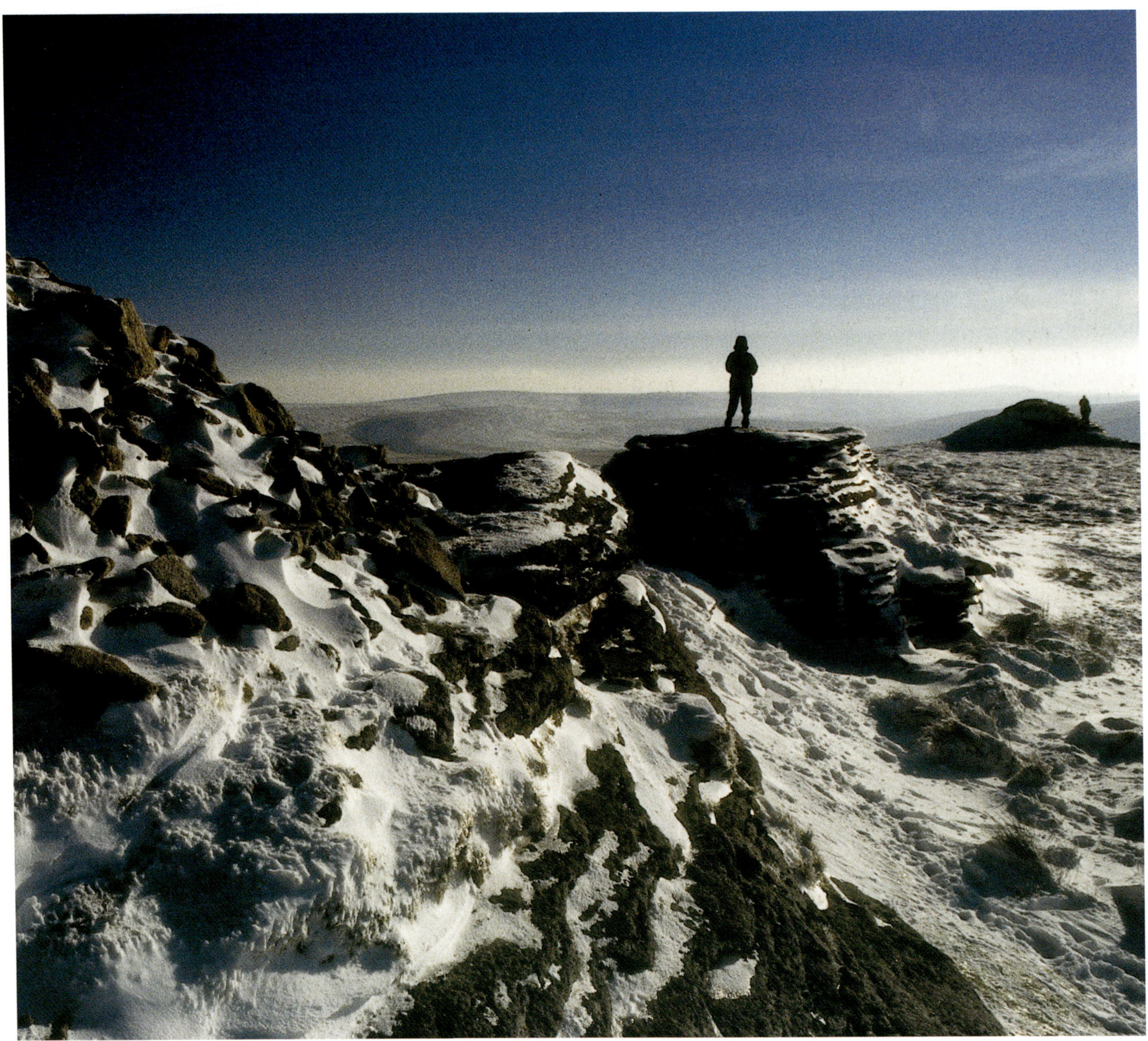

High Willhays, Dartmoor's highest point

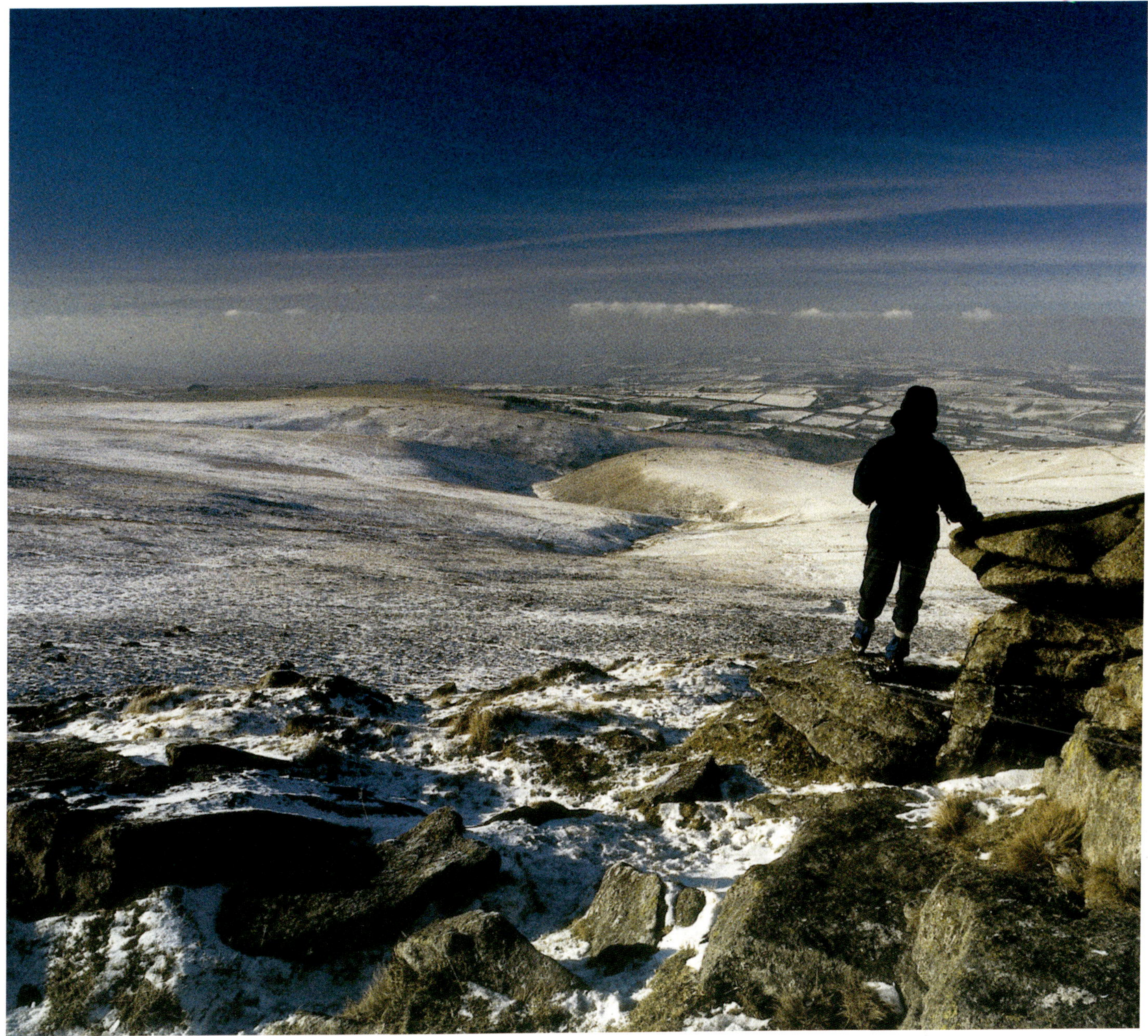

Looking down the Red-a-Ven Brook from West Mill Tor

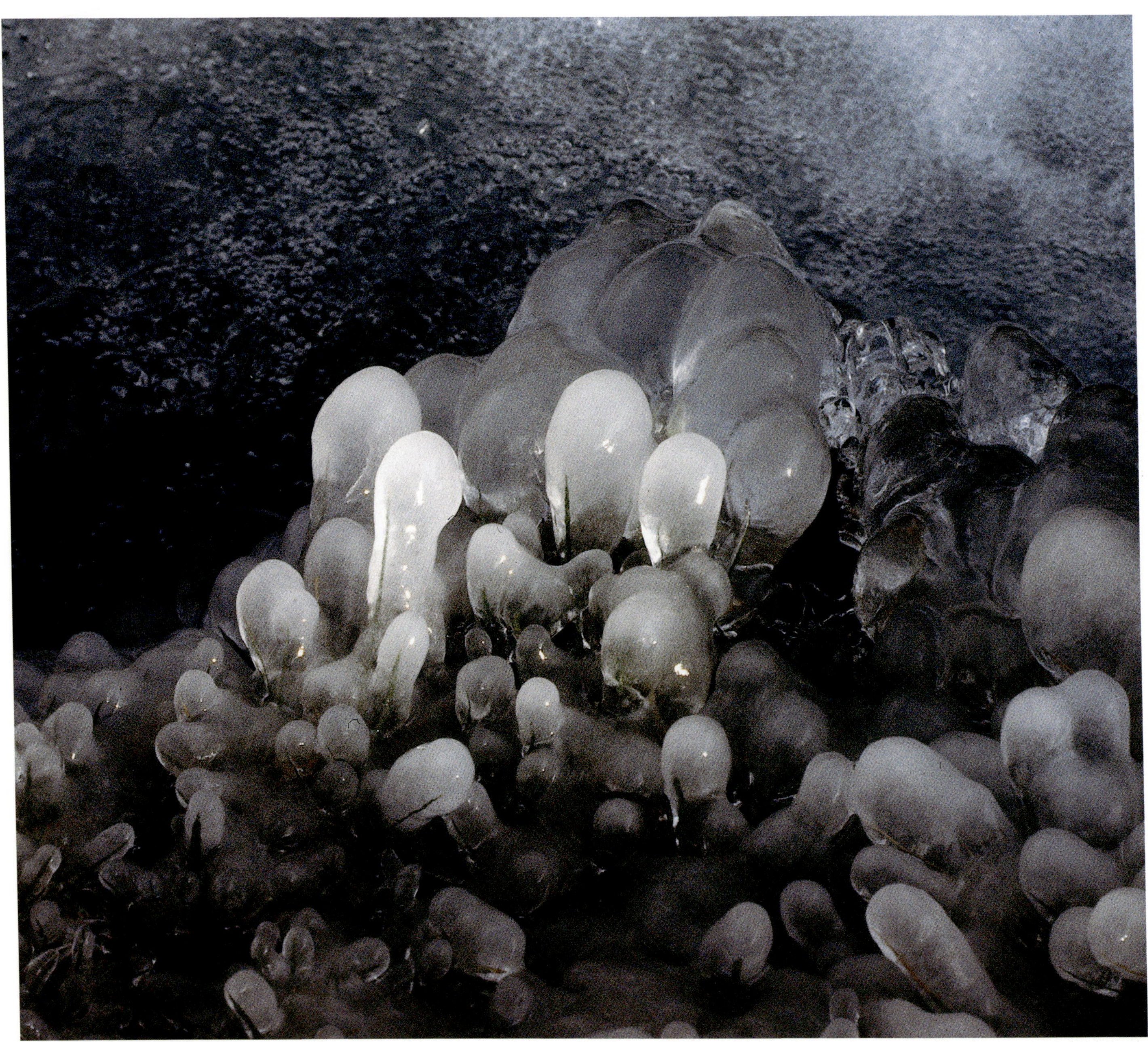

Ice globules by the Dart

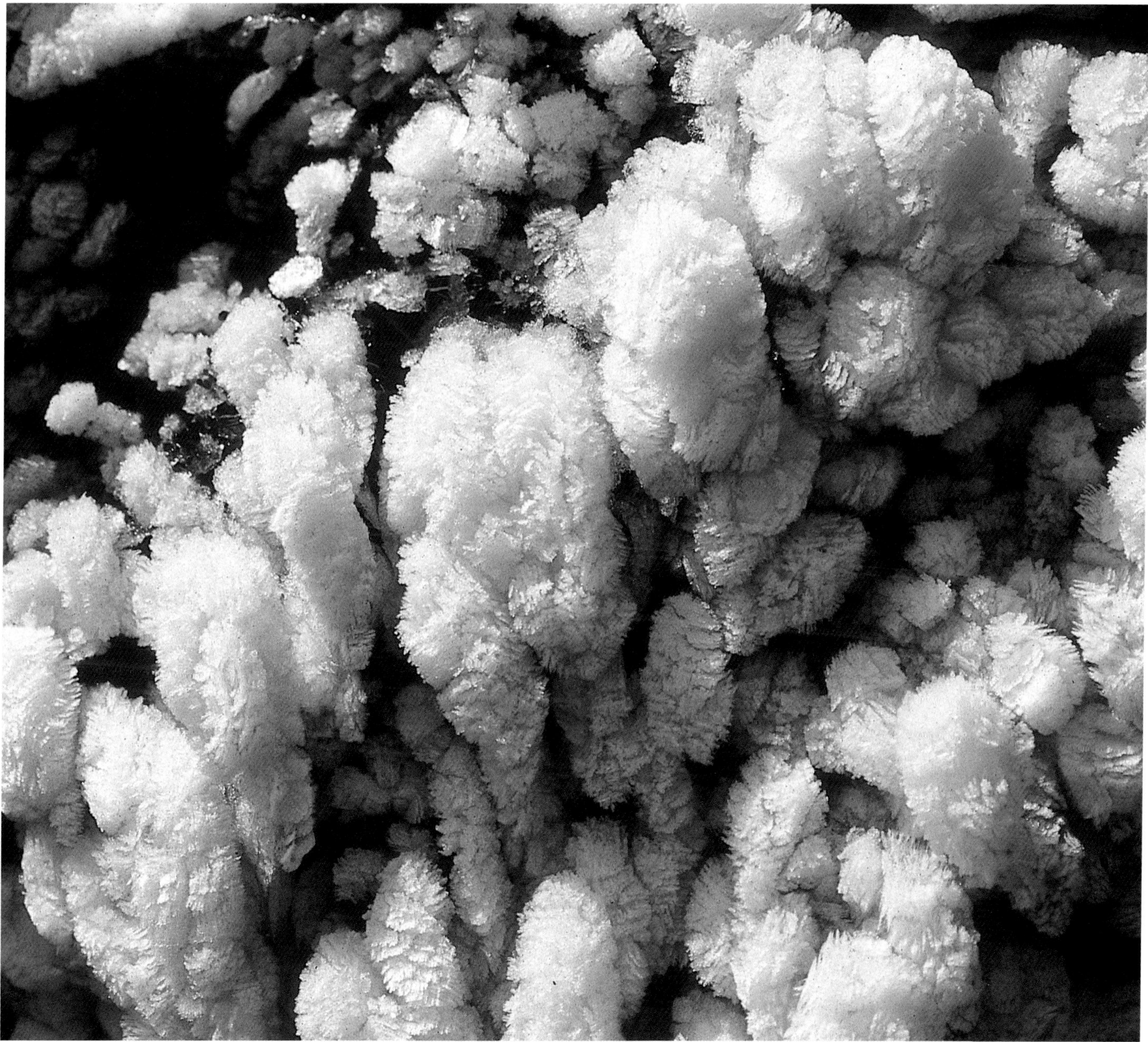

Frosted heather

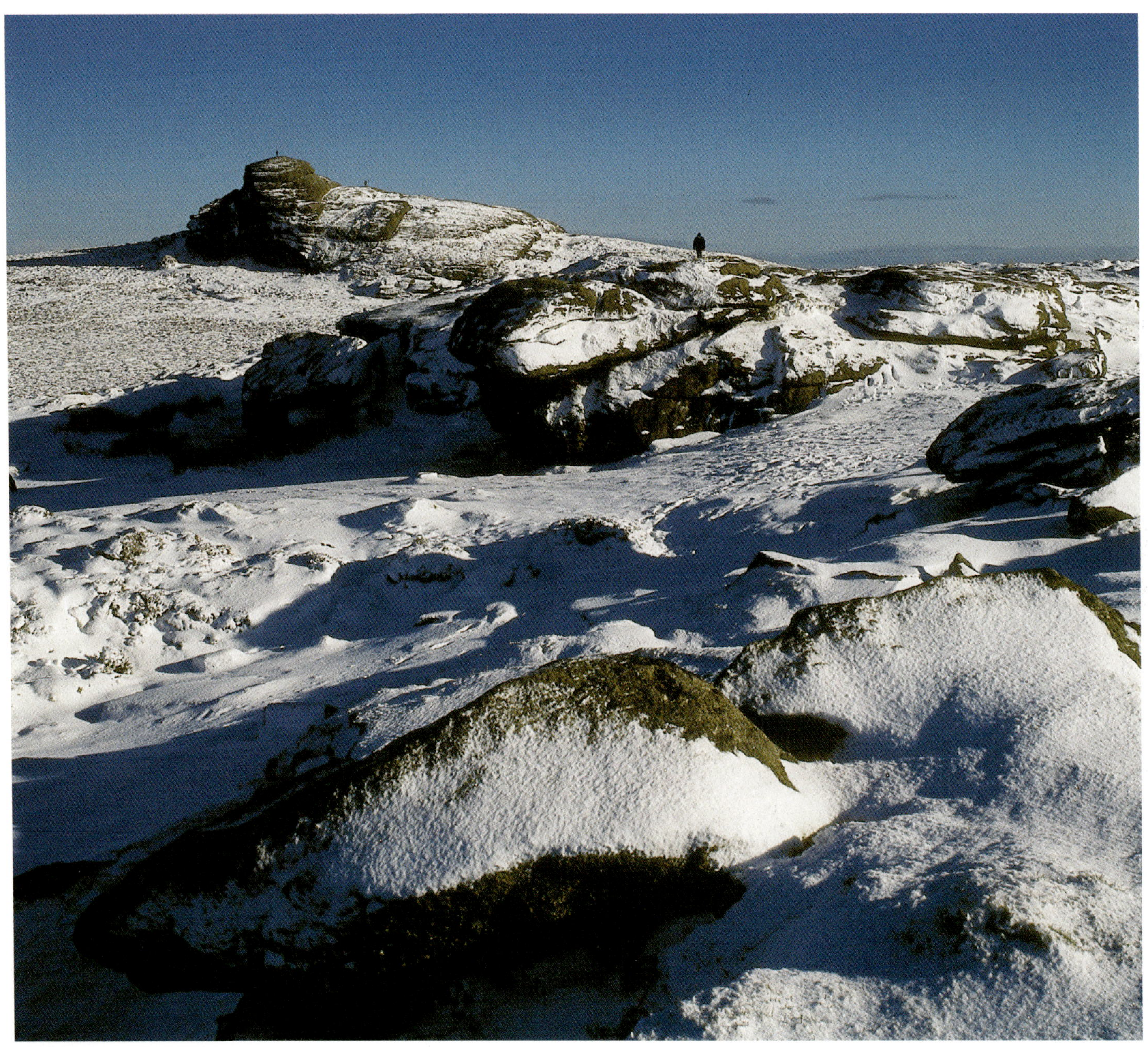

Haytor from near Saddle Tor

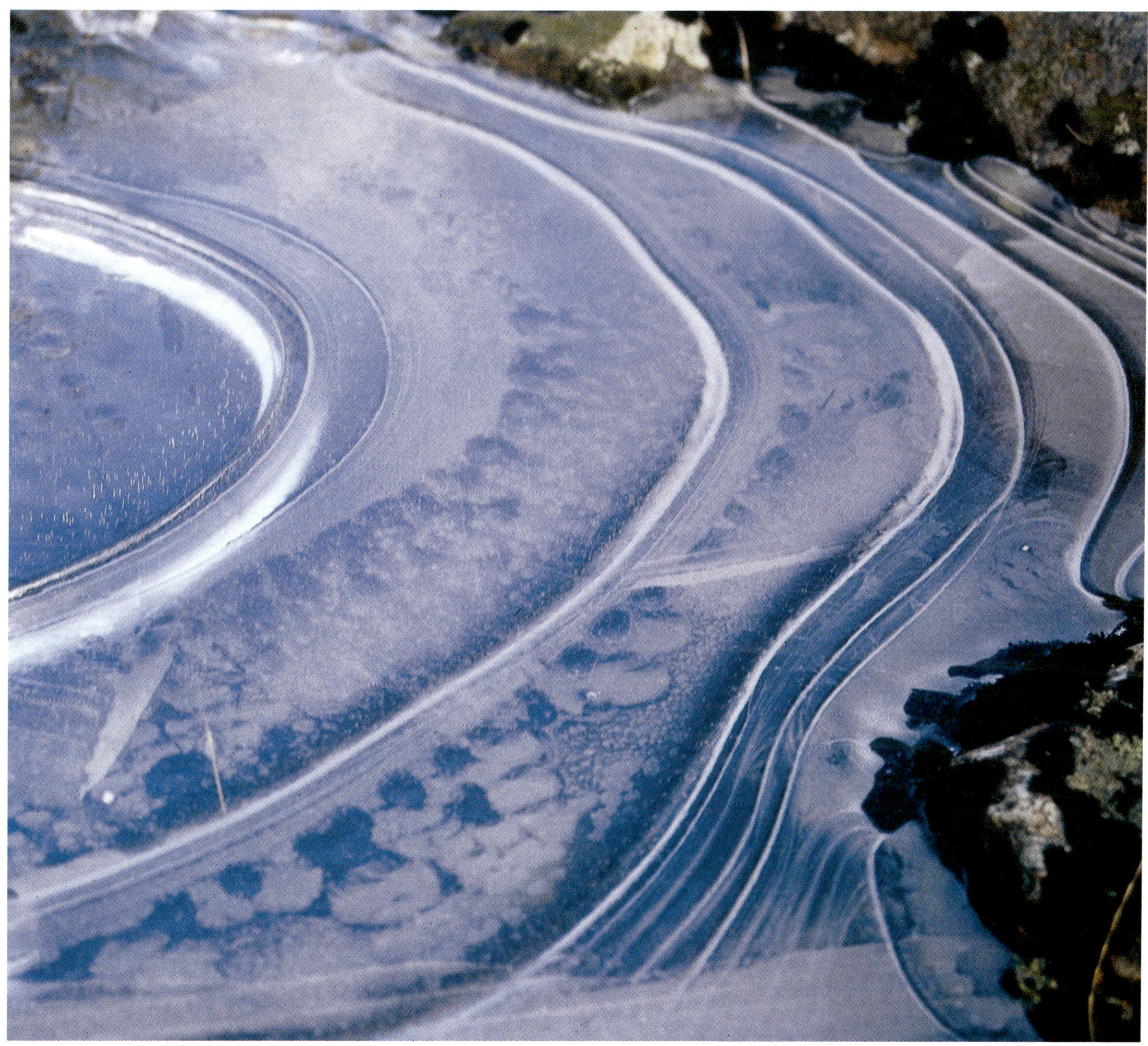

Patterns in a puddle

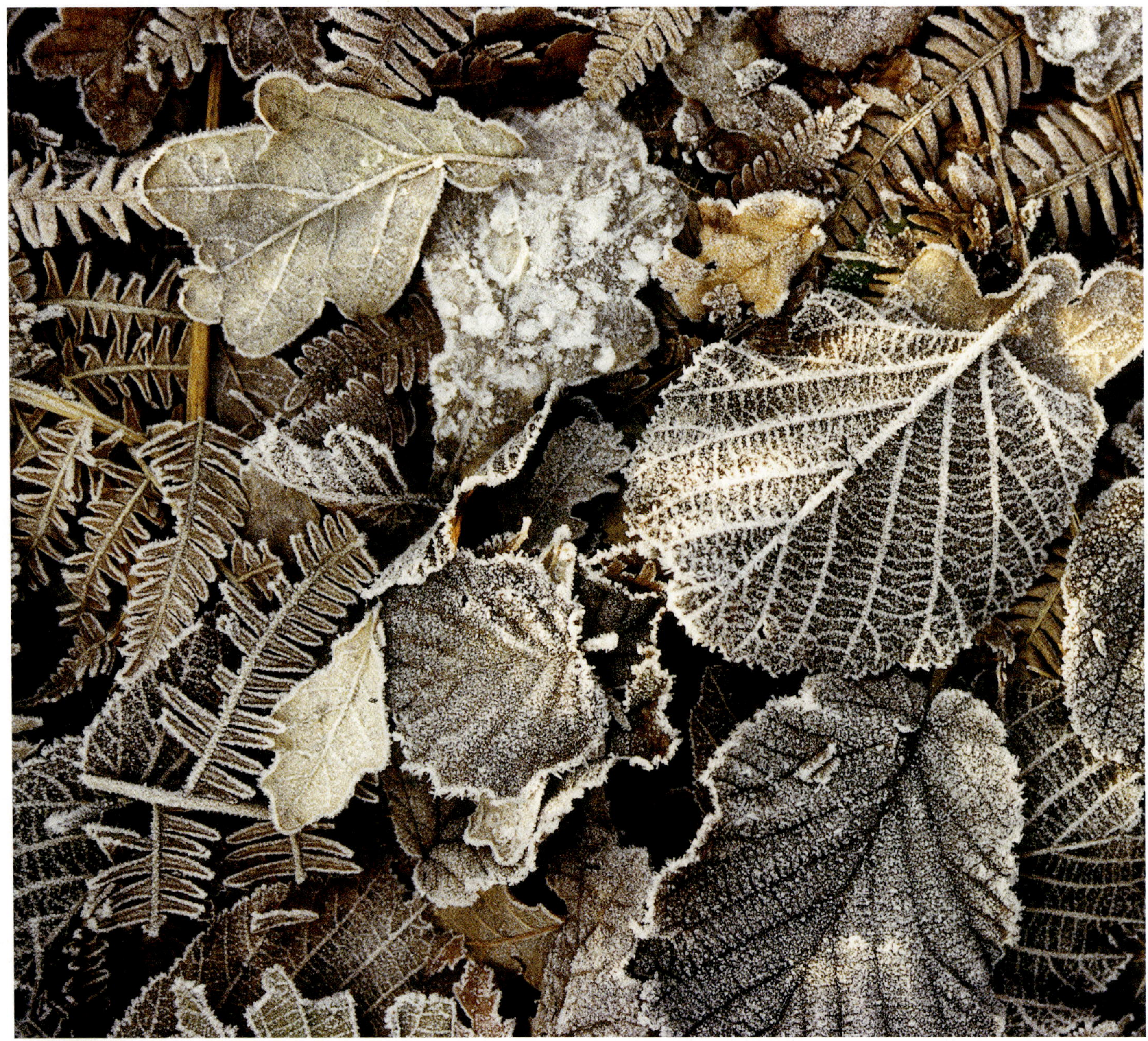

Frosted leaves